Cold War Fighter Pilot

By

HAROLD WADE

National Library of Canada Cataloguing in Publication Data

A cataloguing record for this book that includes the U.S. Library of Congress Classification number, the Library of Congress Call number and the Dewey Decimal cataloguing code is available from the National Library of Canada. The complete cataloguing record can be obtained from the National Library's online database at: www.nlc-bnc.ca/amicus/index-e.html

ISBN 1-4120-3202-4

TRAFFORD

This book was published _on-demand_ in cooperation with Trafford Publishing.
On-demand publishing is a unique process and service of making a book available for retail sale to the public taking advantage of on-demand manufacturing and Internet marketing.
On-demand publishing includes promotions, retail sales, manufacturing, order fulfilment, accounting and collecting royalties on behalf of the author.

Suite 6E, 2333 Government St., Victoria, B.C. V8T 4P4, CANADA

Phone	250-383-6864	Toll-free 1-888-232-4444 (Canada & US)
Fax	250-383-6804	E-mail sales@trafford.com
Web site	www.trafford.com	TRAFFORD PUBLISHING IS A DIVISION OF TRAFFORD HOLDINGS LTD.
Trafford Catalogue #04-1029		www.trafford.com/robots/04-1029.html

10   9   8   7   6   5   4   3

This book is dedicated to those courageous
souls who gave up all their tomorrows
in order for us to enjoy ours.

Foreword

This book is a must for all amateur low-time pilots, who for whatever reason, were not able to ever fly a high performance military jet aircraft. For those of us who would have given our proverbial "right arm" to sit at the controls of such an airplane, this book is almost the next best thing. Harold Wade's writing ability makes the episodes he experienced come alive. One can almost hear the radio chatter, feel the high "G" turns, see the panel instrumentation, and become intense as he relates some very close calls.

In one way this book is not a story. It's a journal, a journal of flying episodes from the eyes of a highly skilled, cool thinking, brilliantly analytical pilot who loved what he was doing. His love of flying was only exceeded by his love for serving his country...a country which gave him the opportunity of being what he wanted to be and to become what he had always dreamed of becoming...a United States Air Force pilot.

Mr. Wade begins by briefly relating his experiences as an enlisted man at a remote, isolated radar outpost in Alaska. The experience of how he and the other men were "discovered" by some Air Force chaplains is very humorous.

From here, he takes us through primary, basic, and advanced flight training. He takes us on assignments as instructor pilot, instrument instructor pilot, and flight examiner. He brings us into the cockpit on a cross country flight, on a target mission, on flights over the frozen Labrador wilderness with iced over windscreen and canopy while low on fuel, and on test flights as he ultimately became a maintenance flight test pilot.

Mr. Wade survived a successful career in a very dangerous profession for three reasons...only two of which he will acknowledge. One, he is a brilliant person with a cool, analytical talent. Two, he admits that the Almighty God had something else for him to do and three, he has a wonderful, loving, supportive wife.

"Miss Kathy" endured many sacrifices, hardships, and lonely times raising four sons so that Mr. Wade could securely do what she knew her husband loved and was intended to do. She is the power in the background that made Mr. Wade's career possible. She never complained. She deserves a medal in her own right. Harold acknowledges this and in retirement has tried to repay her efforts. She now has a comfortable retirement with the husband she, to this day, loves and supports without any reservation.

Harold Wade experienced many successes...as a career Air Force pilot, as a very successful business man, as a father, and as a leader in his church. All four Wade boys are professional and business successes. They are all active in their churches. Success does not come at a higher level than that. Enjoy the book.

Gene Boone

Preface

One of my earliest recollections is from when I was perhaps five years old. Standing in the yard of our house in the cotton mill town of Calhoun falls, SC, I looked up at the biplane clattering across the sky overhead. That excited me. I knew there was a person in that machine making it do whatever it was doing and I promised myself that one day, I, too, would do that.

Family and friends scoffed at the idea when I mentioned my interest in flying machines. In 1935, just about everyone associated with airplanes was looked upon as daredevils or people with less than normal common sense. I was admonished to be content with watching them fly overhead and playing with toy airplanes until I outgrew such foolishness.

No one realized that I had contracted an incurable disease at an early age. Some diseases can be treated, but not cured. The desire to fly is one of those diseases and I never outgrew it.

Without any encouragement from family, and against some pretty long odds, considering my social stratum and lack of formal education, I was able to obtain treatment for my disease through determination, luck, and the grace of God. For a long time, I have endeavored to find a way to describe what it is like for a pilot who knows the satisfaction of being in charge of a flying machine, interacting with it, making it an extension of himself and being able to deal with the infinite variables that are encountered in the process.

I am basically a technical person and not well qualified to describe feeling and emotion, but I am compelled to try.

From Civilian to Airman

The Sabrejet abruptly snapped into a violent inverted spin. The nose went steeply down on the first half turn and was back up almost to the upside down horizon on the second half turn. The transverse G forces were throwing my legs all over the cockpit and slamming my head from side to side against the canopy. I could not get oriented.....and how did I get myself into this mess? Well, let's go back to the beginning.

World War II came a little too early for me. It started for the United States officially on December 7th, 1941 when the Japanese attacked Pearl Harbor. I was only eleven years old, about to be twelve in just under two months.

We had food ration books, because items like butter, meat, and sugar were in short supply. We bought war stamps and war bonds to raise money for the government to finance the war.

My Dad had left the cotton mill in Calhoun Falls and moved to a farm in Georgia and when the war began, our ration books probably allowed us to buy more products than we were accustomed to having, or had money to buy them with. Money in the 1930s and 1940s was a scarce commodity for most people. By that time I had a younger sister, named Faye. I never had a brother.

About the time I entered the seventh grade, we moved to Commerce, Georgia, near Athens, where my Dad worked in the cotton mill. He had given up trying to eke out a living on tenant farms. We then had electric lights to replace the kerosene lamps, but had no car.

Even among school students, the war was a frequent topic of conversation. We boys drew pictures of guns, tanks, and airplanes. We read the magazines in the school library and kept a sharp eye out for pictures and articles about aviators. We all were planning to be pilots when we were old enough. At the time, we did not realize that we could not become pilots just for the asking.

My parents never offered any encouragement regarding a career, and I suppose they were of the opinion that no one should ever try to rise above the level of society he was born into. They accepted the fact that they were poor but my dad would say he wanted my sister and I to do better in life than he had done. To me it was not so much a matter of economics or social standing as it was a matter of doing something I wanted to do and was too naive to know that I shouldn't try.

One of our class, Gene Kellum, hitchhiked the nine miles from Commerce to Jefferson, Georgia and spent his hard earned money from peach orchard work on flight instruction. A little later he got some flight instruction from a local pilot returning from WWII Army Air Corps duty and managed to solo out of a slightly modified cotton patch. If he followed up on that with any more flight instruction, I did not hear of it.

One of our group, Jack Carson, had a strong interest in aircraft and was the only one of us who had the talent, interest, and the funds to build and fly gas powered models. He went on to become an electrical engineer, and as far as I know, never indulged in any flight instruction.

Another classmate, Bill Mize, became an industrial engineer by way of Georgia Tech. While there, he flew with the school aero club and got licensed. He later obtained his instrument rating while at Greensboro, North Carolina. Bill went on to acquire his own flying machine. As far as I know he and I are the only ones from our group to be licensed and to fly our own machines.

By the time I was a senior in high school the war had ended, but that did not diminish my interest in airplanes. The bad news was that in order to be accepted for pilot training in the Air Force, at that time, the Army Air Corps, two years of college was required. College had never been much of a consideration. My parents thought a high school education should be sufficient for just about anyone and at my age I should be working full time and supplementing the family income. There were few, if any, programs for financial assistance.

The navy had a program whereby one could enlist, get two years of college, paid for by the Navy, serve a term as a naval aviator and fulfill the commitment. I went to Atlanta with three other seniors to take the exams. There were fifteen hundred applicants from which two hundred would be selected. I was notified by mail that I was not one of the two hundred.

Since my interest in electronics was almost as strong as it was in aviation, I settled for a deal the Air Force offered. I could get an assignment to a technical school prior to enlistment, provided I met their criteria and enlisted between certain dates.

I submitted all the required documentation, like school grades, letters of recommendation, and applied for radio school. In due time I received approval from Headquarters, Air Training Command. By that time I had graduated from high school and had worked all summer for an uncle who operated a service station.

———

On October 14, 1947, Captain Chuck Yeager, flying the X-1, broke the sound barrier and exceeded mach one at Muroc, later to become Edwards Air Force Base. There was no publicity at the time and I, of course, did not know about it until much later. It was just coincidental that I enlisted the next day.

After a physical exam and some preliminary processing at Fort McPherson, Atlanta, Georgia, I, along with several young men was sent over to Marietta Air Base, later to become Dobbins AFB. There we waited for hours in processing lines, picked up a few million cigarette butts, and swapped stories among ourselves. Everyone was warned about the medical processing and those long, square, or even forked needles. After a few days, we were officially sworn in and put on a train for Texas where we would undergo airman basic training. After a couple of days on the train, we arrived in San Antonio.

The United States Air Force had officially become a separate branch of the military service only a month earlier, but hardly anyone had made any real changes except on paper at headquarters. The uniforms were still olive drab and the drill sergeants still addressed us as "soldiers".

The days were full. Out of the bunk and on the road every morning at five thirty A.M. March to the mess hall. March back and put the barracks in inspection order. Fall in on the road again for drill practice, orientation movies, and aptitude testing. There was daily physical training, Air Force history, firing range and qualification in small arms, long hikes with a heavy back pack, exposure to tear gas, and more drill.

Some guys were homesick. I did miss being in familiar places, with familiar people, but was not bothered much by it. The strict military atmosphere was not difficult for me. Those drill instructors were patsies compared to my dad. He was from a culture that believed in absolute, immediate, and complete compliance with directions.

After a few weeks we began to look like military people. The smallest unit of troops consisted of a group of about sixty men that was called a "flight". My flight was better than average in drill. We knew that toward the end of our training, there would be a wing wide competition for the flight judged best in military drill. The winning flight would be given an airplane ride over the local area. We wanted to win that, but would be competing with several other units. We felt like we had a chance to win the competition, so we entered and won.

So, my flight in military airplanes began with that ride in a C-47, Gooney Bird, along with all the other guys in my outfit, taking in the sights of San Antonio and vicinity from the air. It was a pretty big thrill for a bunch of young recruits.

After thirteen weeks of basic training, the Air Force honored it's agreement to send me to radio operator school.

Radio School

My arrival at Scott AFB, Illinois, by bus must have coincided with the coldest January night ever recorded there; anyway that was the way it felt to me. Coming from the relatively mild climate of San Antonio by way of Georgia for a short leave, the weather was a shocker. There was snow and ice everywhere and the wind felt like it was being blocked by little more than a barbed wire fence.

School was demanding, but I did well and made good grades, because I liked what I was doing. We learned to operate every kind of radio currently in use and learned some basic electronics and elementary maintenance. A lot of communications were still being carried on by radiotelegraph, so we got in a lot of practice communicating by Morse code. I was still holding to at least a little hope of getting assigned as an airborne radio operator.

On the way to Belleville by bus, two young airmen took notice of the very attractive young lady in the seat in front of them. They proceeded to discuss her by voicing dits and dahs in Morse code, thinking that they were being very clever. At her bus stop, as she got up to leave, she turned around toward them and said, "I just thought you boys would like to know that I am a code instructor at the base." The guys were suddenly very red faced and very quiet.

The frigid winter slowly turned to a warm, muddy spring, then to a hot, humid summer. The barracks had no cooling system, but none of us were accustomed to air conditioning and therefore did not miss it much. Refrigerated air conditioning had not yet become a common amenity.

The Federal Communications Commission periodically sent examiners to the air base and I took advantage of my recent training, plus some additional study on amateur radio. I obtained licenses for commercial radio operator and for amateur radio. A lot of my spare time was spent at the base club amateur radio station, hanging out with other hams and building and operating radio equipment.

After thirty two weeks of intense class work and some practice in actual radio communications, my class graduated and we all shipped out for operational assignments.

Andrews AFB, MD

In the late fall of 1948, when I arrived at Andrews, just outside Washington, DC, I had hopes of being assigned to the bomb wing flying B-29s out of there. I wanted to fly and to be around airplanes. However, I was disappointed to learn that my assignment was for a communications squadron which had no connection with the flying activities. We provided all the ground communications facilities for the entire base. We had teletype and phones, but no radio equipment.

At that time, Andrews was also the home of the now famed 4th Fighter Wing, flying early models of the Sabrejet fighters with which they would soon make a name for themselves in the skies over Korea against the MIG 15. At the time, while looking at them admiringly, I could not know that some day I too, would be at the controls of a Sabrejet.

The first sergeant needed a clerk typist and he knew radio operators were trained as typists, therefore he put me to work in the administrative office. I was not happy about being a paper shuffler, but the first sergeant was a nice old guy and promptly got me promoted to corporal, the modern day equivalent of airman second class.

Part of my job entailed a daily trip in our jeep over to the main part of the base to get mail and deliver administrative reports. The trip took me past the end of the primary runway and sometimes I would stop and watch the air traffic. On one occasion, I saw a B-47 approach and touchdown using a drag chute for braking. I had never even heard of such a thing. I later learned that the B-47 was the one that made the record breaking non-stop flight from Washington state to Andrews.

Sometime in the spring, I went home for a few days leave. I was thrilled to get a "hop" on a Mitchell B-25 to Georgia. When I returned to Andrews our squadron had been tasked to set up and operate a radio communications station. I was the chief operator. I never knew why some of the men with more rank were not the chief op. The only thing I would have been happier with would have been a flying job. At least I was doing something I could really get my teeth into.

I really enjoyed my work, but was not entirely satisfied. There was a radio mechanic school at Scott AFB that I wanted to attend, so I applied for that. About that time, the Russians had blockaded Berlin and the United States Air Force was working hard to keep the West Germans from starving. I could have been easily accepted as a volunteer for service in Germany. However, I figured that could wait and I wanted more training in electronics.

Scott AFB Again

In the summer of 1949, I found myself back at hot, muggy Scott AFB, Illinois as a student in the thirty six week school for radio maintenance.

The school kept us very busy. We learned how to troubleshoot and repair every kind of radio the Air Force had in service. That included airborne as well as ground equipment. It was easy for me for two reasons. I liked what I was doing and did a lot of self study, a lot of which was related to amateur radio. Again, I put in a lot time at the club amateur radio facility. As some would say, I was "eat up with it". Consequently, I made good grades without much effort.

In the spring of 1950, my class graduated and my grade average was the highest in the group. My reward was a trip to Alaska, still a U.S. territory; not yet a state. In an attempt to soften the blow, those of us who were ordered to Alaska were told to expect to find a girl behind every tree. Of course, we knew that Alaskan trees were right scarce.

Alaska

The military didn't waste any money on transportation when it came to reassignment. After a long, tiresome bus ride to Oakland, California, I arrived at Camp Stoneman, operated by the army, to await boarding a troop ship for Alaska. Along with a lot of other guys, I waited for a few weeks, wondering when we would actually depart. In the meantime, we low ranking people did housekeeping chores around the base.

Finally, we were loaded onto a troop ship, the USS Hase, along with about fifteen hundred people and some cargo. With the military band on the dock playing "Slow Boat to China" we left Oakland Bay. The ship was crowded and our movement was limited, but we adapted as GIs are usually able to do and after several days arrived at Seward, Alaska. It was well into the evening, but the sun was still shining brightly. Welcome to the land of the midnight sun. Those high latitudes do make a difference in the relative lengths of days and nights.

We off-loaded the ship and boarded an antiquated train. It looked like something out of an old western movie. The wooden seats had no padding and the little locomotive puffed along, badly overloaded. The scenic waters of Cook Inlet were on our left and the steep grades of the mountains on the right. The railroad got so steep in some places, the little engine stalled before getting over the crest and had to back down to the valley and part way up the previous grade, get a running start at full throttle and finally lurch over the crest and go hurtling down the other side.

The train took us to Elmendorf AFB, near Anchorage where we were given unit and work assignments. I now had two Air Force specialties; radio operations and radio maintenance. I was given a choice and still clung to the hope that I might get a flying job, So I chose operations. That got me an assignment to the aircraft control and warning squadron about five miles from the main base.

The assignment could have been a lot worse, and eventually did get worse. Initially, my job was in the radio room, where we provided the off-base communications for all the military throughout Alaska. It kept about five operators busy, continuously. Propagation was just too poor for reliable long haul voice communication, so we used Morse code. I did not mind, and considered the code to be a second language. All our people were well qualified and required little supervision. Protocol was about as loose as it could be, and still have an efficient operation.

One of our radio operators was a little different. Instead of his real name I'll use Smith. Smith was a good operator, but didn't mix well with other people and often appeared to need a bath. One day our chief operator called us all together and announced that he had to provide an operator for an extended temporary duty assignment with an expedition. "Does anyone want to volunteer?" No one did.

I was afraid that I would be selected, since I was the youngest of the group and was not married. However the chief was a fair man and told us all to put our name on a piece of paper and put it in the box he had. Without looking in the box, he would withdraw a name. He did, and then he told Smith, "OK, you will have to go." Smith left and I never saw him again. The chief dumped the box of names in the nearest trash can. After everyone else left the room, I went over and looked at the papers in the box. They all had the same name on them. It was Smith.

———

On 25 June 1950, a lot of things changed. Fighting broke out in Korea. A lot of extra precautions were suddenly taken. We knew that Russian recon flights were in our airspace, especially in the western portion of the territory, but we didn't have much radar coverage out there to track them and see what they were up to.

On July fourth, 1950, I and fourteen other GIs boarded a C-82, forerunner of the C-119, and headed for a destination not yet revealed to us. After a while we touched down on a dirt strip about 175 miles northwest of Anchorage. The little sign proclaimed the name of the location to be Farewell, Alaska. That was our first clue as to where we were going.

Our assignment was to set up a gap filler radar site to help track Russian or other unidentified aircraft in the area. My job was to set up and operate the radio communications facility in order for us to transmit radar plots back to Elmendorf.

We were officially Detachment C-2, 625th Aircraft Control & Warning Squadron and our orders read that we were being dispatched to an undisclosed location on temporary duty for approximately two weeks to set up the site. We naturally assumed that we were just the set up crew and that someone would be along in two weeks to relieve us. The schedule was slightly misleading. When the military says "on or about", the emphasis may be on the "about" Months later we realized that no one was coming to relieve us anytime soon.

Our detachment commander was a first lieutenant and the remainder of us were enlisted types. We had a radar maintenance man, some radar operators, a cook, and a powerman in addition to my crew. I was still in shock that I had been designated as communications chief and still only had two stripes. I had Pfc. Donaldson, a recent grad from radio maintenance school and four radio operators. I had not previously known the radio operators, since they were furnished by other units. I soon learned that when units are tasked to furnish troops to another unit, they don't send their best people.

One had two stripes, was a klutz and a clone of Gomer Pyle. One had three stripes, a buck sergeant, was a good operator, but had a lousy personality and a knack for causing dissension. One guy was an older and mostly incompetent tech sergeant. How he got his rank was a mystery. I had one other operator fresh from school and no experience, but he turned out to be quite reliable.

Upon arrival, our first order of business was to set up camp. There was no housing except for a few buildings belonging to the CAA, the Civil Aeronautics Commission, forerunner of the FAA. They had a radio shack, a duplex for their radio operators quarters, a house for the station supervisor and a shed for equipment. They were supplied by bush pilots who stopped by every two weeks or so, depending on the weather. They maintained and operated a radio navigation aid facility, handled position reports, and provided weather information for air traffic in the area.

The nearest civilization was the village of McGrath, some sixty miles further west. There were no roads, power lines, or phone lines. We were isolated and our only method of communicating with the outside world was with our own radio equipment.

We proceeded to set up our tents on the opposite side of the airstrip from the CAA facility. We had four man tents and after selecting a spot, I started driving tent pegs. The first one went about eight or ten inches into the tundra and stopped abruptly as if there was a rock down there. I moved over a bit and had the same difficulty. After the third unsuccessful attempt to get a peg into the ground, I found a pick and pulled back the tundra to see just how big that rock was. There was no rock. There was ice – the perma frost!

The sun was shining, the temperature was about eighty degrees and the ground was frozen solid! We finally got some pegs into the tundra, but not very securely. The old, well used tent was erected and it had several large holes in the top. Someone must have known that because we had some extra tents. We put up another one over the first one that had holes in different places.

The sun was out about twenty hours a day, but the short nights were chilly and we had some little oil burning tent heaters. The eye in the top of the heaters was just right to place a steel helmet into after removing the helmet liner. We could heat a little water for shaving and a sponge bath. The water came from the CAA well across the way. We had a four hundred gallon water trailer and a vehicle known as a weapons carrier; sort of an oversized pick up.

Our only food consisted entirely of outdated War II C-rations. There was a variety of canned food and some of it was palatable and some of it was pretty bad. I don't know why we had a cook. We did not need a chef to warm a can of beans, so we put him to work as a gofer and general handyman.

With Donaldson's help, I got the radio equipment set up and operating with our portable generator. Our primary transmitter was pretty powerful, but with the poor radio propagation, we needed better antennae than the portable ones that came with the equipment. I had anticipated that and had packed a lot of extra wire and coaxial cable in with our supplies. No real trees were anywhere in sight. A few scrubby pines were off in the distance, but were too short to be used even if we cut them down and brought them to the site.

We found some abandoned power poles that had been left by a CAA crew and with a great deal of difficulty dug some holes in the permafrost. It took us several days since we had to let the ground thaw in the sun, dig down a few inches and wait for more to thaw. We finally got the poles up and strung some fairly efficient antenna systems.

The generator was powered by a worn out four cylinder jeep engine. We had to keep tinkering with it to keep it running and I knew it would not last long. We had a dinky little one lung, rope started emergency generator, but it was not powerful enough to run everything. I started agitating for a replacement of our primary generator, but got no response. I would not let the powerman near our generator. I could tell he did not know a generator from his backside. I knew more about it than he did.

We eventually got a new generator and wore it out, and began on still another one before I left. It's demise was expedited by the carelessness of one of my radio operators in connecting a drum of diesel fuel instead of gasoline. Those field units were simply not designed for continuous service over long periods of time. The unit had been in continuous use for several thousand hours, but we could not shut it down for preventative maintenance in forty degree below zero weather. Chances of getting it started again were slim to none. Once the gasoline powered unit sucked up a load of diesel fuel, we could not restart it. We resorted to our little one lung emergency unit until we could replace the main unit.

If we were not transmitting radar plots or handling administrative radio traffic, we checked in with our control station at Elmendorf every fifteen minutes. I was not getting much rest; being responsible for maintenance and operation with mostly poorly qualified or inexperienced people. Fortunately, Donaldson was learning rapidly and was a hard worker. The corporal and the tech Sgt. and their bungling frequently got me in trouble with the control station at Elmendorf.

We kept the system operating and tracked many unidentified aircraft coming through the area. They obviously were monitoring us, because as soon as our people scrambled the fighters from Elmendorf, the bogeys would turn back toward Siberia. We had no doubt that they were Russian and checking on our radar coverage and our defenses.

In addition to our primary jobs, we had to unload a never ending stream of C-47 and C-46 aircraft, bringing in our winter supply of heating oil and generator fuel. It came in fifty five gallons drums and had to be manhandled off the aircraft onto our recently acquired six by six GI truck.

We were overworked, underfed, poorly equipped, and our living quarters were certainly not representative of a military installation. We slept whenever we could in the tents with sleeping bags, ate C-rations, outdated WWII canned food which we ate cold most of the time. Each person was allowed one carton of food per day that was intended to provide three meals, but they were pretty skimpy meals of mostly poor quality. Sometimes I was able to warm up a can of beans for lunch, after cold cereal and powdered milk for breakfast. Supper consisted of whatever was in the remaining cans, such as watery spaghetti and meat gristle.

We were not informed of our new parent organization and did not know it until much later, but our detachment had been transferred to another squadron for logistical support. Since we did not know of the transfer, messages to the old unit either were ignored or forwarded to someone who ignored them.. Whoever was responsible for us now, apparently did not know what it meant to assume responsibility for logistical support of "Detachment C-2". No one followed up on it and incredibly, no one was supporting us.

Our detachment commander had been replaced by a Captain. It is a mystery as to why he did not inquire about our lack of logistical support. He didn't seem to mind that the troops were being treated so poorly. In fact, he contributed to the problem by requiring us to work for a contractor who had come to Farewell to construct a new building for the CAA. That was not only impractical, it was downright illegal.

We had no real spare time. We felt like slaves and were not getting any rest, so we devised a way to get a letter to the inspector general. We drafted the letter and mailed it inside another letter to an enlisted fellow we knew at Elmendorf. We knew the Captain monitored all the outgoing and incoming mail, and he would have intercepted a letter addressed to any official. The inner envelope was hand delivered to the office of the inspector general at Elmendorf. Each of us had written one letter of the signature, which said simply, "The men of Detachment C-2."

In a few days we received a radio message directing the captain to Elmendorf by the next available aircraft. After several days he was back and obviously quite angry, but subdued. He couldn't figure out how we had made contact with the IG. He then called us all together and demanded to know who had signed the letter. We all denied it, and in fact, no one person did affix the signature. He was frustrated, but did not press the issue any further. He had apparently lost a large portion of his backside and was in danger of losing even more. His harsh treatment of the troops was eased considerably.

We began to look like bums. There was no way to properly wash our clothes. We tried doing them in thirty gallon cans with oil fired immersion heaters, but after a while we ran out of laundry soap and could not get resupplied. Some guys gave up shaving. We dressed in whatever combination of clothing we could, sometimes mixing summer uniform items with winter. We had tried sending clothes to the GI laundry at Elmendorf, but never got them back. No one was responding to our requests for help from Elmendorf. But we had better not fail to report a radar plot or to make a radio check every fifteen minutes.

My GI high top shoes wore out and I was going to need boots for the approaching winter. With the help of one of the CAA radio operators, I mail ordered a pair of boots from Sears. In a few weeks they were dropped off by a bush pilot. I would later experience a lot of pain and misery because of those boots.

We were accustomed to automatically grabbing every available body, piling on the GI truck and hustling over to the airstrip when a military aircraft approached, expecting to unload more fuel. On such an occasion, a gooney bird approached and as we met the bird, we were surprised to see three very sharply dressed U.S. Air Force chaplains step off.

One of them said, "We are circuit riders from Elmendorf and have heard that there are some Air Force men here, can you direct us to their site?" We pointed to our trashy looking tent city and told them we were the people they were looking for. They all stared at us in disbelief. Military men weren't supposed to look like bearded, long haired, dirty, shabbily dressed bums. Our camp would make a scene from a MASH movie look like a five star hotel. We had named ourselves the Farewell Guerrillas.

The chaplains eventually decided to go over and check out our camp and talk with the detachment commander. They did not hold any religious services, and said nothing to us, but instead quickly got back in the C-47. Instead of heading west, on to the next radar station, we noticed they headed back toward Elmendorf.

About three days later, without any notice, aircraft began arriving as fast as we could unload them, and continued arriving all through the day and the next. They were loaded with supplies ranging from food, real food, to new huts for living quarters. We set up the folding, insulated, four man buildings with wooden floors. I had a folding cot to put my sleeping bag on, instead of the ground. We even had a large refrigerator for perishable food, the first we had in months. We put the cook to work and had what we thought was the best meal we ever had.

We never got any official briefing, but heard through the grapevine that the chaplains who visited us, were so appalled at what they saw, they went directly to the Commanding General of the Alaskan Air Command. Evidently, heads rolled and some people were wearing diapers on their backsides.

Some additional bodies were assigned to us and the workload became a little easier. By the time winter arrived a group from the Corps of Engineers had come and built us some even better insulated Quonset huts for about ten men each and heated with oil fired heaters. By normal standards, it was still a primitive environment, but a vast improvement over our initial set up.

AF chaplain teams eventually began to make regular stops at our detachment. We usually had a Protestant chaplain conducting services in one building and a Catholic chaplain doing his service in another building. After the first chaplain visit, of course, the troops compared notes. The Protestant chaplain had used grape juice in his communion service. It was noted that the Catholic chaplain used real wine in his service. On subsequent chaplain visits, they wondered why all the troops were over in the Catholic service.

Living and operating in the arctic environment was a constant challenge. Sometimes the temperature dropped to more than 55 degrees below zero. It was during one of those times that I made the mistake of wearing my Sears boots instead of my mukluks. I had failed to allow room for extra socks and the boots were tight. After being outside too long, I developed frost bite and nearly lost some toes. By that time, we had acquired a medical corpsman. I was able to keep the third set of toenails after my originals came out and the second set were so deformed they had to be removed.

We struggled through the wicked winter, in spite of several feet of snow and paralyzing cold. We kept the radar scanning the skies and the radios reporting the findings to the control center. Pure survival was an accomplishment. Fulfilling our mission was performance extraordinaire.

After a year, my replacement arrived and I lost no time in saying farewell to Farewell, wearing the stripes of a staff sergeant. I had been promoted twice during the past year.

After a few days of rest and administrative processing at Elmendorf, I and Donaldson were happy to depart on an Air Force C-124 for McChord AFB, Tacoma, Washington. My next duty assignment was to Stewart AFB, Newburgh, New York. I was fortunate enough to get a ride on an Air Force C-97 to Kelly AFB, San Antonio, Texas and went on from there to my home by commercial transportation.

Stewart AFB

After some vacation time with my family in Georgia, I reported to a communications squadron at Stewart AFB, Newburgh, New York. My job was easy and I enjoyed and appreciated being back in civilization. Stewart was part of Air Defense Commands 26th Air Division, which covered a lot of territory, including the Northeastern U.S. plus Newfoundland and Labrador. therefore, our communications squadron had a large radio section.

The station chief was Tech Sergeant Lovin. He had been a Staff sergeant and my shift chief on my first job in Alaska. After I went to Farewell, we had no personal contact, but knew who we were dealing with in our frequent radio contacts between my station and his. Radio operators often know each other by their "fist"; their technique when transmitting with a telegraph key. To a layman, it might all sound alike, but to a highly trained telegrapher, each person has his own peculiarities as we all have with a spoken language. Lovin assigned me as a shift supervisor in the radio room.

That was the first easy job I had been on for a while. We were very adequately staffed with well qualified people, and I should have known that anything that good would not last long. It didn't. Some manpower experts came in a allowed we had it too easy and some of us would have to be redistributed to other units. I did not get to experience winter in New York along the Hudson River. Sometime in the late fall or early winter, I packed my bags and traveled to Selfridge AFB, near Detroit for reassignment to another aircraft control and warning squadron.

Maryville, Tennessee

Selfridge AFB does not really count as a duty assignment. I was sent there for processing as per the usual inefficient military administrative procedure. I don't know why I could not have been ordered directly from Stewart to my next duty station. My departure was delayed because a document from my personnel file had been lost. After wasting a few weeks at Selfridge and getting a taste of Michigan winter weather, I arrived at Maryville Air Station in my 1951 Ford for which I had foolishly incurred a lot of debt.

Now I was twenty one years old, a staff sergeant, trained and experienced in radio communications, looking for something to really get my teeth into. Maryville was not exactly what I had in mind. There were no military quarters. We lived wherever we could on the meager allowance we were paid for quarters. The administrative offices were in the local armory. The radar was on the roof of the armory. The radio site was across town on a hill which was part of a cow pasture.

By virtue of being a staff sergeant, and having a supervisory specialty code, I was put in charge of a rotating shift. The communications chief was Master Sergeant Jim Fry and he was easy enough to please. The job was not much of challenge for me, so I looked around for something to do.

I discovered a lot of equipment had developed problems and had simply been put in the back room and tagged unrepairable. I was surprised at that because we had several radio maintenance people in addition to a full time civilian technical representative. During night shifts when there was not a lot of activity, I dragged out the inoperative receivers and transmitters to trouble shoot and one by one, put them all back into operating condition. I didn't talk about it, but the tech rep noticed and was miffed because I had shown him up.

I didn't care. He didn't write my efficiency reports. Jim Fry didn't say much about it either, but I suspect he had a lot to do with my next promotion.

————

Two things of significance happened while I was stationed at Maryville. It was there that I saw the notice on the squadron bulletin board that the Air Force was accepting applicants from enlisted troops for pilot training and would waive the college requirements if an equivalency written exam was passed in order to qualify for the regular aviation cadet entrance exam. I lost no time in submitting an application.

About the same time, I met a young lady whose name was Mary Katherine Hill. I had previously dated several girls in the area, but after meeting Mary K., I dated no one else. More about that later.

————

Our unit was relocated to a more permanent facility at Cross Mountain, near Lake City, or more exactly, close to Briceville. Briceville was a run down community that had been a thriving coal mining area in earlier years. Labor squabbles had resulted in the big companies moving on and leaving a few small private operations. The locals did not like us and made it very plain to us that they didn't, so except for the necessity of passing by on our way to and from the air station, we pretty much avoided them.

Our radar and communications site was on top of Cross Mountain and our quarters were in the valley below. We traveled to and from work by way of a cable car. At times the cable car would be several hundred feet above the dense forest and we could see the plumes of blue smoke wafting up from the fires being tended by the locals making their bootleg booze. Some of them thought we were working for the revenuers, spotting their stills, and would take a few shots at us a we traveled up and down the mountain.

We never got hit, but had some pretty close ones. We really didn't want to hurt anyone, but got tired of their plinking at us, so we put a couple of M-1 carbines on the cable car. The next time they fired at us, we couldn't see them for the dense foliage, but we hosed off a few rounds in their general direction and things became a lot more peaceful.

———

I was surprised to be informed that I was to meet a promotion board at our support headquarters, located at McGhee Tyson airport. There were other staff sergeants in the squadron who were older and had more time in grade, but I would not decline the opportunity. On the appointed day, I reported to the panel of colonels, majors, captains, warrant officers and a couple of master sergeants. After a couple of easy to answer questions, I was dismissed. Two weeks later orders arrived for my promotion to tech sergeant.

Mary Katherine and I continued to date regularly and had talked about marriage. She had completed high school and was working in Knoxville. The Air Force had a strict rule which did not allow aviation cadets to be married, so the marriage plans were put on hold until I completed pilot training.

After a trip to Sewart AFB, Nashville, Tennessee, to undergo a flight physical and some pretty extensive written exams, I was notified that I had passed and the next step would be to go to Chanute AFB, near Chicago, for the written aviation cadet entrance exam and psychomotor exam to test for hand eye coordination and certain physical skills.

Early in 1953, I traveled to Chanute and did all the required testing. After a few weeks, I received notice that everything was in order and a class assignment would be forthcoming. In the meantime, the Korean "police action" was winding down and I was afraid the Air Force would renege on their offer of pilot training. In fact, at one point, I received notice that I could get a class assignment right away if I would change my request from pilot to navigator training. I was not interested in being a navigator. I wanted to be the one at the controls.

My waiting paid off. In July, I received orders to report to Lackland AFB in August for the preflight portion of pilot training as an aviation cadet. I knew that as a cadet I would be taking a severe pay cut and could not afford the Ford. I had traded the earlier coupe for a 1952 convertible. Not a smart move, but young, single GIs don't always make smart decisions. I bought a beat up MG TD roadster and drove it to my parents home in Commerce, Georgia.

In the back yard, I took the engine apart, bought some parts from Atlanta and put the engine back together. My father, always the pessimist, looked at the parts scattered all over the back porch, and allowed that the engine would never run again. It started on the first revolution and never missed a beat all the way to Texas.

Lackland AFB Revisited

San Antonio was not my favorite place. I had not gotten a very good impression of it while undergoing airman basic. It didn't matter, since I would not be seeing much of anything off base for the next thirteen weeks. The only airplanes we would be seeing were those flying overhead or the static displays on the base. I was about to be converted from a tech sergeant to a "Mister". Cadets had no rank.

In the event, I did not complete pilot training, I would revert back to my rank of Technical Sergeant and continue in my specialty. The cadets coming in from civilian life who left the program would be committed to a two year tour in the enlisted ranks, unless they could be shifted from pilot training to navigator training.

The upperclassman who met me at check-in was a little too pleased with himself when he exercised his privilege of removing my sergeants stripes and stripping me of my rank. He probably had little or no prior military service except his first six weeks in the cadet corps. Most cadets came straight from civilian life. Now he had someone he could be superior to and intimidate, so he chose me to pick on for the remainder of his time in preflight. He was diligent in his quest, but I never let him get me flustered. We did not know it at the time, but we would meet again in a different setting.

Military training and discipline was far more strict than airman basic had been, but I soon figured out that the fast paced, demanding routine was designed to frustrate us, wear us down and make us quit. The military drill was excessive in view of the extremely hot weather. I was already trained in that, but the cadet corps made it the centerpiece of the whole program. Hazing by the upper class was a popular sport.

We were graded on everything. There was academics, drill and ceremony, personal inspections and quarters inspections. Even peer evaluations. Any infraction of rules or procedures got us a gig or demerit. Some gigs were because of actual errors. Others were fabricated to make sure everyone got some. If we got over the weekly limit, we walked an hour for each one on the tour path on Saturday and Sunday afternoon under the supervision of an upper classman. There were sixty five cadets in my class.

I decided early on that I would get through this one day at a time and no one could make me quit. I said to myself every day, "this too will end", and at the end of six weeks the upper class departed and we became the upper class. There was a rank system within the corps and to my surprise I was made wing exec. The only cadet who outranked me in the entire wing was the cadet wing commander.

Each squadron had a couple of commissioned officers, called "Tactical Officers". Their job was to make life difficult for cadets. We stayed away from them as much as possible, because any contact, accidentally or on purpose usually led to trouble for us.

———

I was being physically worn down more than I realized. We were not being properly hydrated in the heat, and were not eating enough in the mess hall. There was no opportunity to eat elsewhere. The upper-class harassed us so much during meal time, we could eat very little before the ranking cadet at the head of the table was ready to go and when he left, we had to leave with him and be marched back to quarters. Then, one afternoon we were marched off to the medical clinic for a surprise flight physical. We had all passed extensive exams before arriving at preflight and did not expect another one so soon.

I went through the medical stations without any difficulty, then had to get in line for a weight check. When my turn came, I got on the scales and the medic with the clipboard said to me, "You are two pounds short. You are disqualified." I was stunned. Disqualified for being two pounds underweight? Outrageous! While I stood there, not wanting to believe what I was hearing, the medic said. "I have another group to weigh. If you will get in back of that line I will weigh you again." He didn't have to tell me again. He was giving me a chance to qualify. I raced down the hall and found a water cooler. When I sloshed back up there and got on the scales, I had a pound to spare.

After that I started eating all the bananas I could get my hands on. At the mess hall, there was fruit we could pick up on the way out. We were paying extra for it and it was the only food we could take back to quarters, but I didn't get weighed anymore at Lackland. Strangely enough, each month we were given fifty dollars for food allowance, but had to give back sixty dollars.

Once each month, we received our money at the first table in a long line of tables. At each following table, we gave back part the money. Extra money for fruit in the mess hall, club dues, which we could not visit until our last few weeks, laundry, special assessments of various kinds, usually some charity or savings bonds that someone in the command structure was trying to make points with. After leaving the last table, we had little left.

Mary Katherine was faithful to write just about every day. With my limited spare time, I wrote back perhaps weekly. In those days, people did not communicate by long distance phone except for extremely important or emergency reasons. E-mail had not been invented.

By mid November 1953, we completed preflight and eagerly awaited our assignments to primary flight training. I did not like Texas at this point and hoped for a base back east, but I was ordered to Hondo, Texas, forty miles down highway ninety, toward Mexico.

Hondo

We arrived at Hondo and found a slightly less strict atmosphere for cadets than we had experienced so far. The upper class was busy with flying and academics and did not have a lot of time to harass us.

On the way in, it was impossible to miss the huge sign along side the road. It said:

This is God's country
Don't drive through it like Hell
Hondo Texas

The Air Force had a cheap method of quickly separating the sheep from the goats. Our first twenty hours of flight were in the Piper Super Cub. There was no electrical system except for a starter. No radio or interphone. The instructor sat in the back seat and yelled to the student, or rapped his knees with the control stick. The Pipers flew off a separate runway from the larger, more powerful North American T-6s and were controlled by light gun.

The majority of our class had made it through preflight. Some had not been able to handle the stress and self eliminated. A few had been lost to other various reasons. Only a few of us had any difficulty with the Super Cub. Some could not overcome airsickness. A few could not handle the aircraft to the instructors satisfaction. Hondo was operated under civilian contract for flight instructors and maintenance, but there were military check pilots for periodic check flights to make sure we met all the standards.

We had academics for half day and went to the flight line for half day. In the evenings we studied, did military training, and tried to get a little rest before morning reveille at 5:30. We had classes in meteorology, engineering, navigation, communications, aerodynamics and a few other things. I did OK on most subjects, but was slow on navigation problems. All the math had to be done manually or with a circular slide rule. Electronic computers had not yet arrived. The trouble with navigation problems was that they covered a complete trip. If we made an error early on, that error was carried all the way throughout the entire sequence. Therefore, we could fail an exam because of one mistake.

When we soloed, we were given the traditional treatment of being thrown bodily into the nearest water. If no swimming pool was handy, a large mud puddle would suffice. Although I had soloed earlier as a civilian, and had my shirt tail cut off, I was happy to be qualified for the initiation. We had reached another milestone on our way to being military pilots.

————

Flying training got considerably more interesting when we graduated from the Super Cub to the North American T-6. Designed originally as an advanced trainer, then later as a basic trainer, we were using it as a primary trainer. The "Yellow Monster" was a six thousand pound, 600 horsepower, fire snorting monster with a built in ground loop. It was a good trainer in that it made us work hard to master control of it. Most people will tell you, if they have any experience with that bird, that if you could fly the T-6 well, you could fly anything.

On the ground, like most of the aircraft of it's period, the T-6 nose pointed upward at a steep angle with the tail resting on it's wheel. We would not be introduced to nose wheel aircraft until later. The long nose and the large radial engine blocked most of our forward vision. When moving on the ground, we had to continually "S" turn in order to see what was ahead. The steerable tail wheel was coupled to the rudder pedals if the control stick was held to the rear position.

If the control stick was positioned forward, the tail wheel was released from the rudder control and the wheel went into free swivel mode. A blast of power, producing strong prop wash on the rudder, or differential braking would allow a turn of very short radius. Such turns were usually made when parking in close places, but should not be attempted by a novice, because over control was a strong probability.

When lining up for takeoff, the throttle was advanced slowly, because the powerful engine with it's attendant torque and P factor had to be reckoned with. Right rudder trim and a fair amount of right rudder pressure had to be applied to keep the bird from turning to the left.

For those who don't know what P factor is, the air being pushed toward the rear of the aircraft by the prop, does not travel in a straight line. It swirls around the aircraft in it's rearward travel and by the time it reaches the rudder area, the air impinges on vertical stabilizer from an angle that tends to turn the aircraft. Jet powered aircraft don't have that problem.

That 1340 cubic inch Pratt and Whitney, nine cylinder radial engine belted out a healthy, throaty roar and inspired confidence. The worst thing I had happen to me throughout primary was a generator failure. The battery went down and the radio died before I could land, but that was no big deal. My instructor did experience a total engine failure with another student, but they landed safely in a plowed field.

The T-6 was the only airplane I ever flew that could do a true slow roll. Most aircraft do not have enough rudder. For a slow roll to be done correctly, the nose must be held on a point as the airplane is rotated through 360 degrees around the longitudinal axis. When the roll reached the ninety degree point, the wings were producing no lift and the nose was held on the point with up rudder, requiring full deflection. As the roll progressed to the inverted 180 degree point, the engine died from fuel starvation, because the fuel system did not use a pressure carburetor. That was a bit disconcerting. Forward stick pressure was applied to keep the nose up, and the negative G force made it difficult to keep feet on the rudder pedals. As the roll continued to the 270 degree point, now opposite full up rudder had to be applied and the engine came alive again. Stick and rudder pressures were constantly changing throughout the maneuver.

In normal, level flight, the bird required constant attention and as I recall, had no aileron trim. If there was a fuel unbalance in the wing tanks, constant stick pressure had to be applied to keep it level. Landings required very precise control to assure a smooth touchdown. Most landings were made three point. That meant setting it up to stall just as it touched on all three wheels. Wheel landings, touching down on the main gear initially, required more skill and very precise control with a slight power on approach for a flatter angle.

We learned basic maneuvers, emergency procedures, and of course landings, and a few aerobatics. The instructor was always in the back seat coaching, criticizing or demonstrating new procedures. It seemed that we never did anything to the complete satisfaction of the instructors. Any compliment was rare indeed.

There was so much air traffic at Hondo, we did most of our pattern and landing practice at auxiliary fields. After about ten hours in the bird, we were practicing landings at Rector Auxiliary. Rector was a dirt strip and the outline was marked with old tires painted white, but with age they had taken on the color of dirt and were hard to see. It was a hot afternoon and the red dust being raised by a dozen airplanes making touch and go landings, resulted in very poor visibility. In the pattern, we flew with the canopy open and the dust got into our eyes, ears, mouth and sweaty clothes. The noise, heat, dust, smoke and fuel fumes, combined with the stress of trying to cope with a snarling, unforgiving, 6000 pound monster separated the men from the boys.

My instructor, Mr. Bowles was unusually difficult to please. The back seat was a constant source of harsh criticism and evidently I had not done anything right since we strapped in. I was hot, tired, frustrated and felt that Mr. Bowles was being unreasonable. I had decided that there was no way to avoid a failing grade for the day and had enough. So I keyed the interphone, and said, "Sir, if you have made up your mind to give me a pink slip today, I am going to make this one a full stop and get out." He simply said, "OK, make it a full stop and pull over to the side." I realized that I might have just eliminated myself from pilot training, but he had me so angry, it didn't matter.

There was no more noise from the back seat and I made a respectable landing and pulled over to the side. Then Mr. Bowles said, "Don't shut it down and stay put." He got out, stowed his chute, straps, radio cords etc. and leaned over into the front cockpit. "I am getting out. Go make some touch and go landings by yourself. I was deliberately trying to agitate you into screwing up, especially trying to get you to forget to put down the landing gear. Go out there and make me four or five nice landings. I will be on the radio in the mobile unit if you need help."

I did as he told me and the heat, dust, smoke and fumes did not bother me a bit. I was flying the yellow monster alone. As I taxied back in, Mr. Bowles met me and said, "Don't shut it down. I have to take the mobile unit back to Hondo. You take the bird back solo. I will see you at the flight shack." by the time I got back to quarters that night, my hat size had probably increased a couple of sizes.

———

There was no let up in the intensity of the training in academics or flying. We were introduced to instrument flying, maintaining attitude and position entirely by reference to the instruments on the panel in front of us. It required intense concentration and a rapid cross check of all the gauges. Now the instructor was in the front seat as safety pilot and the student was in the back seat with a hood preventing any view outside the aircraft.

After an hour or so of practicing instrument flight, Mr. Bowles would let me pop the hood and do some aerobatics. That was more my style. I never had any difficulty with aileron rolls, barrel rolls, snap rolls, slow rolls, loops, immelmans, cuban eights, spins, clover leafs et ceteras. The G forces did not bother me and I had no problem staying oriented, whatever the maneuver. Instrument flying was the thing about flying that I liked least, but it had to be mastered. The Air Force was intent on turning out pilots better qualified for bad weather flying than in the past.

The upper class had warned us about the military check pilots. They were bad. We would get two flight checks by them. A transition phase check, and later an instrument check ride. They were prone to trick a student into doing something that would cause him to fail the ride. If a check ride was failed, there would be a recheck by another pilot, but the prejudice was there, and few recheck students survived the program. Eventually my turn came for the transition phase check ride with a stern, gruff, lieutenant. He made it plain that he didn't have much time for students.

After the customary walk around inspection and cockpit checks, we took off with the examiner in the back seat of the T-6. Everything went smoothly, with me following his directions to climb out and head to a particular area on the map. According to his instructions, I had leveled off at 3,000 feet and felt I was doing fine. Then he keyed the interphone and says, "Do me a two turn spin." I said, "Sir, we are prohibited from entering practice spins below 5,000 feet." So the gruff reply was, "Well, climb to 5,000 feet and do me a spin."

If I had set up flight to enter the spin at 3,000 feet even at his direction, he would have taken the controls, returned to Hondo and handed me a pink slip.

I set up the engine controls for climb power and started the climb. The old Pratt & Whitney was hammering away, with airspeed not much above stall, with prop torque and P-factor working on the airplane, it would not have required much left rudder deflection to put us into a spin. I felt pressure being slowly, and progressively applied to the left rudder pedal. I keyed the interphone and asked, "Sir, are you on the rudder pedals?" There was no reply, but I felt the pedal pressure immediately return to normal. If I had sat there, not really feeling the bird, he would have put us into a spin and promptly failed me on the ride.

The remainder of the flight went OK and I felt pretty good about it. My simulated forced landing, my aerobatics, and traffic patterns went OK. We landed and I had some difficulty parking where the check pilot directed me to park, but that was because the markings had been covered with oil drippings. After my second attempt, he was still not satisfied and told me to shut it down where it was because I probably wasn't ever going to get it right. On the way back to our flight shack, I worried over whether he would pass me.

When I returned to the flight shack, Mr. Farmer, our flight commander met me. He said, "you didn't know it, but I was watching from the control tower. If that s.o.b. fails you over the parking problem, I will intervene." A few days later we got my grade from the check ride. It was good!

Night flight was the next challenge, and it was exciting to me. After a blindfold cockpit check and one dual night orientation flight, we went solo, which bolstered our self confidence considerably. Depth perception was poor at night and we learned new techniques for approach and landing. It was very easy to misjudge and flare too early or too late. Most of us did OK with it and moved on to the navigation flights. First dual and then solo, day and then night. There was something special about sitting there with that healthy sounding, nine cylinder engine, spitting out a continuous stream of blue and yellow flame from the short exhaust port.

———

I reckon I just had a good day when the time came for my military instrument check ride. I had been more concerned about that than I had been concerned about the transition check, but it went smoothly. We had figured out that the check pilots were a little lazy, and if we did really well early in the flight, they would abbreviate the rest of the patterns and maneuvers. If the flight was prolonged, we knew they were evaluating our performance more closely. My instrument check was surprisingly short but I knew I had not loused up anything. As soon as I began a particular pattern, I would be told to discontinue it and begin the next one in the series. When the grade came down from above, it was good.

The upper class moved on to their respective bases for their basic pilot training and we became the upper class. My cadet rank was group commander. Our two squadrons did not comprise a wing, so we were a group.

There was nothing of interest in Hondo, so when we had an opportunity to leave the base, we went to San Antonio and began to learn about some of the city's finer points. Actually, we spent very little time off base. All of us were very busy and as group commander, I had other responsibilities that left me very little free time.

My final check ride in the T-6 went OK and everyone in the class had completed about a hundred twenty hours in the terrible half dozen. We had flown patrols over most of the mesquite in the area, done our aerobatics, navigation, hooded instrument flight and a little unauthorized formation. Apparently we had reached the point where we had pretty well tamed the monster and there was not a lot more the instructors could teach us.

In June, 1954, a parade, followed by a ceremony in the base theater marked the end of our primary flight training. I was presented with a certificate which stated that I had attained the highest grade of all the cadets in the class. Officially, it didn't mean much, but it was a good morale builder.

At that point, we could make a request for single engine or multi-engine basic pilot training. Our choice would not be guaranteed, but would be considered. Up until that time, I had pondered what my choice should be. There were pros and cons. After discussing it with Mr. Bowles, I made a decision. He told me that I was too much at ease in aerobatics to pass up a shot at fighters, so I requested single engine training.

I was beginning to dare to believe that my dreams could become a reality and I had a good chance of becoming an Air Force fighter pilot, but there was still a long way to go. There was still a lot of work ahead, and we knew that pilot production quotas were being reduced. We could be eliminated from the program for many reasons, or no reason at all. For the next six months, my performance would be evaluated more critically than ever before.

I also told myself that the odds of my getting out of Texas were pretty good, but the administrative gods thought differently. My assignment for basic pilot training was Laredo, Texas, way down on the Rio Grande. The good news was that the mission of the base was Basic Pilot Training, Single Engine, Jet.

Laredo

It has been said that the military had a general whose job was to survey the country and pick out the most godforsaken places at which to locate bases. He did his job well. Getting a military base established at Laredo must have been one of his most outstanding accomplishments. It was isolated and stifling hot.

The base was a few miles north of the town. To the north, east, and south, there was nothing but mesquite and tumbleweed for a hundred fifty miles or more. To the west, was the Rio Grande, but it didn't have much water in it. On the far side was Nuevo Laredo, the Mexican version. There was nothing in town to interest us. The nearest place to go for enjoying a weekend pass was San Antonio, a hundred fifty miles to the north.

No time was wasted in getting us into the swing of things. Once again, we were the lower class. The upper class was strict, but we had limited contact with them, because they were busy trying to keep up with the program. They held Saturday morning inspections and gave us a hard time, but otherwise, we did not see them a lot.

The commissioned tactical officers went to extremes to find something to gig us for. There was no good reason for us to go through our hang-up clothes every night. We knew they were hung properly and buttoned with nothing in the pockets. Frequently a tac officer would come by, always while we were out, and unbutton something. The next day, he would return, and if the garment was still unbuttoned, he would write up a gig slip. Even more ridiculously, he might place an object in a jacket pocket and come back the next day to see if it was still there.

Bedding not made to their satisfaction would be ripped apart and thrown on the floor. Sometimes they just randomly tore up beds anyway. In the squadron area, we kept a sharp eye out for them and avoided them as much as possible. A shave was never close enough. Shoes were never shined good enough. Three day old haircuts were often unsatisfactory. When we mopped our room floor, we had to back out, mopping as we went, so as not to leave any detectable footprints.

On arrival at the flight line each day, we were always met by an instructor, usually the assistant flight commander, for the required inspection. They knew we led a hard life and their inspection was only a token ritual. Sometimes they even kidded around with us. They never gave us a hard time about appearance unless someone was badly out of line. They were there to teach us to fly. We were getting enough military training elsewhere.

My instructor, Lt. Smith was basically an easy going, low key type, who tried to put us at ease and minimize the tension, in order to maximize the learning process. However, he did not put up with any foolishness or laxness in our effort to learn about flying.

It was extremely rare for a flight instructor to pull a gig slip. They had their own system for keeping us on our toes. It was called the boner system. If we messed up, after being told too many times how to do something, we were charged boners. In our flight, a boner cost ten cents. A mild goof might cost ten boners, and a major one might go as high as a hundred boners. That was a lot of money for a guy making $105 per month, before deductions. The money was kept until the end of the program and then used to finance a big party. The heavy drinkers levied heavy fines.

Right away, we were introduced to the North American T-28 basic trainer. It was a stubby tandem cockpit airplane with tricycle landing gear. That was our first encounter with a nose wheel, and were about to discover how much easier the ground handling and landings would be. The Air Force version was powered with a 1100 cubic inch, Wright seven cylinder radial engine, rated at 800 horsepower. That was 240 cubic inches less than the Pratt & Whitney in the T-6, but it developed two hundred more horsepower.

The T-28 was easy to fly. It handled well on the ground and in the air. We had to be very careful to make prompt changes to cowl flap and oil cooler flap settings when making power changes. The seven cylinder hotrod engine would heat up or cool down very quickly, so we had to watch cylinder head temp and oil temp very closely. If too hot, engine damage could occur quickly. If too cool, it would balk on a throttle advance when power was needed. Not a good situation when you are too low on final approach.

The engine had a very distinctive sound. Three cylinders exhausted out one side and four cylinders on the other. At idle speeds, it made a kapokita, kapokita sound much like a John Deere tractor. It was not as reliable as the Pratt & Whitney had been, but I only experienced difficulty with it on one occasion.

On a warm afternoon, but in fairly smooth air, I was in the back seat under the hood practicing basic instrument flying and Lt. Smith was in the front. It was one of those rare flights when everything was going smoothly and there was not even any remarks coming from the front cockpit. The engine was droning steadily on and all the engine instruments were in the green, the fuel tanks were near full and then, instant silence. There was no sound except the slipstream. The prop was windmilling, the manifold pressure was reading ambient and the tachometer read only the windmill RPM. The engine was dead!

If Smith had been dozing, he was now instantly awake. He was asking, "What did you do?" Practice forced landings usually came without warning, but I had never had the instructor cut the engine while I was under the hood. And when they did have us do one, they only retarded the power to idle. They did not cut the power completely. I said, "Nothing, what did YOU do?" Nobody had bumped the magneto switches or mixture control. Fuel tank selection was good.

I had popped the hood open and was partly scanning the instrument panel for a clue to the problem, and partly looking outside to see what kind of terrain we were over. There was mesquite, rocks and cactus as far as I could see, and the engine would not restart after switching mags and tanks. Smith said, "There is no satisfactory place in sight to land this thing, so I reckon we might as well get ready to bail out." When the engine had died, we had been at about eight thousand feet.

Now, we were gliding and losing over a thousand feet per minute. There was not much time to debate, so we began stowing loose items and zipping up open pockets. Then, just as suddenly as it had died, the engine roared to life and resumed it's steady drone as if nothing had ever happened. Smith took control and made a bee line for Laredo, but the mechanics could find nothing wrong with the engine.

Instrument flight in the T-28 was difficult for me. I never knew why, but I had to really work hard and concentrate to cut it on the gauges. The only pink slip I ever got was on a hooded instrument flight, but that was partly because that ride was with a substitute instructor and he was deliberately impossible to satisfy. Formation flight was hard work, but I did well at it. We did about fifty hours of normal flight, aerobatics, navigation, night navigation, formation and instruments. Then we moved on to the "stove pipe".

––––––––

For my first ride in the Lockheed T-33, two seat, tandem jet trainer, we took off for a demo ride with Smith flying from the back seat, which is difficult for the instructor, and climbed out to forty thousand feet. This "dollar ride" would be the last flight for a long time, during which I would not be working hard. That was higher than I had ever been. We previously had not worked much above 10,000 feet in the recips. Of course, the turbine powered birds really hit their stride at altitudes above 20,000 feet. Everything happened much, much faster than in the prop powered aircraft. This was a different breed of bird.

Up until this point, while flying, our headgear had consisted of a baseball cap and headsets with a boom mike. Now we had to use a hard hat with oxygen mask attached and containing a built in microphone. Our hands were often too busy to bother with a mike switch, so we had a hot interphone system. Conversation between occupants was carried on without any switches being activated. Hearing our own breathing as well as that of the person in the other seat was something to get used to. The radio transmitter was activated by a thumb switch on the throttle handle, which did not require removing the hand.

Although the cockpit was pressurized to some extent, we still needed oxygen at most operational altitudes, and wore the masks from the ground up. They were cumbersome and also required some getting used to. The hoses and radio cords were a necessary annoyance. At some of the higher operating altitudes, the cockpit might be pressurized to an equivalent of 20,000 feet, which was a help, but additional oh-two was required. Anytime we wanted pure oxygen, we could select 100 percent and override the automatic regulator.

After the dollar ride, things rapidly got more serious. We were expected to catch on quickly. Anyone who could not keep up the pace would be eliminated. The academics were increasingly difficult and the flying training more demanding. After having a maneuver demonstrated once, we were expected to do a reasonable job of duplicating it. The academic courses with more engineering, advanced navigation, meteorology, physiological training were tough. The most difficult for me was nuclear weapons. That was because most of it was classified and we could not have any study material or even take any notes. We just had to remember what we were told and shown and then pass exams on it.

Smith flew with me for three rides of about an hour and twenty minutes each. The birds were fueled for flights of about that duration. Except for long navigation flights, we rarely used full tip tank fuel. Many maneuvers were restricted to lighter fuel loads. Rolling high G maneuvers were not permitted with full tip tanks.

With three dual instructional rides under my belt on traffic patterns, landings, some aerobatics and emergency procedures, Smith sent me out to solo. He was in the mobile control unit out by the runway to observe and to render any assistance needed on the radio.

As I became airborne, and the end of the runway went out of sight under the nose, I became fully aware that there was no one in the back seat. I was alone in a high wing-loaded, fifteen thousand pound, unforgiving bird. I would have to do everything right. There was no instructor back there to salvage my mistakes.

The controls were extremely light and sensitive. The elevator was inherently light and responsive. The ailerons had a fifteen to one hydraulic boost, making them very sensitive to stick pressure changes. A flick of the wrist would produce a roll. For most normal control inputs, there was no perceptible movement, just pressure changes. Even at normal speeds, in turns, high G forces were generated and we learned to deal with that now. Previously, in the recips, we had encountered high G forces during aerobatics, but now, in the high performance jet, it was the norm, even in the traffic pattern.

There were a lot of jokes about our first rides, with the instructors demonstrating the 360 degree overhead traffic patterns, requiring a tight turn, called the "pitchout". The standard comment from the student was, "well sir, I was blacked out and didn't see anything until we were on final approach." Unless a cadet was in excellent physical condition, that statement might not be far from the truth.

The fuel system was rather complex and required switching boost pumps on or off to various cell groups to keep fuel going to the engine and to avoid weight and balance problems. A full fuel load amounted to over five thousand pounds. The only fuel gauge was for the ninety five gallon fuselage tank, serving as a buffer tank, through which all fuel had to pass on its way to the engine. We had to keep track of which cells had been emptied and which ones still contained fuel. There was a mechanical counter that had to be set to show the combined amount of fuel in all the tanks. Then it counted backwards as fuel was burned off. It could not show fuel loss by any other means and was not much relied upon.

Fuel consumption rates were incredible compared to the recips and we had to make that a major consideration in flight planning and execution. The only way we knew a cell was empty was when a low pressure light came on or the fuselage tank gauge started decreasing. The tip tanks were pressurized from engine compressor bleed air. If one or both stopped feeding, a wing tank boost pump failed, or something went wrong with the sequence, it was somewhere between difficult and impossible to know how much available fuel was remaining.

The tip tanks could be jettisoned and sometimes that became necessary if one fed out and the other one failed to do so. An extra fifteen hundred pounds out on a wing tip was more than we could compensate for at landing speeds. There were times when both tip tanks failed to feed. An experienced pilot might justify landing with full tanks, but that was not something recommended for a novice pilot.

Fuel was burned so rapidly, changing the weight of the bird, we had to recalculate the pattern speeds each time around. Speed for pattern entry, downwind leg, base leg, final turn, final approach had to be precise. If we were too slow, a stall could result, from which there would not be sufficient altitude to recover. If too fast, we could overshoot the touchdown spot and be unable to stop on the remaining runway.

Getting the power setting, approach angle, airspeed, lateral alignment right all at the same time required a fair amount skill and there was little time to do it. Typical speed over the fence with basic fuel weight was 120 knots (138 mph). With landing gear, full flaps and speed brakes out, the final approach was flown with a fair amount of power on to maintain proper speed and approach angle.

I was blessed by not having any serious problems with landing techniques with any aircraft that I ever flew, although none of my instructors ever did a good job of making the connection between practice stalls and touchdown. Early on, I had figured out that a landing was merely a stall maneuver, timing the stall to occur just as the wheels touched. The principle holds true whether the flying machine is a light plane or a heavy, high wing-loaded fighter.

The turbojet had fewer engine controls than a recip engine. The turbojet had no prop pitch control, no mixture control, just a handle for the throttle, but things happened fast and we were busy. Engine acceleration was slow, so power needs had to be anticipated. Our hands were so busy, it was a blessing to have the speed brake switch and microphone button built into the throttle handle.

The flap switch was alongside the throttle and could be operated with little movement of the left hand. The landing gear handle was more awkward, being on the left side, near the floor, between the seat and the oxygen regular control. Many skinned knuckles resulted from that arrangement.

I managed to make the three or four required landings without any major difficulty and trundled back to the ramp. I was now a jet pilot. Nowadays that doesn't mean much to most people, but back then, there were not many of us and we felt pretty good about it.

The flight training continued, with aerobatics, instrument flying, navigation, and close formation. From time to time we were scheduled for solo flights and were supposed to practice what we had learned so far and increase our proficiency. After having such an easy time of it in formation flying with the T-28, I was in for a surprise when we started formation work in the jet.

————

Lt. Smith teamed up with another instructor and his student to demonstrate a wing take-off. It was a little hairy, steering a 15,000 pound tricycle with the feet, at 120 knots, six feet from another machine on a long roll. After the climb out, we broke off to get some spacing while the other bird went into an easy turn, giving us an opportunity to cut him off and close for a practice rejoin.

I was at the controls, and everything was looking fine to me, closing nicely on the leader and Lt. Smith was saying, "watch that overtake." I backed off on the power a little but kept closing. With the T-28, we could close right up to the lead bird, cut the power and slide right into a good position on the leaders wing. Smith was getting louder with his advice to watch the closing speed. As we got fairly close and I started to back off more on the power to synchronize speed, the lead bird's size suddenly began growing very fast. Then I realized we were way too fast and even with the power all the way back to idle and the speed brakes out, we went flashing under the leader and proceeded with an embarrassing overshoot. It was established procedure for the bird overshooting to pass underneath so visual contact could be maintained.

On the next try, I realized we had to make a much more gradual join-up, and the last few feet had to be controlled very precisely. Much greater judgment was required than had been in the recip. Speed was higher but acceleration and deceleration in the turbojet was much slower.

Holding a position on another aircraft from only a few feet away requires a degree of concentration that most people will never experience. Eyes must be absolutely glued to the leader and his aircraft. If the leader banks, the wingman must bank, however slightly. If the leader climbs or descends, the wingman must do precisely the same. His hand never leaves the throttle except for a moment, putting the landing gear handle up or down. There is no power setting that will exactly hold position. Change is constant. The other hand is always on the stick, adjusting pressure and thumbing the trim button on top of the stick grip.

The "wing" position is normally maintained with about six feet lateral clearance on the leader and about three or four feet vertical clearance. In bad weather, or moonless nights, it may be necessary to hold an even closer position to avoid losing sight of the lead airplane.

The leader is also watched very carefully, for head nods and hand signals which are used to keep down radio chatter. The radio is used very little between flight leaders and other aircraft in a formation. For example, the leader can check fuel remaining by holding up his fist with thumb pointing toward the mask. The other people in the flight respond by holding up a number of fingers corresponding to the amount of fuel remaining in terms of hundreds of gallons or hundreds of pounds, depending on the type aircraft involved.

If weather conditions permit, the leader will normally signal for the wingman to loosen up his position to make needed cockpit checks. The most tiring work I have ever done was to fly close formation for prolonged times at night in bad weather.

––––––––

The number of cadets in the program was dwindling. We had lost some in Preflight, some in Primary for various reasons. We had accidents in primary, but no loss of life. Now the aircraft were faster, heavier, and less tolerant of mistakes. We lost some aircraft and some people. My room mate washed out due to flying deficiency. The instructors were very stingy with grades.

Mary K and I had continued corresponding and making plans for marriage. Our only personal contact over the past several months had been during a leave between primary and basic. Part of our training was an overnight navigational proficiency flight with an instructor near the end of basic. When my turn came to make that flight, my regular instructor was not available and I was paired with one from a different flight.

Our overnight trip was scheduled to include some formation practice as well as navigation and strange field landings. The other aircraft was manned by another instructor and student from our unit. The instructors did not want to remain overnight at McGhee-Tyson airport where I could have had at least a short visit with my fiancee'. They wanted to do the turnaround at Maxwell AFB, Montgomery Alabama. That was fine with the other stud, because his parents and fiancee lived nearby. I led the flight to Maxwell, with Bill Berdeaux, the other stud, on our wing and the instructors in the back seat.

Next day, on departure from Maxwell, with a planned dogleg by way of Tinker AFB, Oklahoma City, the other bird was the leader, so I would get some practice flying the wing position. During the entire trip so far, I had been feeling that my instructor was not very sharp and was perhaps too easy to please. He had allowed me to do everything related with the flight, with no comment or advice. It was rare to fly that much with an instructor and hear no advice or criticism from the other seat. Take-off was around mid day and conditions were typical of hot, humid, South Alabama. The air density was low, the aircraft were at max gross weight, having been fueled for a long cross country flight. The two 230 gallon tip tanks contained three thousand pounds of fuel in addition to the ton of internal fuel.

As expected, we had a long take-off roll and as we coaxed the birds reluctantly into the air, I could tell that my engine was not performing as well as the leader. Nothing to worry about, it happened all the time. Variations in performance were commonplace. It is a normal matter of pride for the wing-man to be reluctant to ask the leader for a power reduction, especially when he thinks he might be able to catch up after getting the wheels and flaps up.

Anyway, we got the wheels up and were struggling to accelerate to 140 knots for flaps up in the hot, low density air. I could not safely look at our airspeed and maintain position on the leader. My cue to retract flaps would be a signal from the leader, which had not yet been given. We were probably indicating no more than 130 knots and falling behind, when our bird shuddered with that sickening wing drop and nose drop that accompanies a stall. I instinctively shoved the stick forward to lower the nose and regain flying speed and rechecked the throttle at full power. We were only a few feet above terra firma, staggering along, barely recovering from the stall. I looked at the flap position indicator and it was just arriving at the full "UP" position.

I knew then that the dummy in the back seat has raised the flaps prematurely. No matter who occupies which seat, NO ONE EVER activates a control without advising the pilot in control. I asked him, "What are you doing ?" He replied, "Just trying to help you catch up with the leader." I was livid. I keyed the radio to ask Bill to back off on his power a percent or two and roll into a turn until I could rejoin. My "instructor" had just come very close to getting us splattered all over the Alabama countryside.

———

As we were getting near the end of basic, Mary Katherine made plans to take a train to Laredo, so we could finalize our wedding plans. Later, her parents and sister Shirley would drive from Alcoa, near Knoxville and my parents would ride with them. We cadets were still working hard in the training program and being very careful not to do anything that would jeopardize our successful completion. We had worked too hard and too long to blow it now.

We were now upper class again. Most of us had cadet officer jobs that mostly involved working with the lower class. I was cadet squadron commander, but fortunately that did not require a lot of my time, and I did not feel like going around looking for trouble.

————

Late one afternoon, I was scheduled for a hooded instrument flight with Lt. Smith in the front seat of the T-bird. It had been a typical long day of academics, physical training, and a previous flight. After more than an hour of concentration and hard work, I was glad when Smith told me to pop the hood and relax while he took control to head back to the airpatch. I was slouched down in the back seat, glad that the work day was coming to an end. We had been in bright sunlight, but now the sun was going down and almost out of sight. Not much light was left and it was getting darker by the minute. For a few minutes everything was quiet except for the muted sound of the engine, the engine driven accessories, and the air going by at 300 knots.

Then Smith, with a tinge of apprehension in his voice, says," Mr. Wade, I am losing my vision." I thought he was kidding. Soon he said, "I'm serious, I can't see much, do you think you can land this thing from the back seat?" I could tell he was serious. We had not been taught back seat landings. There had not been any requirement for it. From the rear seat, forward vision is non existent in a T-bird. The front seat back blocks the view straight ahead and without some training and practice, most pilots simply cannot make a safe landing from back there. By now the sun was down and we were definitely in the twilight, with full darkness rapidly approaching.

I put my hard hat firmly against the right side of the canopy and strained to get some forward vision. At that moment Smith turned his head to the right and I could see a little of his profile. I said, "Sir, have you tried raising your sun visor?" He barked the curt reply. "Mr. Wade, if anyone hears about this, it will cost you one hundred boners."

————

We were beginning to wonder and speculate about what our operational assignments might be. The F-86 Sabre was the premier fighter and any of us would be proud to go that route. Of course, there were others, like the F-84 Thunderstreak, but normally called the Hog because it was reluctant to part company with the ground and become airborne. The F-80 was still common in operational units, but was giving way to newer machinery. The F-100 was coming on line.

I personally had long admired the P-51 Mustang. Debate over whether it or some other fighter was the best of the WWII era will probably never end, but there was no doubt in my mind. Anyone who has ever heard the sound of a Rolls Royce Merlin V-12 and was not moved by it, has no soul. As it turned out, the only member of our class who did get to fly a Mustang was Bill Berdeaux, when he returned to his unit, in the Alabama Air National Guard. Bill later flew F-84 and F-4 types.

With final flight checks and academic exams behind us, we could see some light at the end of the tunnel. The instructors mellowed a little and concentrated mostly on teaching us the finer points of flying and allowing us a few solo rides to sharpen our skills.

Mary Katherine's train was scheduled to arrive on the afternoon of one of my last solo flights. There was no way I could change my schedule to meet her. Someone needed to do that, with her being more than a thousand miles from home, in a strange place where she knew no one except me. I had a friend meet her at the train station.

In the meantime, I could do pretty much what I wanted to do on the solo flight, so I headed north, following the railroad tracks between San Antonio to Laredo. The train was on time and I easily got a visual on it. At altitudes as low as I dared, I flew alongside the train and put on a pretty good aerobatics show. I didn't know if anyone noticed. I later learned that MK had not noticed.

———————

On the appointed morning, November fifteenth, 1954, we stood proudly with the officials by the reviewing stand while all the other troops on the base paraded by to the music of the base band and the roar of sixteen T-33 aircraft passing overhead, four flights of four, in diamond formation. Sixteen cadets of our original sixty five, had survived the program. We were filled with a mixture of relief and pride.

Our morale was further boosted by the arrival of several T-6 aircraft, arriving in formation, from Hondo, piloted by our former instructors who had come to attend our graduation. We greatly appreciated their interest in us as products of their earlier efforts.

From there we assembled at the base theater, and after a speech by a visiting officer, the wing commander presented our diplomas, declaring that we were now officially second lieutenants and USAF fighter pilots. We were also given a pair of silver wings, sometimes referred to by the more irreverent guys as "leg spreaders".

Immediately, following the ceremony, my mom pinned on my gold lieutenants bars and Mary Katherine pinned on my wings, making my shoulders and chest feel conspicuously heavy. We were at the bottom rung of the ladder, commissioned rank wise, but we had made it to the ladder. Some would say I had finally become a gentleman, but it had required an act of congress.

The same afternoon, we gathered at the base chapel for our wedding ceremony. It was a full and memorable day. Later in the day, a class mate and bride used the chapel for their wedding and shared the cost of the flowers. Money was in short supply and using the same flowers was a practical thing to do.

Our parents started their trip home the next day and Mary Katherine and I started our journey to my assignment for advanced training by way of San Antonio. A couple of days there would have to pass for a honeymoon. After Lackland, Hondo, and Laredo, I had guessed the odds my of remaining in Texas were slim to none, but I had guessed wrong again. The orders in my pocket were for advanced pilot training at Perrin AFB, Sherman, Texas.

Advanced Flight Training

Kathy and I drove on up to Perrin AFB in the newly acquired Ford, financed by an accommodating San Antonio bank. We found an apartment we could almost afford and I entered the Instrument Pilot Training Course, Jet, along with several other class mates. We all had instrument ratings, certified by the issuance of a white card. There was a higher rating, indicated by a green card. The green card required considerable experience including at least one hundred hours of instrument flight in actual weather. Hooded instrument time did not count toward that rating.

The class at Perrin included pilots from various sources. Newly rated pilots like ourselves, older, more experienced ones sharpening their skills, and foreign exchange students. The Air Force wanted the overall ability of it's pilots to be upgraded. Aircraft were becoming more sophisticated, and operational missions were requiring more proficiency in bad weather flying.

For six weeks we flew in the back seat, with the instructor pilot in the front seat of a T-33. We had flown entirely by instruments, mostly under the hood, but now flew in actual weather when it was practical to do so. That included intentional thunderstorm penetrations. Since Perrin also operated an all-weather interceptor school, flying F-86D aircraft, we also flew target missions to support the interceptor phase of the school. Our piloting skills were considerably enhanced and we were eager to move on to our operational assignment.

I didn't go anywhere! I and some of my class mates were retained at Perrin to undergo yet another course of training – not progressing into the interceptor phase, but as instrument pilot instructors. For several more weeks, we practiced briefing each other on flight procedures and techniques under the supervision of a standardization instructor. We flew hooded and weather flights, with instructors or classmates, switching between roles as instructor and student. We flew the simulator under all types of weather conditions and practiced emergency procedures.

––––––––

On a day when the weather was really lousy, I was in the back seat practicing precision radar approaches with a standardization pilot in the front seat. We had been in solid clouds, making several approaches for touch and go landings. In spite of the lousy ceiling and visibility, the air was smooth and I was doing well and really not working too hard. Flying a box pattern for successive approaches, we were on the downwind leg, about to turn base leg for another approach. I had the bird nicely trimmed up and airspeed, altitude, heading were all good. We got the command to turn ninety degrees for the base leg. Just as I rolled into the normal bank angle for the level turn, the bird shuddered violently and the nose pitched down. Classic stall indication!

Fortunately we were about fifteen hundred feet above the ground, and by rapidly moving the stick forward and shoving the throttle to the stop, airspeed was increased and we were flying again without losing too much altitude. We were mystified as to why the stall had occurred with the correct airspeed for the gross weight and configuration of the bird, or so we thought.

Having been flying exclusively by reference to instruments, we had not bothered to look outside. The viz was bad and there was nothing to be seen past the wing tips. At this point, we did look outside and the problem was obvious. The wings were covered with ice. The super cooled moisture in the clouds had been collecting on the wings.

Lift was subnormal and there was a lot of extra weight, not accounted for in calculating airspeed. There was no way to determine how much weight. We simply added enough power and airspeed to make the aircraft seem to handle OK and made a full stop landing. That was a lesson I never unlearned. When flying in nasty weather, I visually checked for ice.

The Flight Instructor

We were eventually pronounced qualified to serve as instrument instructors and as transition instructors to check out people coming into the program who were not familiar with the T-33. Every student pilot had to be qualified for front seat solo flight because they were needed to help out with the target flights provided for the interceptor program. By this time, we probably had more specialized training in the T-bird than some of our newer instructors had in basic pilot training.

I was assigned to a flight commanded by Captain Kemp in the 3558th Combat Crew Training Squadron. All the other instructors were old hands at the game, but they treated me well and I am sure I was watched very closely, but it was not obvious. I was not intimidated, but I was very much aware that I was the new kid on the block with very limited experience.

Late one afternoon, after a normal full day, Kemp advised me that he and I would be working late. We strapped on a T-bird with me in the back seat and taking off just at sunset, we patrolled the Red River Valley until full dark and the fuel load was considerably lightened. Then we entered the traffic pattern and I made my first attempt at back seat landings. That is a different ball game from front seat landings. There is zero forward vision and slips are not recommended, especially with 230 gallon tip tanks.

I learned to look out the side, with limited vision and make an angling approach, so that some of the runway was in sight for most of the final approach. At some point, we had to get better aligned and once we were fully aligned with the runway, we couldn't see it. By using all our conscious senses, and maybe some we were not conscious of, we could make pretty decent touchdowns. We often had to do that in demonstrating landings to someone who had arrived in the program and was not checked out in the T-33.

After five good landings and using all our fuel, we quit for the night. Feeling pretty good about it, I asked Kemp if my work was satisfactory. He said, "Sure, but we'll do it again tomorrow night just to be certain you weren't having a lucky night. There won't be a daytime check out, because if you can do it at night, you can surely do it in daylight."

On one of my first flights as an instructor, we took off early one morning for a hooded instrument lesson with Lt. Hargo in the back seat. Hargo was one of the few black pilots I ever came across and he was an excellent pilot. I flew some formation missions with him on the wing and he could hold a position in any maneuver like he was welded there.

Because the weather was good and forecast to remain good for the morning, both training squadrons launched a maximum number of aircraft under visual flight rules. Take-off spacing was in seconds. That meant at the end of the period, approach and landing intervals would be in seconds. That was the norm, unless poor ceiling and visibility dictated instrument approaches and much greater spacing.

About the time we got leveled off around twenty thousand feet, clouds started forming rapidly. At first I figured we would work around or above them. We did not expect to need an IFR clearance. The clouds continued forming at a surprising rate and soon we could not work between them. We started climbing and could not get above them, even at better than 30 thousand. We could not climb much higher until we burned off some fuel. The clouds were getting higher and more dense by the second and I had taken control of the aircraft.

With all my instrument training, I was not alarmed over the conditions, but I knew we had too many birds in the air for control to handle on an IFR basis. I had no choice but to stay in the clouds and begin asking for an IFR clearance. We had leveled at an arbitrary altitude for the time being and were trying to get an assigned altitude. There was chaos on the radio channel. Many other pilots were caught in the same situation and were trying to get clearances. None of us knew exactly where anybody else was and at what altitude.

With so many aircraft in an area of a hundred miles or less, there was serious danger of collisions. The weather at Perrin had closed in with unusual suddenness, and there was no hope of a VFR recovery.

After several minutes and a lot of sweat, control gave us an altitude and advised we divert to Tinker AFB at Oklahoma City. Had I known earlier, we could have done that. Now we did not have sufficient fuel. I declined and asked for an approach time at Perrin. I was given a time well beyond what our fuel would allow so I screamed and begged for a an earlier approach time. Several other guys were doing the same thing. I am sure their seat cushions were being abused, as mine was.

Finally, someone got smart and took from us a list of everyone's remaining fuel. By that time, some of the birds with later take-off times and more fuel had diverted to bases outside the area. We could have made it to Dallas, Fort Worth, or Wichita Falls, but their weather was no better than Perrin. With the fuel list, they revised approaches times, giving the earliest time to the ones shortest on fuel. Approach Control was still saturated and could not give everyone a radar vectored penetration and approach, so they cleared us for a low frequency radio range approach to Perrin.

We had no modern VOR at the time. We were still using the old Adcock radio range which could be used with our automatic direction finder feature or we could fly the "on course" legs by listening to the "A" and "N" signals. In thunderstorm weather the system was not very useful.

We were in thunderclouds, with extreme turbulence, blinding lightning, deafening thunder, rain, hail, and with St. Elmo's fire streaking back over the canopy with it's eerie blue, green glow. The bird was pitching and rolling so badly I could not keep the wings anywhere near level. The altitude was varying up and down by three or four thousand feet. There was nothing I could do to hold assigned altitude with the attitude indicator showing two bar widths nose down and the vertical velocity indicator pegged on an up reading. A few seconds later the situation would be reversed.

I had Hargo get on the controls with me to help keep the bird somewhere near a level attitude. If he was scared, he never said anything. I was too busy to be scared. We were in the worst possible weather conditions to be depending on a low frequency radio facility for a navigation aid. I knew there was no use to even try the ADF. The lightning would have the needle pointing to everything except the station. So, I switched to the manual radio direction finding mode. That meant I would have to use a switch to rotate the loop antenna while listening for a null in the signal. That also kept me from using my right hand on the stick, because the loop left-right switch was on the right console.

I could hear the radio range station between static crashes and noise, and could narrow the bearing to about plus or minus ten degrees. Not good enough, but with the signal volume building I hoped that as we got closer the bearing would be more accurate. The static crashes got worse. The turbulence got worse, if that was possible, and I was beginning to wonder if we would be able to make any kind of a reasonable approach.

Then the signal was slowly fading. That meant we had passed the station and had not gotten an obvious fast fade overhead in the cone of silence. We had missed high station. We reversed course and tried again with the same result. At this time I told Perrin that our last resort was a radar vectored penetration. I had too little fuel for anything else. If we could not get a radar penetration or if our communications radio had failed, we would have no alternative to a nylon letdown.

To my great relief, I was given a heading with instructions to begin our let down. With the throttle back, fuel consumption was eased and I began to breathe a little easier, but we still had a ways to go. As we progressed in the penetration, the turbulence and lightning began to ease up and aircraft control was not so difficult. As we turned inbound, we were switched to the radio channel for a GCA with precision radar.

A few miles out from the runway, with gear and flaps down, on course, on glide slope and the low fuel warning light glaring at me, I starting checking ahead for a visual on the runway. At about a half mile out at about 150 feet, I began to get glimpses of those two parallel rows of yellow lights, bracketing a rain slick runway. They had never looked so good!

Greatly relieved, we parked on our assigned row and went to ops. Captain Kemp met me and told me to go get my travel bag while the bird was being re-fueled. I was going to Wichita Kansas to work out of McConnell AFB. Tornado weather was approaching Perrin. I later learned that while we were trying to recover at Perrin, there had been some monster thunderstorms sitting right over the base.

I and several other Perrin instructors took student pilots to McConnell AFB at Wichita and worked out of there. I did not feel good about leaving a young wife of a few months to fend for herself, but every available pilot was needed to get the aircraft away from the predicted storm area. Sure enough, during the night, tornadoes came through the Sherman, Texas area and trashed the airfield along with several buildings. Debris was everywhere and it took three days to make the runways and ramps useable again. Fortunately, Denison, where Kathy was, had not been damaged.

———————

It was about this time, that we learned, with great sadness, that Norm Hirschman had been the first fatality from our class. Norm had joined us about mid way through basic after being ill and washing back from an earlier class. On graduating, he had gone to Nellis AFB for gunnery training in a day fighter version of the F-86. According to the information we got, he had been killed in a mid-air collision.

Shortly after that, the second member of class 55-D bought the farm. George Munson was killed at Perrin. trying to make a dead stick landing in a T-33 because the engine had failed shortly after takeoff. The student with him did not survive either. George had enough altitude for a flameout landing pattern, but for reasons we will never know, did not choose to drop the heavy, 230 gallon tip tanks which were still nearly full. With nearly 3,000 pounds of extra weight, the stall speed was unusually high and with the loss of lift from banking into the final turn, the bird stalled and spun in from a very low attitude.

———————

Most of the instrument instructor pilots were also graduates of the interceptor phase of the school and I was beginning to feel slighted because I had not been checked out in the F-86D. That situation was rectified when I was sent over to a flight in Phase Two of the school for the all-weather interceptor course. At the time, the F-86D was a first line fighter and was no slouch in the performance department. It's primary shortcoming was endurance. In order to obtain reasonable climb performance, the engine had an afterburner. The entire 850 gallon fuel load could be used up in a few minutes under worst case conditions.

I was getting good experience in the T-bird, but wanted to feel like a real fighter pilot and the Dawg was a real fighter aircraft. It was big, heavy and fast. It had set a speed record at 715 mph in level flight.

After several hours of simulator, I took off on my first flight in a single seater with Captain Kemp as chase pilot. Everyone had a instructor pilot chase on his first Dawg flight, to supervise and to head off any trouble that the new pilot might get into. We did some familiarization air work for about an hour and landed without any difficulty. This was a fine handling bird. Now that I had flown a single seater, I could consider myself a real fighter pilot.

The next flight or two were without a chase. We did some engineering procedures to increase our confidence and familiarity with the bird – things like trying out the emergency fuel control, alternate flight control hydraulic systems, alternate arrangements of electrical systems, and so on. Then the next flight was to be aerobatic with a chase pilot to coach us and keep us out of trouble while doing radical maneuvers.

We took off with my chase pilot in close trail and we climbed out to about twenty thousand. The chase radioed me to begin a loop – a fairly simple aerobatic procedure. I put the nose down and picked up the recommended four hundred fifty knots with the power at one hundred percent RPM, but without afterburner and started the four G pull up. The resultant forces are pushing me down in the seat as if my 155 pound body weighed more than 600 pounds. My arms feel as though they have fifty pound weights attached. I can't think about it now, but my internal organs are being displaced. Tensing leg, thigh and stomach muscles helps to minimize the blood draining from my brain. Otherwise, my field of vision will narrow or become totally blank.

As I approached the vertical, of course, the airspeed was bleeding off. OK, that is normal, pull it on through, and since the horizon is now out of sight, I tilt my head back as far as possible to see the inverted horizon as it comes into view on the back side of the loop. As I was almost inverted, but still nose high, coming over the top, the bird felt like it was in an accelerated stall, so I instinctively released some back pressure on the stick. Actually, it was the wing slats coming out, as they should have, but no one had briefed me on what to expect in that type situation. By my releasing the back pressure on the stick, the bird never came on over the top of the loop. It just ran out of airspeed.

There had been no coaching from the chase pilot. He was now on the radio, saying, "Where are you?" He had lost sight of me. There I was, on my back, nose high, no airspeed, and no response from the elevator or ailerons. Moving the stick all around generated no results. I thought, well, it should fall on through, but it didn't. It just maintained that attitude and then the altimeter was unwinding very rapidly, with the vertical velocity indicator pegged at five thousand feet per minute down and the airspeed indicator was reading zip.

I had a hundred percent RPM but didn't expect to maintain it much longer, because there was no positive fuel flow to the engine. I did not think it wise to try to light the afterburner. I had not checked rudder response and had some reservation about that, but there was nothing else left to do, so I kicked the left rudder pedal to the stop.

The bird abruptly went into a violent inverted spin, oscillating with the nose way down on the first half turn and back up with the nose nearly level with the upside down horizon on the next half turn. The transverse G forces were throwing my legs all over the cockpit and banging my head from side to side against the canopy. I could not get oriented and rather than fight the bird, I just turned it loose. It promptly went into an upright spin on it's own. I knew how to recover from an upright spin, but was now having to decide if I had enough altitude remaining for recovery. The book said if we did not have the bird under control by ten grand, we should punch out.

I applied full rudder against the spin until the rotation stopped, stick neutral, throttle to idle, regaining flying speed, started the pull-out, being careful not to pull too hard too soon and enter a secondary spin.

The recovery was going well, however, true altitude was lagging behind the rapidly unwinding altimeter, but I elected to stay with it. It went through ten thousand under control, but I was considerably lower than that by the time I got the nose up to the horizon again. I had lost nearly 20,000 feet in a few seconds. Later when I briefed my students, I always explained the wing slat function to them.

I never forgot that experience and later when I was the chase pilot, I maintained a close trail position so I knew exactly what the other pilot was experiencing and did not hesitate to punch the mike button and advise him.

On such an occasion, I was chasing a low time student doing aerobatics in a Dawg, when he inconsiderately pulled up into the sun to begin a loop.

Ordinarily, my position would be close behind and slightly below him to avoid the turbulence from his jet wash. There I was, going vertical at better than 400 knots, pulling four Gs, only a few feet behind, and I cannot see him for the blinding sun. As a result, I got into his wash, and my bird pitched up, rolled hard right, then left. At the same time, something whizzed by my head and ricocheted off the canopy and whizzed by again on it's way to the floor. Also, during this time, something crashed into my right upper leg. I did a vertical recovery and leveled to try to assess the situation and told the student to orbit his present position for now. I was puzzled as to what object could be flying around the cockpit.

The recording hands on the G meter were pegged at plus ten and minus three, which was way over the rated limits. There was a lot of pressure on my right leg. I looked down and the right side console fasteners had let go and the entire panel of switches, circuit breakers and various controls had flopped over onto my leg. I shoved it back into position, but had no way to secure the fasteners. I still wondered what had almost zapped me in the head before it hit the canopy and disappeared, but could not see anything that would explain the mystery.

Everything seemed to be functioning properly, but I knew the bird had been overstressed and wondered how much unseen damage might have been done. I looked outside and could see that the drop tank fairings were buckled. Somehow they had stayed on. Not knowing what else might be damaged, I told the student to finish his mission solo and I headed back to base for a bomber pattern. I did not dare pull even two or three Gs in a pitch out for a standard overhead pattern.

After making the smoothest landing I could, I parked the bird and unstrapped. I knew the crew chief would check the G meter and reset the recording hands. They always did, so I told him there was no way I could know how much G forces the bird had actually been subjected to. I wanted to look around the cockpit floor. Under the seat, I found a bucking bar, a chunk of steel weighing about ten or fifteen pounds. They were used to buck rivets and someone had forgotten to remove this one after doing a job.

I took the hunk of steel to my flight commander because I wanted to have one of our operations supervisors contact the maintenance boss and make sure someone lost a portion of their backside. If I had simply left it with the crew chief, there was no assurance that the supervisors would hear about it. Later, I checked and was glad to hear there was no structural damage to the bird. My boss was not happy with me, because of the extra time required to inspect critical structural items, but I felt no guilt over the incident.

On about my fifth flight in the Dawg, I went up to forty grand, put the nose down with full power on and experienced the thrill of watching the mach meter go past mach one. I had been supersonic! I had a chase pilot to verify it and sign the log. North American Aviation sent me a certificate and a lapel pin, proclaiming that I was a "Mach Buster." At that point in time, only a very small percentage of pilots the world over had been supersonic.

Our class went on to cover everything in the curriculum to get familiar with the F-86D. Then we settled down to learn how to use it for what it was designed for; as a weapons platform. We could be directed to the vicinity of an airborne target by ground radar and after acquiring the target on our airborne radar, lock on, complete the intercept, including destruction, with no visual contact.

———

With about eighty five hours of Dawg time in the log, I was assigned to a flight to begin serving as an interceptor weapons instructor. The work days were long, and often began at five o'clock in the morning. There were students to brief, simulator lessons to instruct, target missions to fly, chase missions to fly and grade books to keep up. There were instrument continuation flights with the students in the T-bird. Our training wing was pumping out a steady supply of all-weather interceptor pilots to deal with the manned bomber threat from the U.S.S.R.

Some of the most challenging, but also, most enjoyable work we did was flying chase for the students first flight in the Dawg. We flew a slightly loose formation position on them from take-off to landing in order to coach them if necessary and keep them out of trouble. We had to really be in good form to remain close by but stay out of their way while they were feeling out a bird that was totally new to them. In this manner, if our airspeed was wrong, even in the traffic pattern, theirs was wrong and in need of correction. If their approach angle was not correct, we could spot it early on.

In August of 1955, our son Alan was born. Kathy then had something to keep her busy. I did not see much of him except on week ends. Most mornings I was out and gone before he was up and by the time I returned home, he was sacked out again. That was not an ideal life for a young wife, but she handled it well.

Probably the thing a pilot fears most is fire. In a single engine bird, there is not much he can do about it. When fire is confirmed, the most practical thing is to get out, if there is sufficient altitude, unless the area below is heavily populated. Many pilots have delayed or declined ejection in order to minimize the damage on the ground. Those kind of decisions have to be made quickly and sometimes put the safety of others ahead of their own.

The forward fire warning light is the most serious. If there really is fire in the forward section of the engine, there will be little time to ponder the situation. If there is supporting evidence, such as smoke, unusual instrument readings, power loss, or a report from another aircraft, prompt ejection is the recommended course of action.

When there is no supporting evidence with the light, making the decision is more difficult. In visual flight conditions, rolling into a turn to check for trailing smoke, checking the light circuit in addition to a close check of engine instruments is called for. If conditions allow, a power reduction is in order. If the light goes out, and the push to test illuminates the light, there is a question of whether there was a fire that went out at the lower power setting. Do you continue with reduced power and land ASAP? How do you know control cables are not already partially burned through? How about electrical wiring for critical controls.

If the light does not come on when the test circuit is activated, you have the question of whether the bulb burned out or if the fire warning circuitry burned out and is now unable to warn you? Most pilots will elect to stay with the bird and nurse it to an early landing. I had several fire warning lights that turned out to be circuit malfunctions, but they surely could get a guy tensed up.

The aft fire warning light is less serious, but still not to be taken lightly. The only time I ever dropped a set of tanks was to lighten up the bird immediately after take-off because the aft fire warning light came on. I was pretty sure it was for real, because when I backed off on the power the light went out and when I advanced the power again, the light came back on. Back on the ground, it was confirmed that a clamp joining the tail pipe to the main engine was leaking and the unauthorized stream of exhaust gases was being directed at some control cables.

————————

At least annually, all interceptor weapons instructors had to requalify with live armament. We each went down to Foster AFB at Victoria, near the south coast for that. Foster was a tactical fighter base and had a wing of F-100 aircraft. We had a dozen or so of our instructors on temporary duty there for a week at a time, using the Matagorda range off the coast. In our normal daily training and instruction at Perrin, we carried no live rockets and only went through the motions of firing on a practice intercept. At Foster, it was different. The birds were armed with twenty four live practice rockets. The only difference with practice rockets was the lack of TNT in the warheads. Instead there was an inert, non-explosive substance. They would punch a tidy hole in the target, but would not explode.

We flew the Dawgs without drop tanks to improve the performance and to give us a little edge in the scoring. The distance out to the range was about ninety miles and that doesn't sound like much, but without the two 120 gallon drop tanks, we often returned on the fumes. We wanted to get in at least two scoring passes on the target and sometimes would stay for a third one if something had messed up one of the first two. It was not unusual to run an "accuracy check" on the fuel gauges. That happened when the engine died from fuel starvation by the time we parked, if not earlier. Sometimes we coasted in to the parking area, with the engine already winding down. A fuel gauge was considered accurate if it read exactly zero when the engine died.

The control tower operators at Foster were something less than accommodating. They seemed to be strongly prejudiced in favor of the home folks. I reckon we were just generating extra work for them. Dick Griffin and I had stayed out too long and were returning from the range with too little fuel. He was on my wing and when we entered the traffic pattern we each had about 200 pounds of fuel and I called "flight of two with minimum fuel for full stop landing." We should have been able to assume the tower understood what that meant.

The flight commander of the four F-100s waiting for take-off should have heard and understood also. However, to my astonishment, the F-100 leader called for take-off clearance as I was making the final turn and with even more astonishment, I heard tower clear his flight for take-off. I screamed for the tower to countermand the clearance, but the first element proceeded to take the runway. The second element was beginning to move toward the runway. I had rolled out on final approach and was not about to go around, so instead of barking at the idiot in the tower again, I directly addressed the F-100 leader. I said, "I am on final approach, I AM GOING TO LAND, over you, around your or somehow, unless you move that lead sled."

I knew he would be miffed if he took off with his number three and four birds still on the taxiway, but at that point, I did not care. He made the right decision and started to roll with the number two on his wing. I landed with minimum spacing behind them. The second element was still on the taxiway. I would not have bet, even with good odds, that one could go around and do even a closed pattern with 200 pounds of fuel in a Dawg, but Dick did it somehow, and he had to coast to the ramp.

Another time, I was out on the range alone, and the T-bird target could not get the cable reel unjammed to release the target normally towed about 4,000 feet back. There was no back up target bird so I could not make a firing pass, and I turned back toward Foster. On the way out to the range, once I passed over Matagorda Island, I had set up the armament switches, pulled the safety pins and pushed in the circuit breakers to get ready for a live firing pass. We had a lot of safeguards to prevent an accidental firing.

I was going to have to land with 24 live rockets on board. As I was resetting the switches and pulling circuit breakers, there was a jolt and a thud. The rocket pod was down! I looked down and was just passing over Matagorda Island, which was inhabited, and thought, my goodness, if that pod parted company with me and has hit somebody down there, nobody will ever believe that the pod jettisoned because of a circuit malfunction. I then began to realize that I had a little more than normal drag and hoped that I still had the pod.

I hit the manual "up" switch and was much relieved to feel that thing retract with a satisfying thump.

On my next sortie, I was the first out of the parking area for the afternoon session, so the armament man climbed on the wing and rode out with me to the arming area. He would arm my rockets and remain there until everyone else was armed. Near the end of the runway, I turned away from the runway and the main ramp, with the canopy open, engine running, feet hard on the brakes, and arms up so the armament man could see my hands. What he was about to do was quite dangerous.

If a rocket was going to get loose, this would be an opportune time for it. I nodded my head and he disappeared underneath the bird, activating the external switch for pod extension. With his voltmeter, he would check for stray voltage on the igniter arms, and finding none, proceed to snap an igniter arm onto each rocket motor.

While he was under there the bird bucked hard and trembled, from the concussion, as an earsplitting roar penetrated even my foam covered ear pieces and I assumed the worst. However, there was no smoke and the bird was still running OK. Before I could gather my senses, it happened all over again. Then I looked behind me and saw that a flight of four F-100s had passed behind me and taken the runway. The first two lit their burners and almost blew me away and by the time I looked around, the second pair lit up. The armament tech came out from underneath, retracted the pod, and gave me a thumbs up.

I got my heart back down in my chest where it belonged and went on my way. The tow target was on station and the radar controller gave me a vector for a firing pass. My on-board radar picked up the target at about 14 miles and I locked on, with the range decreasing very rapidly. There was not much time for steering corrections. The target pilots were quite cautious about clearing us to fire because they all had experienced close calls from time to time. It was easy for the airborne radar tracking system to jump lock from the target to the tow plane, especially if they had not been able to extend the cable fully. A pilot doesn't easily forget having to take wild evasive action to avoid being shot down by his friendly attacker. As a result, they sometimes were slow to visually determine if we were locked on to them or the target. They were not going to clear us until they were confident we were locked on to the target.

At this point in the flight, most of my attention must be directed to the radar scope in the lower center area of the instrument panel. A lot of information is displayed there. There is a target blip, of course, in addition to an outer circle with a gap opposite the calibrations for closing speed. A small inner circle, which is sort of a bulls eye. A steering dot which we try to keep in the center of the inner circle. There are calibration marks for target range and angle relative to my heading. At twenty seconds to go, the outer circle begins to collapse and intersects time to go calibrations. Also at twenty seconds to go, the attack computer changes the steering to direct a lead collision course rather than a true collision course. The rocket firing is timed for the rockets to hit the target as we pass slightly behind the target. The scope display also includes an attitude indicator, so we can know our bank angle and pitch attitude without having to divert our attention to the flight instruments.

At about three seconds to go, called phase three, the display changes and the inner circle is replaced by a horizontal line. From this time, we make vertical corrections to keep the dot on the line, but leave the lateral corrections to the computer. The rockets can be fired a little early or a little late, within certain parameters.

My attack display is indicating twenty seconds to go. Check the gun cameras armed. Steer to keep that dot in the center of the inner circle. Keep the head in the scope. Don't look out. That's the target pilots job. Recheck the safety pin removed from the stick grip trigger and all the circuit breakers in. Don't be so tense, after all, you are only on a collision course with a fifteen thousand pound chunk of metal doing 200 knots while you are doing 350 knots in a twenty thousand pound chunk and you want to fire twelve rockets in his direction accurately enough for a good score.

The target pilot calls, "tallyho". He has visual contact. The range is closing and the time-to-go circle collapses to ten seconds. *Clear me to fire!* The stick grip trigger is pulled down one click. That activates the wing root cameras. I will need photographic proof of my hits. I'm working hard to hold the steering dot centered. In a few more seconds, the display will go to phase three, with only a small horizontal line to keep the dot on with vertical corrections. The computer will take care of lateral variations by timing the firing, that is, if I pull the trigger down to the second click. But I don't dare do that until I am cleared.

Six seconds to go. *Clear me to fire!* Just as the display changes to phase three, I hear a distinct "CLEARED TO FIRE" and pop the trigger down. The pod slams down, the rockets leave with a tremendous roar, the cockpit fills with stinking green smoke, the pod slams back up with a thud and I look up just in time to see the dense smoke trails streaking through and around the towed rag. I call the "MA" for mission accomplished and the controller gives me a heading to reposition for another pass. This time I will put the oxygen regulator on one hundred percent oxygen, so I won't have to breathe the putrid smoke on the next pass.

We rarely fired all twenty four rockets on one pass, partly because we wanted to make more than one pass if we could. Also partly because, the rocket motors consumed so much oxygen out in front of the engine, there was a distinct possibility of putting out the engine fire – called a flameout. On those occasions that did call for a 24 rocket salvo, we were poised for an airstart.

————

While at Foster, we usually got in too late to eat dinner at the mess hall and did not want to dress up to go to the officers club. We could usually dig up some kind of transportation and go into town. We frequently ate at a Mexican restaurant called Almond's. The food would make us feel like we had eaten live coals and ice cream was the favored dessert. Next morning, we would be complaining and saying, "come on ice cream", all the time swearing we would never return to Almond's. By nightfall, we were usually there again.

The Cross Country Flight

It is late on a Friday afternoon. I am doing a walk around preflight inspection of the F-86D and have been at work since 5:30 AM. My work days have averaged more than twelve hours all week. Today's working hours will be even longer. I have flown a target mission with a student pilot, flown a radar intercept mission as chase pilot for a student, and instructed two simulator lessons. I have brought my weekend bag with me which contains a change of clothes and a few personal items. The "Dawg" has no baggage compartment, so I stuff the specially made miniature B-4 bag behind the head rest at the rear of the canopy.

A hang-up suit bag could be placed on top of the rocket pod, and the pod retracted, since there is about a four inch space between the top of the pod and false skin on the bottom of the bird. However, the pods have a history of mysteriously dropping down in flight for no apparent reason.

This is my weekend for a navigational proficiency trip, more commonly referred to as a cross country, or X-C, which all unit pilots are required to do periodically. This is my first one to be done alone. Although I am a flight instructor in a combat crew training unit and am certified combat ready, I have not been allowed to go out on an extended trip alone until I fulfilled certain requirements, mostly with regard to time in the bird.

Pilots with low experience levels fly with restrictions that the more experienced jocks don't have. There are things like higher approach minimums and the solo cross country thing. One of the standard jokes is, "If you haven't been there, you can't go."

When I have this trip behind me, I will feel more like "one of the boys". Being a second lieutenant with relatively little flying experience while surrounded by pilots of much more experience and rank often makes me feel more inferior than I really am. Although they are modest, and rarely, if ever, mention it, it is common knowledge that many of the other instructors are veterans of aerial combat and a few are jet aces. The best thing about that is their willingness to offer subtle guidance to a fledgling pilot without acting superior. The stereotype fighter pilot is a fictional personality. Confident and self assured? Yes. boastful? No.

I have been on several extended trips in the venerable two seat T-33 trainer and also on a couple of trips as a member of a flight of three or four F-86s with a more experienced pilot leading the flight. This weekend I will fly several legs to other bases around the country and return by late Sunday afternoon. The F-86D, the all-weather interceptor version of the series, is not well suited for cross country work, but the commander wants everyone to be proficient in getting in and out of unfamiliar airports. In a single seater, there is no doubt as to who does the work.

The flight orders in my pocket indicate a specific itinerary, but also state that I am authorized to deviate from that itinerary for any plausible reason. In other words, I can really go about anywhere I want to, within reason. Tonight, I am departing Perrin AFB, Sherman, Texas and plan to refuel at Columbus AFB, Mississippi and fly on to McGhee-Tyson Airport at Knoxville, Tennessee. Tomorrow, I will decide where to go from there after spending a night with my in-laws who live near the Knoxville airport.

It is late summer and the weather is typical for Northeast Texas; hot and humid. The ramp is very hot, after baking in the sun all day and is reflecting a lot of heat. The metal skin of the airplane I am preflighting is hot enough to damage bare skin, so my gloves are already on. The stench of burned kerosene fumes hangs heavy over the area.

Night flight is not a problem, and the airplane doesn't know it's night time, but it would be nice to get settled down on the first leg of the flight before dark. Also, by the time I refuel and continue on to my destination for the night, it will be well into the evening and the body will be tired. Not a good combination for flight in a single seater which has the highest pilot workload of any aircraft in the inventory.

I have already been by base operations, gotten a weather briefing and filed an instrument flight plan for the first leg of the trip. The weather poses no threat, with the usual scattered to broken cumulus along the way and more so down on the Gulf coast. I can fly over most of that, if not all of it. If not, the bird is, after all, an all-weather interceptor and I am not only instrument rated, but a grad of the intensive Instrument Pilot School, which is a requirement for all interceptor pilots. So there is no sweat on the weather.

I complete the walk-around inspection after finding everything in order. There were a few seeps from hydraulic systems, but that is normal for a bird that uses extensive hydraulics for landing gear, flight controls, speed brakes, wheel brake boost, rocket pod, nose wheel steering, plus back-up systems for the flight controls. The tires and mullti-rotor disc brakes look good enough for several landings. I am ready to fire up and depart, so I pick up my back pack chute off the wing and strap it on – tightly. The hard hat is already propped on the top of the windshield bow – oxygen mask attached.

While doing the pre-flight inspection, the crew chief has followed me closely, ready to answer any questions or to help with anything that might be requested of him. I now ask him, "Sarge, I have reviewed the servicing forms in the 781 (the status book that stays in each aircraft) and everything there looks OK. Is there anything not listed there that I ought to know about ?" "No sir, this bird is good to go."

Somewhere, out on the flight line, or maybe in the air, is an F-86D with my name painted on the canopy frame, but only rarely do I get to fly that bird. The pilots fly whatever bird operations dispatch assigns them as maintenance gives them a list of available aircraft. It is a morale booster to have a bird with my name on it, but then a let-down to hardly ever draw that tail number for a flight.

As I put my foot in the retractable bottom step, you can see the shiny, aluminum streaks on the toe of my black boot. You can identify an F-86 pilot by the toes of his boots. They will have some aluminum color showing where the boots have hit the kick steps on the side of the airplane as he climbs aboard and again as he deplanes. Settling into the seat, I strap on my knee board and place my maps over the instrument panel and behind the windscreen. The early D models have a fair amount of space there, since the space hogging, vision blocking K-14 gunsights have not yet been installed. Instead, a fixed pipper is projected onto the center section of the windscreen. The fixed pipper is so useless, some pilots carry a grease pencil and make their own sight markings on the windscreen.

The crew chief assists with the straps and the powerman starts the auxiliary power unit. (APU). The on-board battery can power the radio while waiting for flight clearance, but sometimes there is a wait of several minutes and the small battery might not last. Better to use the APU. The hard hat is donned and the mask fastened to shut out the noise of the APU and passing aircraft from the built-in microphone. The snugly fitted earphones inside the hard hat shut out most of the external noises so I can only hear a muted roar from the APU.

The interior of the cockpit is scanned in the standard left to right pattern. A host of miscellaneous controls, switches, circuit breakers and fuses and instruments are checked. More than a hundred switches and controls have been eyeballed.

I thumb the little push-button on the throttle grip. "Perrin Ground, Air Force 43863 standing by for clearance." "Roger 863, clearance on request." While waiting, all the cockpit lights are checked, many of them are "push-to-test". Instrument lighting is not needed yet, but will be needed when the sun goes down. I feel the zipper pocket on the left lower leg of my flight suit and check to make sure the small personal flashlight is still there. It is reliable. The issue ones are not reliable and most pilots carry their own personal flashlight. The safety pins from the ejection seat and canopy are pulled, the red streamers rolled up and shoved into the open zipper pocket on the lower right leg.

"863, your clearance is coming through, advise you start now and call when ready to copy." "863, roger." I signal the powerman to standby for the extremely heavy current drain that the starter will require and he gooses the start cart engine. After a wind'em up hand signal I push up the start switch on the left sub panel for engine controls. The sudden heavy, increased load causes the gasoline engine powered APU to bog down, and the cockpit lights dim, but it recovers and handles the increased electrical load with a deep throated roar as the lights return to normal brightness after the initial surge.

The big turbojet engine begins to spin and at six percent RPM the throttle is brought out of the closed position and placed at Start/Idle The bird shudders as the fuel now being sprayed into the burner cans lights off. Several seconds later the engine is idling at 40 percent rpm, and all the engine instruments are quickly scanned and found to be in the green. The meters for the generators indicate normal electrical power is available and all electrical equipment is turned on except the radar, which is left in standby. Flight instruments are scanned and appear to be operating OK. Special attention is given to the gyro powered attitude indicator. At a hand signal from the cockpit, the cable from the APU is disconnected.

The bird is operating on it's own now. While hand signaling the crew chief to observe, the speed brakes are closed with another thumb switch on the throttle and flaps are extended to full down for takeoff setting and I get a thumbs up. There is no flap position indicator in the cockpit. The crew chief hands me the three safety pins with the red streamers for the landing gear, which are shoved into the map case. At another hand signal, he pulls the ropes that remove the wheel chocks.

The throttle is pushed up far enough to start rolling out of the parking row, but not enough to damage start carts and other aircraft as the tail pipe swings through a ninety degree arc on the turn out. Rolling between rows and heading for the main taxiway, power is reduced again to idle and the bird rolls along, with the power nose wheel steering button on the stick grip depressed. If both hands happen to be busy, differential braking could be used for steering, but that would require more power and wasted fuel. With another ninety degree turn the bird is on the main taxiway and falls in line with other aircraft heading toward the runway for takeoff on their local training flights.

"Ground Control, 863 ready to copy clearance." "Roger 863, Air Route Traffic Control clears you to Columbus AFB, direct Paris, then via flight planned route, climb to and maintain Flight level 350, via standard instrument departure, Perrin Number One. Contact Fort Worth Center on frequency 321.4." The clearance is read back as is required to assure accuracy of reception. "863, read back correct, cleared to taxi runway 17 left, wind southwest at 12 knots, altimeter two niner niner seven, contact tower when number one for takeoff."

Keep rolling with the least power possible. To the two birds ahead of me, I mentally beg. Please don't screw around about getting on and off the runway. I cannot afford to waste any fuel. Every gallon I use here, is a gallon I won't have over my destination with which to make an approach with any reserve.

Sweat is trickling down into my eyes and down my legs, making my already damp socks even more soggy. The jump boots and long socks are hot, but necessary equipment. My undershirt is soaked and my salt streaked cotton flight suit is getting wet again. The air conditioning does not work at low engine speeds. The thin goat skin gloves for flash fire protection are soggy with sweat. The heat coupled with the high humidity, then further aggravated by all the big turbojet engines operating in the area, makes for a lot of discomfort, but aircraft control is primary and personal discomfort must not be allowed to distract me.

I switch the radio from ground control to tower frequency and call number one for take off and am cleared on the runway for takeoff with additional clearance instructions to contact Perrin Departure Control on channel fifteen when airborne. The last red warning light goes out when the canopy is closed and locked. The heading indicator is checked against the runway direction and is correctly showing 171 degrees with the nose wheel on the centerline. The other flight instruments are also OK, so heavy pressure is applied to the brakes and the throttle brought briskly up to the military power stop. The electronic fuel control allows the engine to accelerate to full power at optimum rate without fear of a compressor stall as might be the case with other types of turbojet engines.

The rapid surge of power causes the nose to dip as the brakes refuse to let the wheels roll. The tachometer is reading 100 per cent. The fuel flow meter indicates the engine is drinking fuel at the rate of fifty five hundred pounds per hour. The exhaust nozzle indicator shows nozzles are open about one quarter. Oil pressure, hydraulic pressure OK, exhaust gas temp (EGT) reads 685 degrees Centigrade. It must indicate 685 to 690 at full throttle. The generators are putting out 28 volts d.c. and the loadmeters are normal. To get the throttle past the military power stop, it is shoved outboard and forward through the afterburner range as far as it will go. The nose gear strut compresses and the nose dips even more with the tremendous surge of power from the extra fuel being sprayed behind the turbine wheel and burned in the tailpipe. The EGT heads for the red line, but the electronic fuel control does its job and opens the exhaust nozzles to better than three quarters, and the EGT settles back down to 685 C. Several thousand horses are straining and trembling in the harness, eager to go, so the brakes are released and the ten ton tricycle begins to move.

As the bird gathers speed, a light tap on alternate brake pedals keep the nose wheel on the centerline until the airspeed indicator begins to function and shows about seventy knots, when directional control is transferred to the rudder pedals. The takeoff roll has been calculated, using several parameters, such as density altitude, temperature, total aircraft weight, runway gradient etc. The thousand foot runway markers begin to go by with increasing frequency and at around 115 knots, slight back pressure on the stick raises the nose wheel a few inches off the runway. The most critical phase of the flight is about to begin. Too far down the runway to safely abort, and for the next several seconds too low to eject. General Electric, don't let me down now!

A lot of things could go wrong, especially at this point in the flight, but there is no time to reflect on that. The pilot must concentrate on prompt, precise corrections on the controls, while the situation is rapidly changing, yet he must be ready for instant response if anything goes wrong. At lift off, the airspeed will be only slightly above stall and over control must be carefully avoided. The lift being generated by the wings barely exceeds the weight of the bird. Fortunately, thrust exceeds drag and the bird is accelerating and attaining a more comfortable margin above stall speed. Flight is a continuous mixture of variables. Speed changes lift, bank changes lift. Pitch attitude changes drag, speed, and lift, power changes speed, fuel consumption changes weight, and weight and configuration changes power requirements. So many factors, all interwoven. Change one, and they all change.

The white vapor and ice crystals streaming from the air vents in the cockpit are a welcome sight, now that the cooling system is working. For now, the control is set to full cold. That will have to be changed during the climb out as colder outside air is encountered. It seems strange that the surface air can be around a hundred degrees F, while straight up overhead, temperatures drop to colder than forty degrees below zero.

The airspeed indicator passes 140 knots, and a slight amount of additional back pressure on the stick is used to break ground as the six thousand foot marker goes by. The calculated take-off roll of 5,850 ft at 113 degrees of runway temp was about right. The gear handle is shoved to "UP", the gear doors open, the wheels clunk into the wells and the doors thump closed. Acceleration is more rapid now and the flap handle is raised to "UP" as the airspeed indicator passes 155 knots. A moderate climb is maintained and the speed continues to build toward the recommended initial climb speed of 350 knots for a non-afterburner climb as the oil derricks go by more and more rapidly.

In a few seconds, as the airspeed indicator is passing 348 knots, the kerosene handle is retarded out of the afterburner range to the mil detent. The A/B goes out instantly and the decrease in acceleration is abrupt. Noise and vibration decreases as does pressure from the seat back. The exhaust nozzles close back to around one quarter, the tach, fuel flow and EGT fluctuate for a moment and then settle down. The airspeed stabilizes at 350 knots. A quick scan of the instruments reveals that everything is in the green. There are many things that can still go wrong, but the tension is reduced, because now, a fairly safe ejection altitude had been reached. Most fatalities and injuries from ejection problems occur below two thousand feet.

The radio is switched to channel 15 and departure control advises, "....radar contact, continue present heading and squawk mode three low." I comply by setting the IFF transponder to mode three and the power switch to low. At this distance, the normal transponder return will show up on the controllers radar scope as an inordinately large blip and he will not be able to establish an exact position for the aircraft. Therefore the request for "low". "863, radar contact, now turn left to zero niner five and continue climb. Report ten thousand". "863 roger."

As the left turn to the eastbound heading is completed, the airbase is visible, on the left side. Several aircraft are in the landing pattern for runway 17 right and someone in a F-86 with a T-bird chase is completing a practice instrument approach to 17 left as a couple more hold just short of the runway, waiting for takeoff. Numerous aircraft are moving along the taxi strip, and the parking ramps. Looking beyond the airpatch, to the west, the multi-fingered, sprawling lake complex, called Texoma is in view. That is the Red River, backed up by the Denison dam, the worlds largest earthen dam, and the dividing line between Texas and Oklahoma. The river is appropriately named, as its water runs red with silt. The lake provides fishing, boating and other recreation. The air base maintains a recreational facility there, and most pilots don't get to use it much, but they get a view that the local residents do not have access to.

So far, during my short tour at Perrin, three pilots have been lost in Lake Texoma after bailing out and getting tangled in their parachute lines. A little later, another one will be lost in a stock pond. Those are the primary reasons we have starting wearing water wings under our chute harness. We get laughed at by pilots at other bases when they find out we are from Texas and the flotation gear is noticed. Let'em laugh. Better safe than sorry. Too bad the water wings were not worn earlier. Three guys might still be alive.

The climb out continues, with some brief, light bumps as the bird blasts through the scattered white puff balls and small cumulus clouds that contrast sharply with the deep blue sky above. This part of the country is rarely without enough humidity and unstable air to be completely free of clouds.

At this point in the flight, more than six hundred pounds (nearly a hundred gallons) of fuel have already expended, but the fuel gauge is still steady at 3950 pounds of internal fuel. It will not begin to decrease until the 1560 pounds (240 gallons) in the drop tanks is expended. As the base passes off to the rear on the port side, the time keeping is started for enroute time. The first checkpoint will be a visual one, since Paris has no radio navigational aid, but the weather is mostly clear, so that is OK.

Passing through ten thousand feet, control is notified, transponder power set to normal, oxygen quantity checked, regulator settings checked, and the zero delay lanyard is disconnected from the parachute D ring. On take off, approach and landing, and any time we are below ten grand, the dog leash clip is hooked onto the D ring. The other end of the lanyard is connected to the ejection seat, so that in separating from the seat, on an ejection, the D ring will be pulled and the chute deployed immediately. That bypasses the one second delay provided for the chute deployment by the timer. It also bypasses the barometric device that prevents chute opening above 14000 ft. At high altitudes and high speeds, that one second delay is important, providing time for deceleration before the chute canopy is deployed. On the other hand, at low altitudes, eliminating that extra one second delay might make the difference in survival or not.

Objects on the ground continue to shrink, but the roads, villages and major landmarks are still quite visible. The country to the north, across the Red River is very sparsely settled. I look down there and wonder if there are any young men looking up at the silver bird flashing across the sky while they promise themselves that they too, will do that some day. Those people on the ground who only consider us and our noise to be an annoyance, do not understand the price of freedom, much less the satisfaction we derive from risking our gluteus maximus on their behalf.

Control has been changed to Fort Worth Center. Ten minutes into the flight and nine minutes since starting enroute time, sixty nautical miles down the road, Paris is passing under the nose. Fort Worth Center transfers my control to Memphis Center. No radio contact with them yet. The fuel gauge indication has decreased to 3425 pounds. The drop tanks on the wing pylons now contain only air and internal fuel is being used. Altitude is only 20,000. Non afterburner climbs are painfully slow, but provide much better distance for the fuel consumed.

The time is noted on the knee pad and course is changed to 084 degrees for Texarkana, 69 nautical miles away. The throttle is still set against the military power detent for one hundred percent rpm, but no A/B. The forecast winds at this altitude are not strong enough to make much difference on ground speed or course drift.

This is too easy; no high G turns, no wing-man to nurse, no leader to position on, no student to chase, no target trying to evade my attack. Where is the challenge? I am being paid five hundred bucks a month to do this. I would do it for nothing. No, I would pay to do it. However, I must not allow complacency to sneak up on me, as there are many pitfalls awaiting the careless or complacent pilot. Just recently, two of my squadron mates flew into a mountain in California. Just a couple of weeks ago, one of my cadet class mates bought the farm when his T-bird engine died shortly after takeoff and he crashed trying to make a dead stick landing. Over the years to come, I will lose many more friends and acquaintances, some in accidents and some in combat.

The low freq radio range at Texarkana is tuned in but is too weak to be of any help. The Automatic Direction Finder needle is aimlessly wandering around, not pointing at any bearing in particular. Therefore, the only thing to do is to continue on the proper heading and wait. If my calculations are correct, I will arrive over Texarkana at plus twenty one minutes and I still will not have arrived at assigned altitude.

The air route traffic controllers don't like slow climbers taking so long to reach assigned altitudes and using up so many altitudes that they need to keep other traffic away from until they are clear. But, the fuel consumption and distance advantage dictates a non-afterburner climb. Rate of climb is slow, and requires a delicate touch on the stick and pitch trim, otherwise, I will over control and really mess up the airspeed and delay the climb. The altimeter crawls ever so slowly upward. The vertical velocity indicates a climb rate of only a few hundred feet per minute. I am tempted to plug in the afterburner, but common sense prevails.

At plus fifteen minutes, estimating Texarkana in six minutes, the ADF needle starts to settle in on an arc of about twenty degrees whose center is a bearing of about 090 degrees. I turn up the volume and hear a faint identifier. Dah, dah di di dah, dah di dah; T X K for Texarkana. Whatever wind there is up here is not bothering my course much. Also not helping my ground speed. Now the scattered clouds are getting larger, higher, and more like a broken layer than scattered. There is still plenty of visibility but ground objects are less well defined as the altitude increases. The altimeter is nearing 30,000 and the climb rate is getting slower every minute. The traffic controllers must hate us! I am still not at assigned altitude and will not be for several more minutes.

At plus eighteen minutes, the ADF is pretty well settled down on a bearing of 088 degrees and I make a heading change to match. The identifier is strong and steady now. Through the breaks in the clouds, I can see the faint outlines of portions of a fairly large city. Roads and railroads are converging and disappearing into the poorly defined mass. Smoke from the oil refineries helps mark the complex that must be Texarkana.

At plus twenty minutes the ADF needle begins to swing wildly around the face of the compass card, and then stays in the bottom half of the instrument, pointing behind me. I have over flown the low freq radio range station. Maybe I do have a slight tail wind component. I was over the station a few seconds early. Fuel remaining is 2850 pounds. The time and fuel is logged on the knee pad as I take up a heading of 082 degrees. Greenville Mississippi, 155 nautical miles away, at plus forty one minutes total enroute time is my next reporting point.

Several radio calls to Memphis Center bring no reply. Not an uncommon situation, so a position report is transmitted in the blind. Maybe somebody will hear it. There is plenty of chatter on the radio. Other aircraft are making position reports or getting updated weather information from flight service stations. I can hear responses to other aircraft from McComb radio, a flight

service station, although they are farther away than some others. I call Mc-
Comb, and on the third try, I hear my number. So I transmit, "McComb Radio,
this is Air Force 43683, Texarkana, four one, flight level 310 climbing to assigned flight level 350, estimating Greenville zero one. Columbus, over." Another report from an aircraft talking to a ground station some distance away
breaks up their reply. ".........flight level 310 ??" "Roger, flight level 310, climbing
to assigned flight level 350" "683, roger your position report."

Flying well above the clouds, I have a visual horizon and control the bird
partly with regard to visual references and partially with reference to the flight
instruments. Precise altitude and heading can be maintained only by frequent
reference to the altimeter, vertical velocity indicator and attitude indicator. As
I look out of the bubble canopy and view the panorama of fleecy cloud tops,
I marvel, as always, at the aerodynamics that are at work. Those metal wings
are generating enough lift to sustain several tons of high density material as
well as a few thousand pounds of kerosene, and I can make the bird change it's
behavior with only slight pressure on the controls.

———

There are people who can keep the numbers within their critical parameters
and are technically pilots. Then there are those people who can do that and
also feel the bird. If we listen and feel carefully, the bird communicates with us.
Like a sailor getting the sail too close to the wind, if he is attentive, the sail will
tell him before it stalls. He can obtain maximum performance by capitalizing
on that feel, and sailing close, but not too close to the wind. The airplane pilot
can do the same thing. When two pilots, even in identical aircraft, are trying to
out turn each other, one of them will usually prevail, and it is because he can
make use of what the bird is telling him by the way it feels. The loser will pull
too hard and stall the wing, or he will not pull hard enough to get the best turn
rate. That best turn rate is obtained with just enough back pressure on the
stick, so that a barely perceptible increase will push the angle of attack beyond
the critical point. The tricky thing is, that critical angle of attack varies with
speed, gross weight and aircraft configuration.

———

The radio compass needle has been pointing toward the tail of the aircraft for
several minutes and begins to wander around again. I am losing the TXK low

freq station. The identifier is no longer heard. Static in the headsets is quite loud, so the volume is turned down for now.

The throttle is still at max power except for the A/B. I wonder how the internal engine components can tolerate the stress of extreme temperatures, especially for extended time periods. The relatively cool section in the tail pipe where the EGT thermocouples get their reading is still at 685 C, around 1300 F. The turbine wheel and it's 96 blades of exotic alloy metal is spinning at many thousands of rpm, while exposed to temperatures of thousands of degrees. The blast from the combustion of all that kerosene is directed against those turbine blades and causing them to spin and generate a centrifugal force that must be very close to the maximum they will tolerate before disintegrating. That wheel is coupled back to the twelve stage compressor section by way of a shaft, whose bearings are also running very hot and kept lubricated by a special high temp oil.

When flying in close trail with other F-86s at full power, I have been able to look up their tailpipe and see the white hot turbine wheel, spinning at close to 10,000 rpm. A few degrees hotter and the tail section would be instantly sawed off from the rest of the bird. The engine driven fuel pumps, oil pump, the two generators, the alternator, the hydraulic pumps, the fuel boost pumps, are all working hard, and contributing to the noise. The little turbine, running off of bleed air from the fifth stage of the engine compressor, for cockpit air cooling and heating, is turning about 40,000 rpm. The gyro powered flight instruments, such as the attitude indicator, direction indicator, turn and bank, are running at about 25,000 rpm, yet the designers of the instrument panel were concerned about everything being so smooth, they built in a vibrator, so the instruments would not be prone to stick.

The automatic fuel control system includes some black boxes which are full of vacuum tubes. Transistors have not yet come into common usage. Tube failure, due to extreme temp variations, age, and vibration are not uncommon. In my short experience with the Dawg, I have already had occasion to use the emergency fuel control several times. The automatic system has some safeguards built in. Usually if a malfunction is detected, the main fuel control valve is locked in position and a warning light comes on, until the emergency system is selected. In the worst case, the main fuel control valve is driven toward the closed position, but cannot fully close and cause a flame-out because there is a mechanical stop, allowing at least a flow of 600 pounds per hour.

The inverters, running off d.c. generators, provide the a.c. power required for various electronic equipment including the engine instruments. In addition to the two generators, the alternator provides some of the power required by the radar. Even the speed brakes and landing gear are electrically controlled, but positioned by hydraulics. If the speed brakes fail, the only difficulty is in slowing down from high speed flight. Descents from high altitude could require a long time and cover a lot of distance. The flaps are electrically operated. Each flap has its own motor and the two sides are interconnected by a shaft from one side to the other. Total failure is rare. If normal landing gear extension does not work, there is a handle in the cockpit, with a cable mechanically connected to release the uplocks. Then one hopes that gravity will do the rest.

The total noise of the engine, engine driven accessories, and outside air blowing by, in the cockpit, is an earshattering one hundred ten decibels. Thankfully, the foam covered earphones inside my helmet, shut out most of the noise. Also, a lot of the engine exhaust noise is left behind and not heard in the cockpit, but the J-47 engine takes some getting used to. It has some unexplained characteristics in steady state operation in the form of frequent little thumps and rattles and squeaks that are not reflected in the engine instruments or in the power being developed. When we are flying over large bodies of water, especially at night, all these noises seem to become a lot more pronounced, and we are glad to be sitting on a survival pack and a tiny inflatable one man raft.

Passing 23,500 feet, entering the Area of Positive Control (APC) the altimeter was reset to 29.92 to establish a standard datum plane for operating in the flight level system. Atmospheric pressure varies so much with area and altitude, all the aircraft can not keep up with the exact altimeter setting for the surface they are operating over. Therefore, if everyone at or above 24,000 sets their altimeter to the same reference pressure setting, their altitude separation will be uniform.

At last, the altimeter creeps up to the 35,000 mark. Indicated airspeed up here in this thin air is only 255 knots, but true airspeed is 440 knots. Fuel remaining is 2025 pounds. I have used the majority of my fuel to reach cruise altitude, but have traveled nearly 200 miles. I could have reached this altitude with an afterburner climb in about six minutes, but in less distance and much more fuel. Memphis center responds this time when I report on assigned altitude. Since I have radio contact, I request current Columbus weather.

"Air Force 64683, Memphis Center, Columbus weather twenty five hundred broken, visibility four miles, haze, scattered showers, wind southwest twelve, gusts to fifteen, altimeter 29.95 over" "683 roger."

I reduce power slightly, now that the long climb out is completed, and give the engine a little break, and reduce fuel consumption a bit. I turn the crank on the radio compass control box to a new frequency, looking for Greenville. Some pilots refer to the tuning crank as the coffee grinder. A faint identifier is heard through the static and the needle points mostly toward the nose, but wanders too much to indicate an exact bearing. I will continue with the pre-calculated heading and make any necessary corrections when closer to the station.

Off to the south, on my right, the clouds are larger, higher, and more dense. The radio compass needle, occasionally swings off to the right for a few seconds before returning to it's primary indication, toward the nose. That is a strong indication of lightning from the clouds down on the gulf coast. The low frequency radio compass' long suit is pointing toward thunderstorms.

It has been a long day, and fatigue is beginning to rear it's ugly head. Why am I flying with total manual control? The Lear autopilot isn't much more than a wing leveler, but it can help. I hold the stick firmly in my left hand with a finger on the autopilot quick release. You never know if the thing will engage smoothly, violently, somewhere in between or not at all. With my right hand, I punch the "engage" button and with a slight deflection of the ailerons, it engages and stays steady. It will hold my heading for me, but there is no altitude "hold" that a full featured autopilot would have. I will have to watch the pitch attitude and use the pitch control wheels to make necessary corrections to maintain altitude. Better than nothing. Pitch trim corrections have to be made rather frequently. As the fuel burns off, weight and balance changes at a rate of about forty five pounds per minute, so the bird becomes lighter and will climb unless trim is changed or power is reduced – or both.

―――――――

The Greenville identifier is getting stronger now and the ADF needle is staying fairly close to the proper bearing set in top of the compass card. I am still above all the clouds along the route and I cannot see much now except the fleecy tops as the sun moves toward a lower angle in it's descent to the west. There are no anvil shaped cloud tops except those far to the south. Full grown, mature thunderstorms have anvil shaped tops, and they are usually spewing hailstones out of the top for a distance of several miles.

At plus four zero, the ADF needle gets very nervous, the volume diminishes rapidly, and the needle spins quickly to the bottom of the compass card. I am in the cone of silence, directly over the station. There is very little radio energy transmitted straight up over this type of radio nav aid. Seconds later, the volume builds again and the needle points steadily toward the tail. I note the time. Fuel remaining is eighteen hundred pounds with one hundred twenty five miles to go for high station over Columbus – seventeen minutes and seven hundred pounds of fuel. If they don't give me the run-around on the letdown and approach, I will be fat on fuel, an unaccustomed luxury, but on a strange field instrument approach, I don't need the added stress of sweating the fuel.

Greenwood is next along the route and only thirty six miles away. I Immediately retune the radio compass to the Greenwood frequency and get a fairly solid signal. With the radio compass needle again pointing toward the nose I take up a heading of zero nine two degrees. Five minutes later the needle is spinning and pointing at the tail again. After having made a position report over Greenville, I don't need to make another one this soon, but I note the time and fuel remaining on the knee pad. Fifteen hundred and seventy pounds showing on the fuel gauge. Eighty eight miles and twelve minutes to high station. In later times with better radar coverage by the area control centers, I would probably receive clearance shortly for an enroute descent and handover to approach control which would save a bunch of time and fuel. That time has not come yet, so we will do it the hard way.

The procedure is to report over the destination radio fix and get cleared for a tear drop shaped descent that takes us out several miles away from the radio station fix and back in as we reach approach altitude. At half the altitude loss, the two hundred degree turn is begun back to the station. Upon arriving back over "low station" we either take up a timed track for the airport or begin to follow instructions for a radar vectored approach. Without the radar, we begin the time over the station, as a known fix and descend to the published minimum altitude for that particular approach to the runway. Hopefully, the runway will come into view before the time expires. If it does not, a missed approach is executed. Each approach has it's own published procedures for a missed approach. On a missed approach, low on fuel, a Dawg pilot can find himself in serious trouble.

The sunlight is coming from toward the tail now and as I look ahead, over the cloud tops, the sky is getting darker to the east. I know that underneath the clouds, there will not be a lot of light, but official sunset is still several minutes away. I don't need any lights yet. It would be nice to know what type approach I will be making at Columbus. I have some time to study the letdown plates now. By the time I find out, I will be busy and will have to quickly interpret the plates and follow the instructions.

———

Memphis is calling me. "Air Force 64683, descend to 20,000 and contact Columbus approach on frequency 319.5" "Roger Memphis, 683 out of flight level 350 and leaving your frequency." I dial in the new frequency and call Columbus. They answer: "683 what is your position?" "683, descending to 20,000, estimating Columbus radio at one eight." "Roger 683. maintain 20,000 ft, report over the station, cleared for immediate penetration on Columbus ADF approach number two." "683 roger, 20,000." I have thumbed the speed brake switch on the side of the throttle handle and dropped the nose. The power is back to seventy five percent rpm and the EGT decreases to about 300 deg C. I don't want it any cooler because I would be inviting engine trouble.

From the map case I grab the Southeastern Letdown Book, showing all the published instrument letdowns and approaches in the Southeastern United States, and flip the pages to the alphabetical listing of Columbus. Then look for the page with the number two letdown chart. It is a run of the mill penetration and approach. Over the station, turn to a designated outbound heading, descending at 5,000 feet per minute or better at 250 knots; after losing half the altitude, begin a 200 degree left turn to an inbound heading back to the station. Level at 2000 feet. Over the station turn to a heading listed for the runway and descend to 600 feet. The distance and times are listed from low station to the airport for several typical approach speeds. Instructions for missed approach are listed.

I switch on the pitot heat for the probe that senses pressure for the airspeed indicator, because I will most likely be in some clouds during the penetration and maybe ice up the pitot tube. I also switch on the engine anti-icing system. Hot air is routed from a rear stage of the compressor back up front to keep ice from coating the intake area and then breaking off in chunks to damage the rotor blades. I have windshield anti-icing hot air available, but at this point, I don't need it. I can even route hot air underneath the leading edge wing slats if conditions warrant.

On time and at 20,000 feet, remaining fuel at a little over a thousand pounds, the ADF needle spins and I turn to the outbound heading, again retarding the power to 75 percent, dropping the speed brakes and keying the mike to report leaving high station. The noise and vibration of the air past those slabs sticking out from the sides of the fuselage, called speed brakes, coupled with the turn, radical altitude change, and attendant pressure change, makes me a candidate for vertigo. I am in the clouds now and strictly on the gauges. Changing head position to recheck the info on the letdown chart doesn't help either. At half the altitude loss, the teardrop turn is begun. The vertical air currents in those cumulus clouds generate some pretty hard bumps, some of them banging my head against the canopy.

Fighting the vertigo and forcing myself to believe the gauges rather than my feelings, the turn is completed and heading corrections are made to continue tracking inbound to the station. For a while, rain rattles against the windscreen, but soon ceases. The zero delay lanyard is reconnected to the parachute D ring. At about 2600 feet, I break through the bottom of the cloud layer and level at 1500 feet above the ground. I have a reason for not descending to the authorized minimum of 600 feet.

Now, I have broken out below the clouds and it is still daylight, but there is very little sunlight coming through the clouds. Everything looks dull and poorly defined through the haze, but I can see a vague outline of the airpatch up ahead. I punch the mike button and tell approach control I am going VFR (Visual Flight Rules). I have already looked up the tower frequency and noted it on the destination block of my nav log. I quickly dial it in and increase airspeed to two hundred seventy knots indicated – normal pattern entry speed. Check the utility hydraulic pressure. I don't want any surprises involving speed brakes, landing gear, or wheel brakes.

Columbus tower clears me for a 360 degree overhead landing pattern. I particularly wanted to do that rather than do a bomber type straight-in instrument approach. Columbus is a pilot training wing with cadets and student officers, many of whom have likely never seen a high performance jet other than a T-bird. Knowing that some of them might be watching and admiring, I do a snappy, three G break, retarding the power and popping the speed brakes. Roll out on the downwind, put down the gear and flaps, pushing the power back up to eighty five percent to maintain a hundred and seventy five knots in the base turn. Check the pressure on the pedals for the wheel brakes. When I have to look back over my left shoulder to see the approach end of the runway, it is time to begin a descending turn on around to final approach. Lining up with the blacktop, power is reduced to seventy five percent to maintain a hundred forty knots until I am over the fence.

At that speed, about 160 mph, there is not much time to make adjustments for misalignment with the runway or for the approach angle. It has to be pretty close to correct on rollout from the turn onto final approach. There is time only for a minor correction or two, and a final glance at the panel to make sure I have three green lights for wheels, one last check on airspeed, and if anything doesn't look right, a go-around is in order. So, I literally go smoking along on final and pull off the power as the tires "chirp chirp" on the asphalt at my projected touchdown spot, about 300 feet from the approach end. Not bad for a brown bar lieutenant.

The tower advises me to go to ground control frequency, which I do and am given instructions to taxi to the transient servicing area. Like most USAF bases it is almost in front of base ops. When I shut down, the fuel quantity gauge is reading 550 pounds. I hand the landing gear safety pins to the guy in the white coveralls, and tell him that I have no maintenance problems and want fuel, oxygen, oil checked, and wipe the windshield. (seriously, bugs accumulate at low altitude) I install the safety pins for ejection seat and canopy, unstrap, and after logging my flight time and type of approach, head for base ops. There doesn't seem to be any activity in the traffic pattern or on the flight line.

Being Friday evening, the flying training has apparently been shut down for the weekend, or at least for the day. If anyone was thrilled to have a real fighter land here, they are not in evidence. The ever present smell of kerosene that is characteristic of an airpatch used by turbine powered aircraft is quite strong. You cannot get away from it.

The sky is lead gray now and the haze is thicker with sunset only a couple of minutes away. The next leg may not be as easy as this one was. After a stop to check out the men's room, I toss my copy of the flight clearance form to the sergeant behind the ops counter to insure that my flight plan was canceled and there is a formal record of my safe arrival. I don't want the USAF to be making a search for me, because some knucklehead did not record my arrival. If things were done right, the tower has already informed all concerned, but foulups have been known to happen.

There is not time for a real sit down meal even if the mess hall is still open and it probably is not. I cannot go to the officers club dressed as I am and don't have time for that either. The standard option is the flight line snack bar and the standard people fuel is a hamburger and a milk shake. Quick, cheap, and full of calories. Back to the ops planning room to check Notices to Airmen for McGhee Tyson Airport, Knoxville, Tennessee. There is nothing of significance.

I did a preliminary nav log for this next leg before leaving Perrin. All I have to do is get the upper air winds from the meteorologist on duty and a briefing for enroute and destination weather. Using the upper wind speed and direction, I use my pocket plotter, which is really a circular slide rule, and compute ground speeds and drift correction. By applying the wind factor, true airspeed is converted to ground speed. Ground speed and distance provides time. The time provides fuel consumption figures.

My nav log is complete with headings, checkpoints versus times and fuel remaining and total enroute time. Some of that info is entered on a flight plan clearance form to be filed with ops. The weather officer on duty fills in the section on enroute and destination weather plus forecast weather for destination. I am what is known as a slick winged pilot, no star or commode seat as a senior pilot or command pilot. Therefore my flight plan must be reviewed and signed by at least a senior pilot. The captain on duty scans it and scrawls his signature. He is probably a flight instructor in the training wing taking his turn as duty officer. His only comment is: "Have a good flight Lieutenant," as I shove my copy in a zippered breast pocket. The sergeant on dispatch duty takes the other copy to phone in the clearance request to Air Route Traffic Control.

———

Outside, it is now fully dark and the airbase is quiet and less hot than earlier, but the air is still heavy. Except for the base ops people and transient maintenance crew, most everyone is probably kicking back for an evening of relaxation or beginning a night out. Visiting air traffic is usually slim at training bases on weekends, except for the occasional transient, bumming fuel, as I am. These types of bases are most all located in areas of little interest to visitors.

I climb up the kick steps and get the forms book lying in the seat. According to the entries, all required servicing has been done. Fuel tanks are full, a little engine oil has been added and oxygen tanks filled. Hydraulic systems didn't need topping up. The amount of fuel added matches what the tanks should hold. Just to be sure, I do a walk around and open the filler caps for the drop tanks. They are full. Since there is no gauge for the drop tanks, that is the only way I can be sure they were serviced. I get out my little pocket flashlight and check the tires, brake rotors and discs. They look OK. While underneath, I also shine the light up into the wheel wells where I can see the charging indicators for the hydraulic accumulators. They all show normal.

Although there is a secondary engine driven hydraulic system, and even a third, electrically driven system for the critical flight control operation, I like to see that all of them are operational prior to flight. There is no way to control the ailerons and stabilator mechanically on this airplane. Without hydraulics, there is zero flight control operation. Except for the rudder, there are no mechanical connections to the flight controls.

The transient alert crew is vigilant and as soon as I start to climb aboard, they leave their shack and head my way. The APU is brought up and the long black snake that provides electrical power is plugged into my bird. As I am strapping up with the aid of one of them, the other one starts the APU and my cockpit lights up. After a few minutes, the start and taxi out routine is complete and I have a clearance for my next leg.

On the way out, the blue, green, and red boundary and taxiway lights are very colorful, standing out in the dark, and as I take the runway, the dim, yellow, runway marker lights down each side are rather dull. At the far end, they disappear into a black hole. Technically, the field is still VFR, but in reality, one must be on the gauges when breaking ground and boring holes into the darkness.

In getting my clearance from Air Traffic Control by way of the local tower, I have engaged in the unspoken contest frequently initiated by clearance delivery. They know we are handicapped by single-handedly controlling the moving airplane, keeping a watchful eye on various objects and other traffic to avoid, and copying the clearance, which is often long and complicated. The game rules are: They talk fast and if we have to ask for a fill or a repeat, or get corrected on the read-back, they win. If we read it back correctly, with no errors, we win. We all have our own brand of short hand to record the info quickly and accurately.

I have been cleared direct Birmingham, direct Chattanooga, direct Knoxville at 37,000 feet. This is to be a relatively short flight, but I will still conserve fuel by making a non afterburner climb. However, I will use the burner for take-off. It would not be using good judgment to risk a marginal takeoff to save a few gallons of fuel. With full fuel, I am near maximum gross weight. The only other load that could be added would be rockets in the pod, which we don't carry on this type mission. The calculated gross weight is near 20,000 pounds and the bird would roll a long way before becoming airborne without the A/B.

Again, the nose wheel is on the white centerline with the nose pointed straight down the runway. My landing light changes tilt angle and becomes a taxi light when there is weight on the nose wheel. To my rear and to the sides, the darkness is displaced by several feet of blue and yellow flame as the A/B lights off with a surge and abrupt roar. I'm thinking ," I'll bet that rattled some windows and everybody on the base and some beyond, heard that. That's no T-bird."

The gauges all look good, so the brakes are released and all that surging power is allowed to begin pushing nearly ten tons of assorted metals and fluids down the invisible black strip. Guided by the white centerline and the row of lights on either side of the runway, the bird is traveling straight and gaining speed at an ever increasing rate. At liftoff, my attention is directed primarily to the attitude indicator for pitch and bank control and to the directional indicator because the outside visual indicators are disappearing. Thank goodness for gyro powered instruments. I can see nothing straight ahead through the windshield. It might as well be covered with black cloth.

The inner ear contains three fluid filled semi-circular canals that detect motion around the three axes and send that information to the brain. Unfortunately, very slow rotation around an axis is not detected and the brain is not informed of the position change. It gets worse, when correction is made at a faster rate, and is detected, the brain thinks the correction is made to an erroneous position. Then the mental battle begins. The eyes may be getting information from the flight instruments that does not agree with what the brain is getting from the inner ear. The struggle can be so severe that sometimes pilots actually develop nausea from it.

The solution is to concentrate on the info from the eyes and ignore what we feel. Incredibly, the flight instruments, although usually provided by the lowest bidder, are more trustworthy than our own senses under those circumstances.

I get the gear and flaps cleaned up and start a turn for the outbound heading. At 350 knots, throttle back to a hundred percent military power and shut down the fuel guzzling afterburner. Inside the cockpit, there is a warm glow from the instrument lights and various indicator lights. Outside the cockpit, there is not much to be seen. Even the reflected light from the flashing red and green nav lights on the wing tips looks fuzzy. Since immediately after take off, the haze has gotten more dense and visibility is very restricted, even looking straight down. Only a few lights around the countryside are in view and they are just dim little pin pricks of light on a dull black cloth. There is no light from the stars or moon breaking through the clouds and haze. There are no discernible terrain features.

I still have the Columbus low frequency radio beacon tuned on the ADF and figure I might as well use it to fly an accurate course outbound, so I turn up the volume and am surprised to hear mostly static with a very weak and fading signal. I don't expect to be able to receive Birmingham yet, so here we go again. Just hold the course, corrected for the forecast wind. There is no visibility, even when looking straight down now. The haze has merged with the clouds and it seems I am alone in the world. I am not receiving any radio nav aids and I cannot see anything outside the cockpit except reflections from my own running lights. The bright/flash mode is very distracting, with so much reflection, so I switch to dim and steady, instead of bright and flash.

The gyro horizon or attitude indicator, is the primary flight instrument. Keep the wings level and the nose slightly high to maintain course and sustain the climb. The directional indicator is also frequently checked, along with the airspeed. Vertical velocity, airspeed and altimeter indications are closely related. Angle of bank on the gyro horizon is cross checked against the turn needle. The information provided by these instruments is inter-related. If one gets out of kilter, they all will. Watch for minute changes and make minute corrections, before big changes require big corrections. Periodically include engine instruments in the cross check. If something is going wrong, I want early warning. Watch the oil pressure, hydraulic pressures, fuel flow, exhaust gas temp, rpm and nozzle position. Check the generator load meters and check the oxygen pressure. I don't want to go to sleep from hypoxia up here. Keep those eyeballs moving. Knowing that even expensive gyro instruments can go awry, I occasionally check the directional indicator against the mag compass. The mag compass may bounce around and be difficult to get an exact reading from, but it is not dependent on electrical power and complex circuitry.

Climbing through about twenty six thousand, I break out on top of the clouds and there is a low, weak, partial moon, reflecting a little light onto the cloud tops as I continue the climb. Birmingham is only twelve minutes from Columbus, so at plus six minutes, I tune the ADF to the Birmingham frequency. Surely, I can get a bearing from this distance. Only static – loud static – no radio signal. The ADF needle wanders aimlessly. Nothing is attracting it, so I turn down the volume. I don't need to have that useless noise beating on my ears.

Maybe the Birmingham radio beacon is out of service. The NOTAMS listed nothing about it. Maybe my ADF receiver has died. Here I am, unable to see anything except clouds, no way to verify my position. In those days, the control centers did not have radar nor were tied in to powerful military radar systems as they were later. Anyway, I am not lost – dead reckoning will work – to an extent. But how about the letdown? It is extremely dangerous to let down without knowing precisely where I am. OK, I will cross that bridge when I get to it. Right now, just hold precise headings and keep an accurate check on the time.

———

This is a lot different from air to air combat practice. Sitting here exposed to the force of one G, maintaining level flight as opposed to trying to keep several other maneuvering aircraft in sight, trying to anticipate what they are going to do, while I am on my back, grunting, gasping, sweating, and pulling four G's or better. A guy can be pretty busy, keeping track of altitude, fuel, the leader, if you are the wing-man or if you are the leader, making constant snap decisions that may well determine whether you win or lose, live or die. If you don't like challenges, choose another occupation. You would have to spend a lot of money for drugs in order to experience all the weird sensations you can have during just one night formation flight in bad weather.

———

At about two minutes to estimated time over Birmingham, I see a dull glow through the clouds, almost straight ahead, just a little off to the left. The aeronautical chart indicates that the city is a little to the north of the radio beacon. That tallies with my course, relative to the city. The only metropolis around that could generate that much light, would have to be Birmingham. As I pass over the southern portion of the glow, the ADF needle spins around and points to the tail. I turn up the volume and sure enough, through the static, I can hear the identifier – Birmingham. I have just passed it and the ADF could only receive it while I was right on top of it.

Some radio propagation! When I need the radio the most, it's performance is at it's worst. The signal has faded and the needle is wandering aimlessly again. There is nothing to see ahead – just total darkness. The airplane does not know it is night time, but it sure makes noises not heard at any other time.

Chattanooga is next. The time and fuel is going according to plan. For a few minutes I can see a very large area of glow through the clouds in the distance off to the right. I reckon that would have to be Atlanta. I cannot receive any navigational radio signals. The static level is incredibly high. If I can dead reckon to a position directly over a radio beacon, the darned radio can confirm that I am over the station. I feel even more alone and vulnerable than I did earlier.

Two years earlier, I was the assistant non-commissioned officer in charge of communications at the radar station atop Cross Mountain. That Air Force Station is located about forty miles northwest of Knoxville and operates a powerful air defense radar. They are not required to provide flight following service, but have the capability and sometimes will accommodate a pilot in the area. It is not likely that anyone I know personally is still there, or if they are, may not be on duty. Anyway, it can't hurt to ask for a little nav assistance. So, I request Atlanta Center for permission to leave their frequency temporarily. They give me the OK.

After a couple of radio calls, I get a reply. I make my request and give him an estimated position between Birmingham and Chattanooga. He has me "squawk flash", that is, push the ID switch for the IFF transponder. That provides a large return on his scope for a sweep or two. He verifies my position and I feel a little a better about my situation. I am thinking, "He can direct me to right over McGhee-Tyson Airport and hand me over to approach control."

After another couple of minutes, the voice on the radio says, "Air Force 64683, flight following is terminated – out". No explanation. I don't have any way to know if he got busy, was tired, lazy, or had equipment problems. I switch the radio back to Atlanta Center and inform the controller that I am back on his frequency. All I have to look at is a panel full of instruments, and none of them can tell me exactly where I am.

———

The F-86D has a reputation as a widow maker among some pilots, mostly by those who have not flown it. It is quite a hand full, being a very complex machine that has a lot of equipment and systems that can fail. It is always short on fuel. It is heavy and unforgiving, if not handled properly, to a much greater extent than the day fighter versions, but those of us who do fly it must have confidence in the machine and in ourselves. Pilots in the all weather interceptor school get more training than in any other advanced flight school.

The complexity is partly a result of it's all-weather interceptor role and partly because of it's redundant systems. If the pilot knows the systems well, he can work around a host of equipment problems. We have all done a lot of that in the simulator, and perhaps at least a little bit for real in the bird. In the simulator, we never have the luxury of just flying around and making intercepts. The instructor continuously induces problems to be dealt with in a realistic manner. More often than not, we complete a sim flight more sweaty and wrung out than we would in a real flight.

The result is, when a real problem does surface, we have already had practice in dealing with it and there is no panic. Usually, we actually forget that we are in the simulator and that the flight is not real. Our minds become geared to the concept that everything is real and we react accordingly. Often we are brought back to the reality that we have been earthbound for the past hour, only when the instructor pops the canopy and he is standing there beside the cockpit, telling us, "Lets go, the lesson is over." As far as our mind is concerned, we have been flying.

So far, I have not turned on the radar in this bird. In addition to the attack display, it has a ground mapping mode and I decide to turn it on and check it out. The scope between my knees lights up and the antenna in the nose is scanning back and forth in Auto Search. There are some returns there, but nothing very well defined. If we are over a combination of land and water, like a coastline or large lake, the contrast shows up quite well, but over all land there is not much intelligence indicated. I can't see anything that helps with the navigation, so I turn it off again to reduce the electrical load.

The Birmingham scenario is repeated as I pass Chattanooga. As the glow through the clouds fades behind me, I am again looking at solid black wall all around. So I continue to play the same game. Hold my calculated heading, watch the time and wait. All systems are doing fine except the ADF and I think any problem there lies with the weather and the radio wave propagation. I have been at my assigned 37,000 feet for a few minutes and the fuel situation is good. In a few more minutes I will ask Atlanta Center to release me to Knoxville Approach Control.

———————

Sitting here, alone, strapped in this hunk of metal, with a big blowtorch pushing it along, I feel like I am not part of the real world. I am detached from it. It is seven miles below me and my only connection with it is an occasional distant voice coming through the headphones from someone I have never met and probably never will. They are the only people who even know I am up here. The closest friends I have right now are those glowing dials on the panel in front of me. I must trust them. Otherwise, I will not know how high I am, how fast I am traveling, what direction I am going, or even if I am right side up. There is no physical sensation of speed, no visual horizon for orientation, no feeling of height. I don't even know yet how I will make the transition back to terra firma. Knoxville Approach has not informed me.

I do know that just outside this aluminum, magnesium, and plastic tube is a very hostile environment. The temperature is minus forty Degrees. There is very little air and I am dependent on the aircraft oxygen system for survival. I am protected from all that by a few thousandths of an inch of aluminum. As the air for the engine progresses through the multi-stage compressor, it becomes very hot, and some of it is bled off and fed into the cockpit so I don't freeze. That thin air accounts for the fact that the bird is moving at four hundred sixty knots and the airspeed indicator tells me it is only about two fifty.

Judging from the low level of radio activity, air traffic is light. Atlanta sends me over to approach control. Approach clears me for immediate penetration from high station. Most of these guys deal with enough jet fighter traffic that they know we can not spend much, if any, time in a holding pattern, and are pretty good at minimizing the delays in getting us down. The letdown book is opened to McGhee-Tyson and the flashlight allows me to see the letdown procedure I am cleared for. I can't see much of the book with the red cockpit flood lights and I could turn on the white thunderstorm lights, but that would destroy too much night vision.

The headings are different, but the procedure turns out to be pretty much the same as it was at Columbus. As I throttle back, drop the nose, and put out the speed brakes, I think about the commitment I am making. Once I let down to approach altitude, I will not have enough fuel to climb back up again and go to an alternate airfield. The ceiling and visibility at Knoxville is reported to be high enough so as not to pose a problem. The turbulent airflow around the speed brakes generates the usual noise and vibration as I go through my penetration checklist. Without those drag devices, it would require too much time and distance to descend without excessive speed build up.

It gets darker as I plunge into the cloud tops and I am strictly on the gauges again. There is not much turbulence from the clouds and I am able to hold the bird steady on the correct headings. The vertical velocity indicator is showing nearly 5,000 feet per minute descent at 250 knots airspeed. The altimeter must be read very carefully as it is changing very rapidly and I know it is lagging my real altitude somewhat at this rate of descent. Therefore, I must lead the level off by several hundred feet. Nearing the published initial approach altitude, I begin to break the rate of descent

Inbound to low station, the clouds become ragged and thinner and I can begin to see some lights on the ground. Since it is dark and I am not familiar with the local VFR patterns, I continue inbound with the instrument approach, crossing low station and taking up a heading for the primary runway at minimum published altitude. Speed brakes are out, flaps down, landing gear down and showing three green lights on the panel. The instrument lights have been set to a fairly dim setting and all the indicator light lenses in the cockpit have been rotated mechanically to a dim setting.

The approach is looking good, tower has cleared me for landing. The threshold lights for the runway are about to disappear underneath the nose, and I am about to begin backing off on the power to plant the bird on the runway numbers, when, ZAP!!! The cockpit is filled with dazzling bright yellow light and the beeping of the inner marker signal is pounding my ears. Beep! Flash! Beep! Flash! Beep! For a split second, I thought the aft fire warning light was on, but then I realized that it would be steady and not flashing and I would not get a beep from it.

I cannot see the runway clearly. It is an out of focus blur with all that bright light hitting me squarely in the eyes from it's upper panel position. My night vision is destroyed. I slam the throttle full forward, as I pull in the speed brakes and try to focus on the attitude indicator for the moment. While I am pulling up the wheels with my left hand, I hit the mike button on the stick grip with the other hand to tell tower I am going around, can they clear me for a closed pattern? "Roger 683 closed pattern approved." That means I can simply fly a box pattern around the airpatch and come right back around to the final approach again.

With the bird under control and at a safe altitude, on the downwind leg, I reach up and try to twist the lens on the offending light to the dim position. It won't move any further clockwise, the dim position. The dimming mechanism has jammed. There is no switch to turn off the marker beacon receiver. It is hard wired on and I cannot safely look now to see if there is a circuit breaker for it under the consoles. Many of these breakers control items in addition to what they are labeled for anyway. I cannot make a safe flare and touchdown if that thing comes on again when I come back around. I can't cover it up, so I simply reach up there and screw the entire lens assembly out of the holder and remove the bulb. With that stuff in my pocket, I come back around and make a respectable landing.

After shutting down and making sure my clearance is canceled and that base ops is sending a RON (remain overnight message) to Perrin, I telephone my father-in-law to come and get me for the night. When we hang it up for the night, we always keep our home station informed of our whereabouts.

―――――

It was right here, about two years earlier, that my first flight as a student pilot took place, in a sixty five horsepower Aeronca 7AC, commonly referred to as an "Air knocker". I was a Staff Sergeant and my boss was Master Sergeant Jim Fry. He was the NCO in charge of communications for our unit. We got along well. I was single and Jim was divorced, and we often bummed around together, sometimes double dating

We were stationed with a radar squadron, in Maryville, about three miles from McGhee Tyson Airport. Our unit was part of the early warning air defense system, operating a long range radar with operational control of the interceptor aircraft at McGhee Tyson. This was the unit that later moved to Cross Mountain, near Lake City.

Jim was a licensed pilot and certified flight instructor. To keep up his flying proficiency, Jim frequently went out to Cooks Flying Service at the airpatch. I had some inclination to obtain a pilots license, but was not managing my money well enough to pay for the training. We had to live on the local economy and our allowance for living expenses was less than the actual cost. There was no military housing or messing facilities. Because of that and my foolishly paying too much for a late model automobile, as young men are prone to do, there were no funds for flight training. My dream of becoming a military pilot did not appear to be coming true.

At that time, I held FCC licenses for commercial radio operation and repair, but could not find a local, part time job because of my rotating work schedule. Jim talked with Mr. Cook, owner of the flying service without my knowing it, until Mr. Cook approached me with a job offer. It seemed that he had a lot of radio problems with his fleet of aircraft, but could not get anyone to keep them working. Evidently Jim had recommended me because of the work I had done in the communications section of the radar squadron. Mr. Cook asked me to work for him, with no set schedule. I could just come to work when I wanted to.

The short version of that story is, that I jumped at the offer. I enjoyed getting all his radio equipment in good working condition, and being around the pilots and the airplanes. After accumulating some pay credit, I started flying lessons when one of the instructors had a slack period. Using my credit on their books, I had no out of pocket expenses. Sometimes Jim gave me some instruction and we only paid for the airplane, since Jim did not want to charge me for the instruction. I eventually soloed, but did not have much hope of becoming a military pilot.

However, my appetite was whetted, and I didn't care what kind of flying I did, as long as I was airborne. While hanging around the flying service, I sometimes could scrounge a ride in addition to my irregular lessons. If a pilot invited me to go along on a test flight, I jumped at the chance to go. Sometimes we invented a need for a test flight after working on the radios. If a plane just needed to be moved around the ramp or hangar, I volunteered. Starting up and trundling around the ramp put me at the controls even if I could not get airborne at the moment.

―――――――

The Dawg I have just shut down is light years ahead of the Aeronca I flew here earlier. The puddle jumper had no engine starter, no battery, no generator. We hand propped it to crank the engine. The radio was receive only with it's own internal battery – no transmitter.

On the ground, we acknowledged the control tower light gun instructions by moving the stick from side to side so the controller could see our ailerons moving. In the air, we rocked the wings. The instrumentation consisted of an air speed indicator, altimeter, tachometer and oil pressure gauge. The take off and landing speed was about 50 miles per hour and the max speed, level flight, was about eighty five mph. The Dawg won't even stay in the air at less than a hundred forty knots. (161 mph) and has set a speed record of seven hundred fifteen mph.

The light aircraft is a trainer and a fun machine. The F-86 is a machine for serious business. Seven hundred ninety two MIG 15s shot down with a loss of seventy eight F-86s is not a bad score by any standard. According to some of the Russian and Chinese pilots the score was in their favor, but they have been known to cheat.

Any real flying machine is a quantum step up from the toys and models that I hand carved with a pocket knife as a young boy. I was frequently chastised by my dad for wasting time on such foolishness. I don't think he ever understood what it was like for person to have serious aspirations toward any significant accomplishment, and to be willing to put forth whatever effort the objective might require. I was too naive to understand that I wasn't supposed to dream those kind of dreams.

––––––

It was also here in the Maryville-Alcoa area about three years earlier, that I met a young lady by the name of Mary Katherine. We hit it off very well from the beginning. She needed to complete high school and I could not be married if I wanted to get into pilot training. So, we waited and were married the day I graduated from pilot training. My Dad always said that she pinned on my pilots wings at ten o'clock in the morning and she clipped them at two that afternoon. She was nineteen and I was twenty four.

––––––

After a night of rest with the in-laws, it is time to do some checking on weather conditions around the country and decide where to travel to next. I have telephoned home and everything is OK there. I have Dad drive me out to the airpatch and we look at the F-86D. He has never seen the bird close up and certainly has never seen the inside of my office. He climbs up far enough to get a good look, but for some reason, does not want sit in the seat. He is in awe of all the dials, switches, and various controls. His main question was, "how do you keep track of all this?"

I go in to the weather office and find that the entire eastern half of the country either has big thunderstorm activity or soon will have. I can deal with thunderstorms, with assistance from ground radar for navigation, but as mentioned earlier, when on my own for navigation, the ADF just does not cut it. I have a long hard week behind me with another one coming up. Not being fully rested, I decide to delay until afternoon and check weather again. I would like to go to Charleston S.C., but the thunderstorm activity is worse there than any other area.

In the afternoon, I telephone the weather office. The storm activity has not improved. In fact, it has worsened. I decide to wait until Sunday and just head back to Perrin. Ops will not expect me to risk beating up the airplane with hail and take unnecessary chances. On an operational mission, those risks are justified, but not on a trip just bumming around the country. Wing commanders worry about their careers. Their careers depend to a great extent on pilots like me not breaking airplanes.

Sunday morning : The weather looks better, so after brunch, we go out to the airpatch again. Greenville, Mississippi looks like a good place to refuel. There is another pilot training wing there. Air traffic should be light on Sunday and the weather is clearing up all across the country. The trip is only about four hundred nautical miles, and weather conditions won't require an alternate landing spot. All I will need to be legal is a fuel of reserve of twenty minutes over high station.

That leg of the trip is easy. I can see most of the land marks and the radio compass works fine. The sky is mostly clear except for some occasional scattered cumulus and some very high thin cirrus clouds. I can see Greenville AFB long before I get to the radio fix. Being lazy, I cancel the IFR and start descending straight toward the base from about thirty miles out. I contact the control tower and get instructions for pattern entry and a 360 overhead pattern. With a snappy break and my best, tight, hundred and eighty degree turn on to the downwind, I put down the wheels and flaps, then continue right on around for another one eighty onto the final approach for a normal landing.

———

The airbase is very quiet. I don't see or hear any other air traffic. The transient maintenance crew should be able to service my bird promptly. I go to the flight planning room and look at the big U.S. map that all base ops have on the wall. There is the string, anchored at Greenville and hanging down to be picked up and stretched across any location in the states. You hold your thumb on the string at that location and transfer the string to the mileage scale. Bingo, you have instant direct mileage from here to wherever you want to go.

With this good weather, maybe, I should dogleg around and get in another flight to make up for yesterday. Well, on the other hand, the day is passing on by and tomorrow will be another hard work day. The lazy side of me wins and I make up a nav chart for Home. It should be a short, easy trip. I have not been with my wife much for several days and I think about how she has been slighted.

From the early days of our courtship, I had emphasized to her that my love of airplanes would continue to occupy a position of high priority in my life and she understood that. Now that we were married, she was finding out the hard way that nothing had changed, but she handled it well. I have seen too many woman agree to a mans plans, set the hook, and then go about trying to change him. I am grateful that my woman accepted me as I was and would continue to do so. I had a disease, that demanded treatment, but would never be cured. That's about as much as I ever understood, concerning my attraction to flying machines.

———————

Dispatch says transient maintenance has not called in to report my bird being ready and I wonder why. I get on the line with them and find out, they have put my bird on a red X because of a tire problem. The right main has a spot where the tire is worn beyond allowable limits. Strange, I have not been on the brakes hard enough to skid the tires on a landing roll. That will almost always wipe out one or both main gear tires. In the status block of the aircraft form, an "X" in red pencil grounds the aircraft until properly cleared.

At home, a service truck carrying wheels already built up would have re-placed tire, wheel and brakes, if needed, while the refueling crew was doing their thing. It's a five minute job, at most. While flying with the Air Defense Alert Unit, during heavy activity, I have had the bird serviced with fuel, oxygen, oil, hydraulics, both main gear tires and brakes and been airborne again in under ten minutes. Then I have to understand, the guys here are highly experi-enced on T-birds, but nothing else.

I trudge down the flight line to where my bird is. The maintenance people are sitting around. I ask why they are not changing my wheel and tire. "We don't have that type wheel or tire." I ask, "Do you have a T-bird tire." "Yessir but not this type wheel." "OK, take my wheel down to the tire shop and put a T-bird tire on it. "Will that work?" I explain that it will work, but due to the twelve ply cord, instead of fourteen, I will be allowed only one landing on it. With that I go back to ops to have a coke and cool my heels.

About an hour later, I call down to maintenance to find out if my bird is ready now. "No sir, we still have a problem." Again, I walk down to where they are. "What is the problem now." "well sir, we haven't removed the wheel yet because we can't find the parking brake to shut off the hydraulic fluid while the wheel and brake assembly is removed." While trying to keep a straight face, I inform them that the reason they can't find the parking brake is because the F-86 does not have a parking brake. The brake line has a valve that will automatically seal off the line when disconnected from the brake assembly.

They finally get the wheel, tire and brake assembly back from the tire shop and get me ready to roll. As I taxi out for take-off, the sun is quite low on the western horizon. This is a short leg and I plan to use the afterburner for take-off and also the climb to cruise altitude. With everything looking good again, on the take-off roll, the control tower calls and says the base ops officer would like to have me do a high speed pass over the field if I can afford the time and fuel. I reply that I will oblige. Those guys at that country airpatch might as well have their excitement for the week.

The weather is clear and I can maneuver unrestricted in the vicinity of the airport. After take-off, I climb to about ten grand and shut off the burner, do a ninety/two seventy reverse and look down at the runway, straight ahead at about five miles. I can pick up a lot of speed in the diving approach, but can not go supersonic. People get riled up over sonic booms, unless we do it in an approved area.

I point the nose at the approach end of the runway and leave the power at one hundred percent rpm, but without burner. Leveling out at about twenty feet above the ground, I go streaking down the runway with the airspeed indicator showing about five hundred and fifty knots. (that's about 630 mph) and shove the throttle into the full afterburner range as I start easing the nose up. At that speed and with all that air being crammed into the engine, it lights with a boom, and shoves me against the seat back. They may have thought the blast of the burner lighting up was a sonic boom. I continued climbing at about a forty five degree angle until I figured I was out of sight and then lowered the nose for normal climb and turned toward home.

Tomorrow, I will be back at work, teaching other guys to fly this machine and to use it as a weapons platform.

More Routine Stuff

Dick Griffin had also been retained at Perrin as instructor. His parents lived at Long Beach, on the south side of Los Angeles and with military airport locations being what they were, the closest practical place for him to land was at Marine El Toro, Santa Anna.

On a Friday afternoon, he and I departed Perrin in a T-bird for El Toro and refueled at Roswell, New Mexico, and Tucson, Arizona. It would be late when we arrived in California.

Approaching El Toro, the weather was good and we could see the lights of Santa Anna ahead. We got clearance for a VOR penetration on arrival at high station, and were advised that a fog bank was rapidly forming off the coast. There was a fair amount of moonlight and in the distance we could see the fog bank, but were not concerned because it was not close by.

We crossed high station, and Dick, being in the front seat, began our descent. I was in the back seat, minding the maps, nav logs, radios and let-down charts. We were OK on fuel, but did not have much reserve. Early in the penetration, approach control advised us the fog bank was moving rapidly inland. We were committed now, with too little fuel to go anywhere else, and besides, who's afraid of a little fog?

About half way through the penetration turn, our visibility abruptly disappeared and we could see nothing past the wingtip nav lights. Now approach control was advising that the airfield was zero-zero. No ceiling, no visibility. The dense, rapidly forming fog bank extended to the ground. We were advised to execute a missed approach and divert to March AFB, for which we did not have adequate fuel and we knew it would be futile to try.

So, I told approach control that we were electing to continue the approach, knowing we had already been promised a precision radar final. We would not be legal, making an approach to an airport known to be below authorized approach minimums, but it was the logical choice. The controller had fulfilled his legal obligation to advise us.

We were switched to the precision radar controller's channel and he did a good job of directing us down the glide slope and keeping us on the centerline. At two hundred feet, he was advising us to go around if we had no visual contact. Dick was flying the bird and actually let the bird slip a little below two hundred on short final, but could see nothing – not even any lights. Not surprised, we went around, already on the last of our fuel. The fuselage tank held ninety five gallons. It was the only tank with a gauge and it was dropping rapidly. There was nothing in the other cells with which to replenish it. The low pressure lights were on for the tip tanks, main wing tanks and leading edge wing tanks, but we left all the boost pumps on in the hope of draining any fuel that might have been sloshing around in there.

We requested another approach. Dick asked me to take control from the back seat so he could concentrate on making visual contact from the front. We came around again with the low fuel warning lights glaring at us while the controller did a great job and I worked hard at following directions precisely. We were running out of time, fuel and ideas. He was saying what I wanted to hear. "On glide path, on course, steer right two degrees now, going ten feet high, increase descent slightly......" and so on.

All the while the distance to touchdown was shrinking at the rate of 120 knots. As we got close in and our height above ground again went below 200 feet, I was asking Dick if he could see anything. "Nope, not yet." The controller was telling us to go around, but I knew we would flame out from fuel starvation shortly after any go around was established. So, I continued the glide path. The controller's voice was betraying a little more concern as he was forcefully directing us to go around. Again, I asked Dick, "Can you see anything?" At that moment the wheels made their Chirp Chirp sound contacting the asphalt and Dick, said, "I have it.!"

We could barely see the yellow runway lights on each side through the fog, but we were on the white center line illuminated by our landing light. Dick braked some but let the bird roll until there was a line breaking off to the right, indicating a turn off to a taxiway. He turned off the runway and stopped. We could see nothing in any direction. I felt like we could cut that fog with a knife. Ground control sent out a Follow Me truck to find us and lead us in to the parking area.

We never heard anything about making the approach to an airport below published approach minimums. Actually, it was no big deal to Dick and me. We were all weather pilots. That was what we had been trained to do.

In the course of normal training operations, we flew in a lot of bad weather. After all, we were training all weather pilots and we rarely stood down because of weather. During one winter, we began to experience a high incidence of flame-outs with the T-birds; sometimes as many as three or four a day. Most of the engines died at altitudes well above the freezing level and often at better than twenty thousand feet. That gave us time to work on making an airstart and after switching the fuel control to the emergency system the engines would start up.

The emergency fuel control was a fairly crude system and a lot of care had to be exercised to avoid rapid throttle movements because it bypassed the more sophisticated features of the main fuel control. However, we were glad to settle for any system that would work after having lost all power. We continued to be plagued with engines winding down with no warning while a lot of work was being done to identify the source of the problem. It almost always happened while flying in clouds.

Little, by little we discovered there was no single problem, but a combination of several things. Water was getting into the main fuel control and then freezing, and blocking the fuel flow. Much care was taken to keep the fuel moisture free, but surprisingly, kerosene does have a strong affinity for water. The flame out problems were occurring early, mostly during the first flight of the day. Many times when a bird returned from it's last flight of the day, say around midnight or later, no refueling was done until early morning, in time for the first flight of the next day.

While sitting on a relatively cool ramp all night, with tanks filled mostly with moist air, the moisture condensed and mixed with the fuel when the morning crews readied the bird for flight. It didn't take a lot of water to make ice once it got to the complex fuel control, operating in air below freezing temperatures. Refueling the birds immediately on return from a flight eliminated at lot of condensation, but we still had some problems. It was finally determined that ice and supercooled water coming into the engine air intakes was impinging on a component of the main fuel control itself. A simple shield was installed in front of the control and our problem was diminished but not totally eliminated.

The T-33 was equipped with an alcohol tank, but we had never thought that we needed to use them. Now we changed our minds about that and started servicing the alcohol tanks with straight alcohol. As we ran up the engine for takeoff, we would activate the alcohol pump for a few seconds to melt any ice forming in the system. While airborne, we would periodically give the system a shot of alcohol and enjoy a flight without having to make an airstart while on the gauges.

Meanwhile, the evaporation problem with the alcohol in storage got to be larger than it should have been. We were using pure grain stuff and it must have been mighty tempting to the ground crews. It sure smelled good. The people in charge started labeling the drums with a skull and cross bones, plus a label that warned that the juice had been cut with at least ten percent wood alcohol. There was an immediate decrease in the evaporation rate.

Since we were operating the school with first line interceptors, and as pilots certified combat ready, the Air Force was not going to let us be just a training facility. We were assigned to an operational unit in the Air Defense Command as augmentation forces. Periodically, we were called upon to deploy to another location, sometimes several hundred miles away.

Because of the constant requirement for deployment availability, we were kept on a short leash. When off duty, we could not leave home without notifying our flight commander of our whereabouts, even if it was only across the street. Going to the lake, would not excuse us from notification. When a recall came, the base helicopter was dispatched to fly up and down the lake, dragging a banner. We were expected to be in position at the deployment base within three hours. Initially our deployment base was in Minnesota, so far away it required a refueling stop and was totally impractical for a lead time of only three hours.

Eventually our normal deployment base was changed to Little Rock AFB, Arkansas. We could easily make that in one flight. The deployment exercises usually came at times that would least disrupt our training schedule. Those times often turned out to be at Thanksgiving and Christmas when the students were enjoying time off. The war games were usually terminated on Christmas Eve and we hustled to get home. Many of the birds were flown with problems that should have grounded them. We flew in good weather or bad, good birds or sick birds. As long as we could get them in the air, we flew and wrote the up maintenance problems as having occurred on the last flight. Get-home-itis sometimes overrode proper procedures.

———

Our flight graduated a class and picked up a new group of students. One of them was Landon, who had made it a point to harass me in preflight. He and several other members of his class had originally gone to an operational unit that had been dissolved and they were now to be retrained as interceptor pilots. Landon was obviously concerned to learn that he was assigned to me, although I had nothing to do with it. It was a random assignment. I let him stew about it for the first couple of days of preliminaries before we got into the actual flying.

He approached me and voiced his concern, wondering if we could get along. I did not want to prolong my revenge and figured there was no point in causing him any undue difficulty. I told him that it would not affect my treatment of him, but if he thought he would feel better by being paired with another instructor, I would suggest the change to our boss. To Landon's credit, he elected to stay with me and I was true to my word, but there was some satisfaction in seeing the shoe on the other foot for a while.

———

After a while, I traded my battered, not so shiny brown bar for a silver one. I was now First Lieutenant Wade with a fair amount of experience as a pilot and as a flight instructor. At least there were now some newer guys below me on the totem pole. Not that I needed to feel superior to anybody, but it was nice to feel more like one of the old hands.

One of our additional duties was to take turns manning the mobile control fishbowl out between the parallel runways. We had a senior controller, an assistant and a student for each shift. The senior oversaw all the air traffic coming and going and was there to advise by radio anyone who was having difficulty. The assistant kept a close check on aircraft in the landing pattern, using binoculars to spot any apparent signs of trouble, particularly in regard to flap settings and landing gear. The student pilot kept a log of all take offs and arrivals by time and tail number. The control tower issued take off and landing clearances, but when a pilot was in difficulty, the mobile controller was in charge.

With so many aircraft in the air, with low time pilots, it was a rare shift when there was not an opportunity to assist someone. Also, when there was no chase pilot, advisories were issued to improve patterns and landings. It was not uncommon for a T-33 pilot and a Dawg pilot to be having difficulty at the same time. We sometimes had to think in terms of two different systems and performance parameters at the same time. If there was a serious problem, such as engine malfunction, we had to make split second, life and death decisions.

On some occasions, there was no time to render any assistance. We had some pilots eject, because there was no time to discuss the problem by radio. Some were successful and some were not. On a particularly dark, moonless night, I lost a student, and have always wondered what I should have done to prevent it.

As mentioned, the F-86 had no flap position indicator. Looking back, we could visually check the position, in daylight, that is. However, at night an experienced pilot could tell by the feel of the bird if the flaps were down in the landing pattern. It was important, because they decreased the stall speed by about twenty knots. The thing that sometimes led to the mistaken belief that the flaps were down was the operating handle, alongside the throttle.

The handle had three positions: Up, off, and down. Normal procedure called for the handle to activated, then returned to "off". In actuality, it was not unusual to raise the flaps after takeoff and leave the handle in the up position without returning it to off. It caused no problem, because the limit switches turned off the electricity when the full up position was reached. Upon preparing for landing, the handle was moved to the down position; that is, if moved one click from off to down. That control was one that we did not look at. It was positioned by feel.

If the handle had remained in the up position throughout the flight and moved one click from up to off, one might think he had really moved it from off to down. My student entered the pattern, made a normal pitchout, rolled out on the downwind leg, looking good, and proceeded to roll into the turn to final approach. About half way through the base to final turn, the bird snap rolled and nosed down. A second later, we had a huge fireball off the end of the runway. No time or altitude for recovery or bail out. Sifting through the wreckage, we determined that the flap motors were up and the handle was in the off position. No doubt the handle had been moved one click from up to off, thinking it was being moved from off to down. My personal technique was to actuate the flaps by moving the handle to the full extent of it's travel. Then it didn't matter where it started from. That is just one example of how seemingly small things can kill.

───────

Sitting in the front seat as coach and safety pilot for a student under the hood might seem like a dull and boring job, but that was not always the case. We really had to be on our toes, especially on take off. I would put the aircraft on the center of the runway, and advise the student that he was in control. "You have the aircraft, you are cleared for takeoff". The student would get on the brakes and run up to eighty percent RPM, checking flight instruments and engine instruments, particularly comparing the directional indicator with the known runway magnetic direction. Variations of a degree or so were significant, because on the take off roll of several thousand feet, the bird had to be kept rolling straight, initially with differential braking and as speed increased, with rudder.

When everything checked OK, the brakes were released and the throttle pushed up to 100 percent. Steering was critical and if the aircraft was getting too close to the edge of the runway, I would advise, "correct right a degree or two" or whatever I thought would keep us from running off the runway. In the meantime, my left hand was on the gear handle in the floor, my left knee propped against the throttle, right hand poised just behind the control stick and feet lightly on the rudder pedals. That way, he could not raise the wheels prematurely, the throttle could not creep back, and he could not jerk the stick back and cause a stall on lift-off. If he was in real danger of running off the runway, I could apply pressure to the rudder pedals and keep us on the runway.

Upon lift- off and reaching 125 knots airspeed, the stud would call, "gear up" and if it was safe, I responded with "clear" and transferred my left hand to the flap handle, preventing him from raising the flaps prior to attaining 140 knots. After accelerating to climb speed and gaining some altitude, things were much less tense. Those were some of the self preservation habits we acquired. Then, on a hot day, the turbine cooler would begin doing it's thing and give us some relief after we had roasted in the broiling Texas sun.

Hooded takeoffs were made to simulate a departure under conditions of zero visibility. Likewise approaches and landings were made under the hood for the same reason. If a student was doing well on approach, we let him continue right on to touchdown. It was a good confidence builder and prepared him for the time when it might be a necessary procedure.

––––––––

As instructors, we were given check rides for all the normal procedures plus the additional requirement of performing aerobatics under the hood. Skeptics might think that is an exaggeration, but we did it, with an instructor in the front seat. On our periodic check rides, or no-notice standardization flights, we did all the maneuvers that were mandated by Air Force regs, and as instructors were required to perform additional demonstrations of proficiency. I liked doing aerobatics, even under the hood. The aircraft were equipped with non-tumbling gyro flight instruments and with proper reference to them, plus the airspeed indicator and the G meter, we did pretty well. We did not expect to do aerobatics under normal instrument flight conditions, but the capability gave us added confidence in ourselves and the aircraft. We were conditioned to fly a single seater in extreme attitudes in extreme weather conditions.

––––––––

In February of 1957, we got a special valentine. Our second son Jeff, was born on the 14th. Kathy now had double trouble, but she handled it well. I still was not much help on the home front. We worked from early to late most days, and sometimes at night time. Training flights usually continued until midnight or later. Then we instructors, after debriefing our students, had grade books to catch up on, daily flight activity reports and aircraft requests for the next days operations. Schedules were made with little regard for crew rest.

On the late schedule, we reported for work around noon or shortly after, then might make it home by two AM. When our schedule changed from late to early, we sometimes got home in the wee hours and reported back to work on the early schedule at 5:30 AM. It was a demanding job, but I don't think any of us would have traded jobs with a non flying type. There is something satisfying about coming home, dead tired, but knowing you have done something well that most people cannot do at all.

The Dawg afforded the pilot a fair amount of personal comfort as fighters go and flight duration was relatively short. Not so with the T-33. Being an adaptation of the F-80, the cockpits were not made for large bodies. Space between the armrests measured seventeen inches. The occupant had to fit his bottom into that amount of space - period. The consoles and canopy rails were very close on the sides and left little room for shoulders and arm movement when reaching for switches and controls. At least, the rudder pedals were adjustable and could accommodate long legs. There was little head clearance with the canopy, and a tall guy would be bumping his head, even with the seat adjusted down.

When strapped in, there was no movement of the butt. Discomfort set in and became increasingly noticeable after a few minutes. The seat pack chutes were uncomfortable, but most of us had to wear that type as opposed to back pack for lack of knee clearance from the windshield bow. Leg length in excess of a certain amount, would guarantee contact with the windshield bow on ejection.

A typical sortie lasted two hours or more, sometimes up to two and half hours and we swore we could by feel, count the stitches in the straps we were sitting on. After two sorties a day, plus other chores and being subjected to so much tension, hard work and bodily discomfort, we were extremely tired and often went home with sore tails. As much as we loved flying, some of us felt like we were being scheduled too heavily on a continuing basis, in the T-bird.

The group weenies took this into consideration and issued some guidelines. T-bird time would be limited to 85 hours per month. Squadron commanders could exceed those limits if they felt there was a bona fide requirement. Therefore, nothing really changed. There was always bona fide need. I often went home and ate supper sitting on a pillow.

During my tour at Perrin I had several flight commanders, but the majority of my time was with "A" flight, commanded by William G. (Bill, Whale Tail) Dixon. The only part of Dixon that did not match the typical fighter pilot was his appearance. He was a large, awkwardly built person, and wore thick glasses, but appearance can be deceiving. You would not want to be his opponent in aerial combat. He wanted his flight to be the best in the squadron. He didn't want us to just think we were the best, he wanted us to be the best and he put forth a lot of effort to make it true. To match our performance, he wanted us to also look the part. Somehow, he got permission for us to wear black flight suits, with our white "A' patch on one shoulder and our 58th patch on the chest. We wore white silk scarves bearing our nicknames in red and our red 58th baseball caps when not flying.

Bill wanted us all to grow Clark Gable type mustaches and we all tried, but gave up after a while. They were just too uncomfortable under the oxygen masks, and besides, the wives did not like them.

Much of the rules and advice regarding safety was window dressing and CYA for the officials. That was especially true with regard to unbriefed dogfighting. Since most of our flying was done with students, we welcomed the opportunity to fly with other instructors and more so if we could get in some plain old dog fighting. Such sorties were supposed to be planned and properly briefed. The maintenance people didn't like it, because under high G maneuvers, we sometimes damaged the gimbal mounted radar antenna in the nose cone.

Under the local rules, if we were scheduled for a chase mission and the student aborted, we were free to go ahead and fly a personal proficiency sortie. When that happened, we were always on the look out for anyone else who was freelance at the time. We had some good dog fights, more challenging than dealing with students. Our 58th aircraft had a red ID stripe on the vertical stabilizer. The sister squadron, the 56th, always the competition, had a blue stripe on their aircraft.

Naturally, we were always on the lookout for stray aircraft with a blue tail stripe. It didn't matter who the pilot might be. We would take our chances on it being one of the brass. In most cases, even if it was, they were also willing to engage. Only rarely did anyone get into trouble over that and even so, no one I knew was officially admonished.

Ever so often, our ops people would schedule themselves and several other instructors for four flights of four, supposedly for practicing a sixteen ship fly over for parades and special occasions. Strangely enough, the 56th would so the same thing at the same time. We would just "happen" across each other out in the local area. Some massive inter-squadron battles resulted.

––––––

The physiological aspects of military flying are not accurately addressed in books, movies and media material. The stresses incurred by the body are highly variable and often extreme. When I entered flight training, my neck size was fourteen. After two years it had grown to size sixteen and there was no fat, just more muscle. Due to a lot of head movement with a heavy hard-hat, complete with mask and visor, and frequent high G maneuvers we all developed large necks. Most of us also developed an occupational disease; hemorrhoids.

Some flight operations require little physical exertion and others require tremendous strength and endurance. Combat maneuvers generate very high G forces. The average Joe can not even keep his feet on the rudder pedals in a high G situation, or lift a hand to actuate a control. In providing orientation rides to ROTC students, I noted that some of them could not get their head back up off their chest after looking down during a hard turn. Extremes of heat and cold, coupled with great physical effort, intense mental concentration, in complex situations, where there is no margin for error, can tire a person to a degree most people will never experience. Sweat soaked flight suits were the norm.

After a long, hot, afternoon and evening when all the aircraft were down for the night and we were finishing up the paperwork in our stuffy flight room, Dixon would send a student up to the O. club for a case of cool ones. The cans would be left in various trash cans in the ops building.

One afternoon, our operations officer, Captain Clees, came in to our flight room and advised Dixon that he wasn't banning the pleasure of a few cool ones, after hours, but would prefer not to see any more cans in the trash containers. It just didn't look good and some people might get the wrong impression of our squadron.

The next morning, Clees came to work, and sure enough, there were no cans in sight, anywhere in the building. When he sat down at his desk and opened its drawers, they were filled with cans. He took it well, but no one pressed their luck by doing it again.

A lot of harmless pranks were performed by people with a sense of humor. The favorite one in our flight was to put a fictitious pilots name on our status board in our flight room. The squadron commander had personal knowledge of every pilot, or thought he did. On his occasional visits to our flight room, he would of course, peruse the name board and on seeing a name he didn't recognize, would wonder why he couldn't recall meeting one of his pilots.

If he asked about it, he would reveal that he had either forgotten about meeting someone or that he was wondering how someone had gotten assigned to a flight without him knowing about it. I suspect there were times when he really knew what was going on and just didn't say anything.

———

We had received a lot of physiological training, which included altitude pressure chamber flights with rapid decompressions. At pressures equivalent to 5,000 feet we were usually subjected to explosive decompression to the equivalent of 25,000 feet. It was no big deal, we knew it was coming.

The F-86 had three settings for cockpit pressurization. None, two point five for combat, and five pounds per square inch for normal. We always selected the 5.0 setting in order to be more comfortable at high altitudes. One night while working out of the Alert Unit, I had led a flight of two on an intercept mission, and when finishing up, at 38,000, the wing-man was a couple of miles back. I rolled into an easy left turn to help him rejoin for the RTB. My lights were on bright/flash. As he moved in closer, it was time to change my lights to dim/steady, otherwise the brightly flashing lights on the wing tips would make it virtually impossible for him to hold a good position in close formation.

I was looking back over my left shoulder, to keep a close watch as he completed the join up. I had to hold the stick in my left hand, in order to get my right hand way back on the right rear console where the light switches were. I counted the switches by feel, and BANG!! I blew up, or so I thought for a moment. My mask was pushed away from my face by the strong involuntary exhalation. My Mae West inflated underneath my chute harness and felt like I was being squeezed in a big vise. The cockpit was full of vapor, looking like smoke, but it was clearing out. All the instruments were normal, except for the cockpit altimeter, which was reading 38,000, matching the flight altimeter.

I had miscounted the light switches and dumped the cockpit pressurization. The dump switch was next to one of the light switches. The pressurization had instantly gone from fairly comfortable to 38,000 feet where there was virtually no atmospheric pressure. It didn't take me long to close the dump valve and repressurize, but it took me a few minutes to stop shaking. I don't remember what we did on the intercept mission, but I vividly remember the explosive decompression. I never, ever, miscounted the switches again.

───────

The Dawgs had accumulated a lot of flight time and several additions to the cockpit layout had left it cluttered in an unorganized fashion. The turn capability at high altitudes was not what we needed it to be. Even with the leading edge wing slats, in our haste to make a correction in a high altitude attack, it was too easy rush the turn and get into an accelerated stall. The solution, to some degree, was a modified version of the bird, the F-86L.

There were no L models manufactured by North American. They were all converted" D" models. We flew our "D" models, a few at a time, out to Fresno, California to be modified. Most everyone got a turn at a ferry trip. On such a trip, I was the number four man in a four ship flight. We departed Perrin fairly late in the afternoon, and had an uneventful trip to El Paso. We did not like refueling at Biggs AFB, because it was a SAC base and experience had taught us that they would treat us like the Jews treated Samaritans in biblical times. That was true of SAC bases in general. They did not refuse service outright, but there was so much foot dragging and shabby treatment, we got the message.

We landed at El Paso International, knowing that the civilian operators would be quite happy to sell us a few thousand gallons of kerosene. All we had to do was to sign the bill. Additionally, their courtesy van would drop us off at the bridge and we could walk across the Rio Grande for a little shopping in Juarez. We could haggle with the shop owners and get bargain prices for jewelry and trinkets for our wives. We could also get a great steak dinner for very little money.

The next morning, we decided to take off individually, in trail, and join up after getting airborne. That was during the time that our afterburner operation was restricted to emergency use. There had been several instances of major engine damage while operating in A/B and no fix had yet been forthcoming. We would take off at military power, knowing the roll would be quite long because of the high elevation and a runway with marginal length. We did not need the added problems of wing takeoffs in close formation.

Being the last of the four, I watched as one, two and three made their roll, using all the runway and staggering into the air from a runway almost a mile high. I was reconciled to taking my chances with the burner if I developed any doubt about getting airborne without it. I hung the tail pipe out over the end of the runway and released the brakes. Every foot of runway was valuable. Due to the elevation, acceleration was predictably slow and the runway distance markers were going by terribly slow. I needed 140 knots and wasn't getting there. Just as the end of the asphalt was getting close and I was about to hit the burner, I had almost 140, so I eased the nose up another notch and staggered off over the dirt overrun.

I slammed the gear handle up and hoped the extra drag of the doors opening would not be the straw that broke the camels back. The wheels clunked into the wells, and the doors thudded closed, allowing the bird to accelerate a little better. Watching the tall buildings going by and making sure I wasn't headed for any of them, I looked around for the other birds. In the distance, I could see that our leader was making a turn for two to cut him off, and three had his bird cleaned up and closing on them. I still needed to see 155 knots on the indicator, in order to get my flaps up. Finally, I got it and got my bird cleaned up, cutting way inside the turn the other guys were making. Two was on the leaders left wing, three, my element leader was on the right wing. I joined on his right wing for fingertip formation and we proceeded with the climb out, headed for Williams AFB, Phoenix, Arizona.

We had no difficulty in getting to Williams, and being a training command wing, they gave us prompt service. Everybody got fuel, oxygen and maybe oil, if needed. We filed a flight plan for George AFB, Victorville, California. That was not on a direct route to Fresno, but it was fairly early in the day and our flight leader wanted to visit a friend there. We all strapped up and began the start routine. Number one, number three and I, as four, all were fired up and waiting for number two. He was not fired up yet.

Finally, he came on the radio and announced that he had a sheared starter shaft. We all shut down and dismounted for a huddle. Williams had no starter for a Dawg. It would take too long to have one brought in from Perrin. The remaining three of us could have justified going on and leaving him with the problem, but he was begging us not to leave him. After a bit of brainstorming, someone remembered seeing a North American Aviation bulletin about air starting on the ground. None of us had ever tried it, or seen it done.

We decided to try it. Rounding up a few more bodies, we pushed the broken bird to where we aligned it as well as we could with the number one bird and about twenty five feet back. The number two pilot got in, closed the canopy and stood by. The lead pilot fired up his bird and advanced the power as much as he dared. His exhaust was cooking the bird behind, but two announced that he was getting some windmill rotation of his engine. After what seemed like too long, with the back bird getting black from smoke and all of us worrying about heat damage, we saw smoke and heat waves coming from his tail pipe. He had gotten it lit off.

He then announced that the RPM was hung up and he could not get it up to normal idle. Up to that point, he had been very gingerly manipulating the fuel flow on a manual start with the emergency fuel control. A normal start procedure on the automatic fuel control would not have worked and a slip of his hand would have severely overtemped the engine. We finally realized the air entering his intake from the front bird was too oxygen poor and motioned for the leader to pull away. He did and the engine speed came right up to normal on number two.

Three and I scrambled back into our birds, got started up and the four of us departed for Victorville. Aircraft number two would be operating on number two generator only, since the starter became the number one generator at normal engine speeds. However, he would not need his radar and with proper management he could work around the shortage of electrical power by using only the number two generator. He could safely fly the bird.

We all landed safely at George AFB and got fuel service but still needed oxygen. As we watched, the airman with the oxygen cart made a turn at high speed and the cart rolled over, doing massive damage. We asked about another cart and were told there was not another one. I think that was true of transient maintenance, and they were just not interested in getting one on loan from one of the operational units on the base. We conferred about what to do.

The last leg to Fresno was fairly short and fuel would not be critical. Therefore, we decided to fly at ten thousand feet, where we would use more fuel, but would not use oxygen. We also knew that it was getting late in the day, and the sun would set before our arrival. We all had a little oxygen left in our tanks and figured we should use it on arrival at Fresno, to insure we had normal vision and judgment, especially for a night landing at a strange airport.

We pushed the number two aircraft into position behind the leader for another air start. That attracted a crowd of on-lookers who were wondering what we were doing. We were now old hands at it and got number two going again with some added soot and possible heat damage. This was the last leg, and if we could make that, we didn't care. We made a formation takeoff in elements of two and proceeded on our way.

A few minutes out from Fresno, the sun was down, and as expected, it was full dark, with no moon. The leader reminded us to turn on our oxygen and to close up the formation in order to look sharp for anyone observing from the ground. Roaring in on initial approach, in echelon, he pitched out for a 360 degree overhead fighter pattern, calling for three second spacing on the break and we all followed suit. Up until that time, my focus was on my element leader and I had not had a look at the airport.

I remember following number three around to the downwind leg, base turn and onto final, trying to adjust so that we were all about equally spaced. Lead touched down on the left side, two on the right, three on the left, leaving me the right side. My landing light picked up a very high fence just short of the touchdown end of the runway and my approach was a little too shallow for that, but I goosed the engine for a couple of seconds and cleared the fence, then dropped rapidly to avoid a long roll on a fairly short runway. We all turned off and were directed to the parking area.

Even before we had completed our shutdown procedure, workmen were removing panels from our aircraft in preparation for the modifications we had delivered them for. We had delivered all four aircraft together in spite some difficulties.

Next day, we flew back to Dallas by way of commercial airliner. The last leg back to Sherman was on an old feeder line DC-3. We were in uniform, carrying our canvas bags containing our flight gear. The other passengers noticed the parachutes and gave us some mighty strange looks.

We got our airplanes back as converted L models which had a little more wing area and a much better organized cockpit. They also had more modern navigation radios. Turn performance at the higher altitudes was noticeably improved. The downside was no changes in the engine. With the larger wing and greater lift, there was also slightly more drag. Therefore, the old D models were slightly faster. For a long while, we had mix of both types on the flight line.

The dispatchers thought they were doing the instructors a favor by assigning a newer "L" for chasing a student in the older "D" model. It actually made it more difficult for the chase pilot. We had trouble keeping up with the students in some situations. It did not sound good for us to have to request a power reduction, so on radar intercept chase missions we followed the smoke trails and cut them off in turns to catch up.

We had a lot of foreign student pilots. I flew with pilots from Scandinavia, Greece, the Philippines, Korea, Japan, China and maybe some others. We had exchange pilots from the RAF, Navy, and the Marine Corps. The language problem was not supposed to be a problem, but it was. Someone was sending us foreign students who had been certified as qualified in English, but in reality could speak and understand very little. Oriental pride complicated the problem. They did not want to admit that they did not understand.

Even if they spoke some limited English, when things got sticky, they reverted to their native language. We could not learn all the various languages we were dealing with. Yet they were there for us to teach them how to fly the airplanes our country was planning to give their countries. After my Phillipino student almost hit me on a right break when I called a left break, I did concede and learn "left" and "right" in Spanish.

Our family experienced two fairly long temporary duty assignments. One was to Maxwell AFB, Montgomery, Alabama for squadron officers school at the Air University. The course was mostly academic and kept us terribly busy for three months. By virtue of being flight instructor rated, I had the additional duty of flying with other students who needed flight time, but were not current in the T-33. That was done after school hours, but I worked it in and was able to maintain my own proficiency in the T-bird.

The other temporary duty was down to James-Connally AFB at Waco, Texas. The family did not accompany me, and I drove home on most weekends. Although I had already been serving as a flight instructor for many hundreds of hours, this was an opportunity to attend the premier flight school for instructor pilots. It was the USAF Instrument Pilot Instructor School. It would not hurt to have that "I" prefix on my specialty code, permanently. We also received training as academic instructors. After ten weeks of highly refined flight instruction in the T-33, I returned to Perrin AFB.

Eventually, the F-86 was no longer a first line fighter. All of ours were now converted "L" models. The '58th would have their Sabres replaced with the F-102. The '56th would continue with their Sabres for the time being. Having been there for an extended tour, some of us were not allowed to check out in the "Deuce". It was felt that it would not be cost effective if we were on short time. Besides the '56th could use us. So with deep misgivings about our treatment, we shuffled down to our sister squadron and former rival.

I did my best to fit in and do a good job. I was probably as well qualified as anyone in the flight, but the flight commander treated me like an orphan, and although I never did anything to deserve it, he wrote me the worst officer effectiveness report I ever got. I got all the work that nobody else wanted and got more additional work assignments than anyone in the flight. One of those jobs was working with some of the slower foreign students.

We had a Korean Air Force Lt. Colonel who had badly damaged a T-bird on a night solo target mission. The guy didn't like flying target missions although everyone else, including we instructors, did it. It was too demeaning for him, but a student was a student. They were all treated alike, regardless of rank. Somebody had to do it and we all took our turn. Since he had an aircraft accident, it was required that he get some remedial flight training, which fell to me. He had sheared off a T-bird nose gear as a result of a bad landing.

First thing one morning, we were scheduled for a combination target and transition training mission. He was disdainful of USAF people and especially of anyone with lesser rank. He was arrogant and aloof. He would not engage in any conversation except what was absolutely necessary and connected with the flight. I was polite, but firm. I was the boss. The instructor pilot was always the boss, regardless of rank. We briefed for a flight with him flying from the front seat for one period as a target and returning for landing practice during the second period. Normally, the target aircraft remained on station for two periods of intercept activity, since the T-bird had fuel for about twice the endurance of the interceptors.

We got airborne and he did fine on the climb out and running the target track for the first batch of interceptors. After about an hour, or so, I normally would have taken control of the bird for a while. Partly to give him a break and partly because I liked to drive, but I didn't. He was a certified jerk; sullen and cooperative only to a minimum degree.

When the first wave of interceptors made their last pass and headed home, the controller released us as planned and I told the Korean to RTB and enter the traffic pattern. By this time our tip tanks were empty, but we still had our internal fuel, which would be enough for several touch and go landings. He complied and drove us back to home plate and entered the traffic pattern. The entry, pitchout, and the downwind leg were OK, but approaching the final turn, we still had too much airspeed. There was still time to correct that, but he continued on into the final turn too high and too fast. I was coaching him to slow down and to establish a proper approach angle with the correct airspeed, but he continued on, high and fast.

As we got over the touchdown point, obviously high and fast, he was trying to spike it onto the runway. That was what had gotten him into trouble the night he dinged an airplane. I told him to go around and he did, without touching down. His problem was identified. He was trying to fly the T-bird with F-86 pattern airspeeds. On the way around back to the entry point, I reviewed proper pattern speeds with him for our fuel load.

The next time around wasn't much better, so I took control and flew a little ways out from the traffic pattern at about 5,000 feet. I calculated our stall speed for the present fuel weight and slowed to about two knots above that, in landing configuration. Wheels, flaps and speed brakes down. I added just enough power to maintain our speed in level flight. Then I asked him, "Are we flying ?" "Yes". "Are maintaining level flight?" "Yes". "Then why won't the bird fly at 120 knots descending ?" No answer.

"Take control and go do me a decent landing." The next one was a little better, but he was still having a lot of trouble dealing with the lower airspeed, so I took the bird and demonstrated a pattern and landing with a another touch and go. I gave him back the bird and the result was only slightly better. By this time all the fuel cells were empty except for the 95 gallon fuselage tank. We had low fuel pressure lights for the main wing, leading edge, and tip tanks. He wanted to do a full stop, but I made him go around.

The next time around the fuselage tank was down to about forty five gallons and he was saying with a fearful voice, "Low fuel warning light on". I said, "I see it, go around." "BUT LOW FUEL LIGHT ON". "GO AROUND!" as I shoved the throttle to the stop to insure that he went around. I told him, "We are going to stay at it until you get it right!" I knew we were cutting it close, but also knew my capability and was confident of a safe landing the next time around. In any case, it would have to be the last, but at this point the Korean wasn't sure of what I would do and if he was scared, that was fine with me. That time he came pretty close to getting it right and made an acceptable landing. We went in and parked. I figured the crew chief would wonder why it took 806 gallons to refuel a bird with a capacity of 810 gallons.

I told the boss that the Korean was making progress, but would need another dual flight before I would recommend him to go solo again. We finally turned him loose and he didn't break any more airplanes. We continued with the usual grind. Simulator, instrument continuation flights, day, night, mobile control, radar chase rides, formation, more new students and checkouts.

———

Many situations developed where disaster was averted due to skill and experience. In other cases, there was no explanation except that someone was looking out for us. One night on returning from a mission in a T-bird, I entered the landing pattern, pitched out, rolled out on the downwind leg and put down the gear handle. I got a green light for the left main and nose gear, but an unsafe light for the right main. I could tell by the way the bird was trying to yaw to the left, that the right main was really not down. The lights weren't lying.

Continuing on around the base to final turn, I recycled the gear and by the time I rolled out on final approach, I still had the same indications as before, so I went around. On this particular flight I had returned with a little more fuel than usual, as we often had only enough for one go-around, if that much. I re-entered the pattern and activated the emergency hydraulic pump and it's one shot reservoir of fluid. I didn't expect any improvement because the utility hydraulic pressure was normal, but I was following procedure.

By the time I was on a short final, there had been no change, but I continued the approach to touchdown on the left main and deliberately hit a little hard, thinking perhaps I could jar something loose. Nothing changed, so I went around again. There was no other action I could take to remedy the problem. I had enough fuel for two more patterns and made the next pass right by the control tower after asking them to use their white light and binoculars to check if they could see anything that might explain the situation. They could only confirm that the right main appeared to be up and locked.

It was decision time. I could eject, but the situation did not justify that. I did not want to lose the bird and I had never been anxious to test a parachute. I could pull up all the wheels and land in the grass between the runways to minimize the damage, but I elected to land on the asphalt and hold up the right wing as long as possible. With the last of my fuel I rolled out on final with the right main wheel still not down and locked, hoping the right wing would not dig in and cause the bird to cartwheel. I figured there was a pretty good chance it would stay right side up and I could get out before any fire got too bad. That was another reason I wanted to land with little or no fuel on board.

I was on a very short final, lined up with the left side of the 150 foot wide runway, to allow for a slide to the right, beginning the flare, when I got a THUMP! The green light for the right main came on and I touched down smoothly on both main wheels. I let the bird roll to a stop at the end of the runway and called for maintenance to come out and install the safety pins before I made any turns to taxi in. I wrote up the discrepancy in the form 781.

Next morning I was in our flight room, getting ready to fly with a student, when a maintenance supervisor came looking for me. He wanted to know how I had gotten the right main gear down. I told him what I had done, and wondered what they had found. He then told me he could not explain it either. The bolt that attached the hydraulic cylinder to the right main strut was missing.

There was no apparent way to get it down with the actuating cylinder unattached and hanging in the breeze.

———

Our third child was on the way and after two boys, we were sure this one would be a girl. We named her Jonathan Scott. No girls for us. By this time, we had learned to like Texas. There were worse places. We had a lot of civilian friends in town and at church where we attended in Denison. Except for the extreme heat and humidity and periodic tornadoes it was not a bad place. If I could get a little time off, we could go to the base rec area on the lake.

———

My time as a lieutenant had been served and along with my Laredo classmates still at Perrin, I pinned on my railroad tracks, denoting the rank of captain. I was still not entirely comfortable with being a member of the '56th. I reckon I had been in the rival '58th too long, but they had disowned me. I think it influenced some of the '56th people to some extent also. That problem was soon solved.

Air Defense Alert Unit

The Air Defense Alert Unit would no longer be manned by rotating pilots from the training squadrons. It would be permanently staffed by pilots drawn from the 3556th training squadron. I was sent down there as a flight commander. I had four excellent, highly experienced pilots who needed little supervision. We had a unit commander, an operations officer and an enlisted staff. We were under the operational control of Air Defense Command.

We had no duties outside the alert unit, but if some time hog wanted to, he could still go down to the training squadrons and fly with them. My little band of pilots was responsible for flight operations half the time. Another captain and his four pilots was responsible for the other half. The training wing furnished us with aircraft, including a T-33 each day for target flights, proficiency training, check rides and so on. I retained my instructor and flight examiner status and if anyone in the unit needed a periodic standardization flight, we could provide it.

Our normal alert requirement was two interceptors on five minutes. When joining other units in war games, we sometimes had more birds on five minutes. That meant, after being notified, we were expected to be airborne in five minutes or less. We had some other shorter time requirements that were sometimes implemented during higher states of alert by ADC. Two minutes, required being in the aircraft, strapped up and ready to roll from the barn. Runway alert meant being on the taxi strip next to the take off end of the runway, with engines running. That was not practical for extended times because of the fuel problem and pilot fatigue.

Some might wonder why an alert facility was maintained in Northeast Texas. At that time, our intelligence sources knew that the threat of an attack by Russian long range bombers was real. Some of the attack routes would be over the pole to various destinations in the U.S. Some would be up through Mexico after staging out of some South American country. The USSR was more serious about world domination than many people could believe.

Our intelligence also indicated that in the event an attack did come, it would come from multiple routes and that we would be facing massive numbers of bombers. It was likely that we would expend our armament and still have targets to neutralize. To that end, we had tactics that involved ramming them with our aircraft, hopefully in a manner that would allow us to survive. Our bird was our twenty fifth rocket. We were probably going to run out of fuel and have to dead stick to a landing or eject anyway.

The only deterrent to an attack was the fear that they would not win. If they could feel confident they could win, they would come. The scenario was described to us by intelligence: Each morning, the chief of Soviet Intelligence comes in to brief the head man, and each morning, he says, "Sir, today is not the day." If he ever comes in and says, "Sir, today is the day," the attack will be launched. We and many others were the reason that "the day" did not come.

———

Each shift we did practice scrambles, operating in pairs, on SAC aircraft coming through the area, on our own daily T-bird or sometimes fighters from other units. When the klaxon horns blared with their ear shattering brrrp, we did not know if the scramble was practice or for real. There would be an announcement on the PA, but with so much other noise being generated in the hangar, we pilots would have to get the info later. Our "hot" birds were armed with twenty four rockets, with live warheads.

It was common for us to practice intercepts on SAC B-52 bombers coming through our area. They were a little bit of a challenge, due to their powerful electronic counter-measures capability. Their electronic warfare officers could about burn a hole in our scope with their jamming. The only way I ever found to outwit them, was to run my radar through its limited tuning range, with the ECM guy tracking it, and then turn mine to standby, to make him think I had tuned away from him. When he went looking elsewhere for my signal, I would turn mine back on and have time for a sweep or two to see him before he found me again.

We played dirty with their tail gunners. Usually, after a couple of radar intercepts, the B-52 crew would request gunnery passes to provide practice for their tail gunner. Gunnery passes meant making lead pursuit attacks, exposing ourselves to the stinger in the tail. We usually had an agreement between the two interceptor pilots as to which one would go low and which one would go high as we crossed over after initiating our attacks from opposite sides of the bomber. The gunner could not track both of us.

If someone was sick, or on leave, I filled in. Sometimes I filled in just to keep proficient and to give somebody a day off. Our commander and ops officer were both combat ready pilots and they sometimes filled in. During large exercises, we might have every pilot in the unit working. Except for short stretches, no one worked terribly hard. What a break from the past!

———

As always, flight endurance was the major problem with the Sabre. After making an afterburner climb to high altitude, we had enough fuel for perhaps two passes on a target Then we had to find a place to put it down with minimal delay. We flew many forty five minute sorties and landed with empty tanks. We practiced intercepts. We assisted lost pilots. We identified aircraft that could not be identified by any other method.

One of our pilots, was scrambled to intercept a student pilot in a T-33 out of Big Springs, who had gotten disoriented and lost at night, was scared and low on fuel. He was smart enough to get on the emergency radio channel and lucky enough to be picked up by our primary control. They vectored our Sabre pilot to a join-up with the student and led him to Carswell AFB for a safe landing.

One day, with really lousy weather, we were scrambled and climbed through solid weather from the ground to forty thousand feet to be joined up with an F-51 pilot who was lost, had instrument malfunctions and had no other way to safely penetrate the weather and land. We were trained to intercept and assist airliners who had experienced radio or instrument failure. Our own safe recovery was a secondary consideration.

———

One night, I was scrambled to intercept and identify an unknown aircraft off to the southwest. In the back of my mind, I always pictured the possibility of finding a Russian Bear sneaking up from Mexico. My wing man had turned back with aircraft trouble. The radar controller got me within a few miles of the target and we figured they must listening on our radio frequency. Every time I would get close enough to see it on my airborne radar, the target would turn, climb, and descend, doing a pretty good job at evasive action. We were in and out of clouds, making it hard to get visual contact.

After several minutes of the cat and mouse game, I finally got on him and radioed the controller that it was a USAF B-47. We didn't know what his situation was and could not establish radio contact. The big problem was that there had been no flight plan available to ADC that would help establish a friendly radar track. That was why we had been scrambled in the first place. At least now, we could classify it as friendly. As I broke off, the controller gave my pigeons, distance and bearing for home.

I was shocked! I had been chasing this B-47 for too long without being informed of my whereabouts. Under the circumstances, a single person could not fly the airplane, operate the radar, play games with a target in bad weather and have any time to keep track of his location. That was primarily the responsibility of the ground radar controller. He was supposed to make periodic fuel and oxygen checks to insure we had enough to return or be able to land at a suitable base.

I was almost to Louisiana. My choices for a recovery base lay between Barksdale, Fort Worth and home. They were all about the same distance, but theoretically, I didn't have enough fuel to make it to any of them. I quickly decided that if I was going to be on the fumes, I would rather be in familiar territory and turned toward home. Along the way, I was weighing my options and remembered a county airport at Greenville, Texas would be on my route. I had landed there previously in a T-33. They didn't have a start cart big enough to restart a Sabre, but at least it was a place to set it down.

The fuel consumption was going a little better than I had originally figured, and decided that if I had as much as 600 pounds over Greenville, I would continue toward Perrin. I could really conserve fuel in a letdown with the power back for the last forty miles. If I had less than 600 pounds over Greenville, I would land there. The cloud cover was breaking up and I could see Greenville and I still had 600 pounds of kerosene remaining.

The controller was sweating as much as I was. He would have to share the responsibility for any problems on getting down. He had given me a vector directly to Perrin, and I had the VOR tuned in, confirming his directions. Shortly, I could see the rotating beacon at Perrin and told the controller I was changing the radio to Perrin tower. I told them I was making a straight in approach and could not, repeat, could not deviate or go around. There was no other traffic at four in the morning. I made the straight in approach from the south to runway 35 Right, and coasted off on to the scramble strip to the alert hangar just as the engine died from fuel starvation. No big deal, just another nights work.

———

We had agreements with several military bases around the southwest that would allow us to get expedited service in case we did land there while on an air defense mission. They were to give us priority for fuel and oxygen. ADC also had an abbreviated system for getting us in the air without the usual pile of paperwork. When seconds counted, the paperwork could come later. Base operations in other commands had difficulty understanding that the flight clearances were taken care of by the controlling ground radar facility.

Our unit commander sometimes had a pair of us who were otherwise off duty, make a no-notice flight into one of those bases to check their response to a request for expedited service. Between personnel changes and memory lapses we sometimes found that the people in charge did not know what we were talking about, or pretended not to know. One of those bases was Tinker AFB, Oklahoma City.

One afternoon, Paul Strickland and I took a pair of birds up there and only after we were entering the traffic pattern, did we identify ourselves as Air Defense Command aircraft with live armament on board. You would have thought we had leprosy. On landing we were parked as far away from the main ramp as they could get us. It must have been two miles to base operations and the normal transient parking area.

We got a ride in on a maintenance truck and told the duty officer that we expected to be ready for take off in a few minutes. He thought we were trying to be funny and had no intention of having our refueling expedited. Finally, we did get notice that we had fuel and told him we needed a ride back to the parking area. He snidely informed us that we had not filed the necessary flight clearance forms. When we told him, we didn't do paper on ADC flights, he really got his dander up. He thought we were a pair of lunatics!

We told the duty officer goodbye and that we were going out to fire up our birds. His reply was that we could not do that. We said, "Bye". We strapped in and called the local ADC radar control site on the radio, which was fairly close by and knew what was going on.

By the time we started engines and called Tinker Tower, we were told that we had scramble orders and were cleared for expedited takeoff. The funny part would come later when ADC headquarters had some official at Tinker on the carpet because his guys were not complying with the agreement. They didn't know it, but, in a few weeks we would be dropping in again to find out if there had been an attitude adjustment.

––––––––––

John Foster and I dropped in on Little Rock AFB for quick turnaround and they did pretty well, especially for a SAC base. On the way out to the active runway, we were blocked from turning from the taxi strip to the runway by a B-47. They were partially facing us and the pilot and co-pilot with their bubble canopy had a clear view of us trying to get by. We sat there for several seconds, thinking they would move, but they did not. John was leading our flight, so I said nothing on the radio, knowing that John shortly would. We could not afford to waste any more fuel.

So, John punched his mike button, and said, "B-47, how about moving that monster and letting us be on our way." With their heads facing in our direction, a voice in a mocking tone said, "Why should we?" John replied, "Because we have forty eight rockets pointed right at you." Without further comment, the next sound we heard above the sound of our own engines, was the whine and roar of six J-47s winding up and the B-47 began to move.

Scramble

The air base is quiet at 2:30 AM. There is not much activity at this time of night. The two pilots on duty in the upstairs lounge of the alert hangar are reading, but barely awake. The airmen are downstairs, most of them playing cards, and draining the ever present coffee urns with their contents something closely akin to battery acid. Their maintenance chores are caught up for now. Two all-weather interceptor aircraft are "cocked", one in each bay on opposite sides of the center section, and two more in the outer bays. Those are spare aircraft, available for increased alert status or for replacement in case there is a malfunction in one of the primary birds. All four have been fueled, armed and checked by the crew chiefs and the pilots.

The weather is below minimum ceiling and visibility for normal flying operations. Rain is pelting down from clouds almost on the ground. The weather briefing, when coming on shift, indicated solid clouds from less than a hundred feet all the way up to 40,000 feet. There will be no practice scrambles tonight. The birds are walking.

Suddenly, the klaxons blast out their raspy, buzzing sound and everyone instinctively jumps up to sprint to their place of duty. No one picks up the direct line to control to ask if the scramble is for real. The pilots bound down the stairs and burst through the doors leading to the bays containing their aircraft. The powermen are starting the auxiliary power units and the crew chiefs are already on the wing of their bird to assist the pilot aboard. Scramble instructions are coming over the PA system, but no one can understand them, because of the deafening noise from the start cart engines reverberating in the closed hangar. The massive hangar doors are opening. There is an air of excitement, and everyone is moving quickly, but being methodical and precise. They know their business well.

The lead pilot bounds up and over the side of his mount and settles in the seat. The crew chief helps him with the chute straps, shoulder harness, lap belt, radio cord and oxygen hose as the pilot lifts his hard hat from where it has been parked on top of the windshield. The master switch is on and all the cockpit lights are on. All eyes are mindful of the indicator light that will tell them when the electronic fuel control has warmed up sufficiently to begin the start procedure. The pilot is still working with his mask and chin strap when the lock-up light goes out, so the crew chief hits the switch to engage the starter.

The initial surge draws many hundreds of amps and the start cart engine groans, loses speed and then begins to recover as the starter brings the engine up to speed. With a shudder and rumble, the fuel lights off in the burner cans and the engine continues to accelerate. The engine noise changes from a whine to a roar. As it accelerates through about forty percent RPM, with all gauges reading normal, the pilot pushes up the throttle, closes and locks the canopy, and signals the crew chief to pull the chocks. The powerman has pulled the electrical cable from the side of the aircraft and is moving well away, because he knows the throttle is being advanced to full power to get the bird moving quickly. There will be a major blast from the tail pipe. The crew chief does not have time to get out of the way, so he just crouches down and holds onto his cap as the bird roars out of the bay, generating noise well above the pain threshold.

As the lead pilot emerges from the hangar onto the ramp, he looks over his shoulder and sees the wing-man coming out of his bay. The leader will lose face if his number two beats him out of the hangar, and he will try. The leader punches his mike button and tells the control tower, "Kilo Papa Zero One rolling." Next he hears, "Two checking in." Tower responds with, "Kilo Papa flight, this is an active air scramble, you are cleared for take-off on runway one seven left, wind light and variable, altimeter two niner eight four, scramble vector two two zero, angels forty. Contact Adcock on channel twenty."

By this time, the pair are nearing the end of the scramble strip and are approaching the runway at an illegally high taxi speed, but no one will complain. Just don't roll a main gear tire off the wheel in the turn. With full fuel and armament, these birds weigh a over twenty thousand pounds, with most of that weight on the two main wheels. Lead makes sure his light switches are on dim/steady for the benefit of Zero Two and continues checking things like secondary hydraulic flight controls and a dozen other things as they barrel down the strip.

The leader pulls onto the right side of the runway and Two pulls in close on his left side, slightly to the rear, in position for a formation take-off. The rain obscures almost everything except the dim runway marker lights which extend as far as one can see in the rain. The other end of the 8,000 foot runway is not visible. It is too dark for hand signals, but Two knows One is already on the brakes and holding at full military power, so he does the same and with a quick final check of his instruments, he says, "Two ready." Lead says, "A/B now," and they both pop the throttle handle into the full afterburner range and release he brakes. As they start rolling, lead reduces his power slightly to give Two a little extra power in case he needs it to keep up.

The abrupt roar of the afterburners, splits the night in two, rattles windows for miles around, and awakens the wives in their quarters adjacent to the base. They know their husbands are on a serious mission and pray for their safe return. The children whimper and go back to sleep. The wives watch the clock.

The birds roll and gain speed, spewing fifty feet of blue and yellow flame, as the wheels splash water from the wet runway and rain splatters against the windshields, the wing-man strains to see and maintain position on his leader. A few thousand feet down the runway they become airborne, and before the gear doors clunk closed they are engulfed in thick, dark clouds. There are no outside visual references. The leader is solidly on the gauges. Two is hugging lead from no more than six feet away. If he gets any further away, he will lose sight of the leaders running lights in the murk. They change radio channels to check in with control. Two must count the clicks on his channel switch, because he cannot take his eyes off the lead bird and they start their right turn for a heading of two two zero degrees.

The time is the nineteen fifties and the aircraft are all-weather versions of the Sabrejet, first line fighters of the period and a variant of the Sabre that cleared the skies of MIG 15s against great odds in the Korean conflict. The leader is a captain with over nine hundred hours in this type aircraft plus several hundred hours in other types. The wing-man is a first lieutenant with only slightly less experience. They could be making a lot more money as commercial pilots.

"Adcock, this is Kilo Papa Zero One, climbing through angels four, heading two two zero." "Roger, Kilo Papa flight, this is Adcock one five, radar contact, continue vector two two zero, climb gate (max power) to angels forty one." (One five identifies the individual controller) "Roger, climbing to angels forty one. (forty one thousand feet). "Kilo Papa, this is Adcock, your target is 20 degrees left at one hundred forty miles." The response from the pilot is two clicks of the mike button.

Airspeed is four hundred knots, the vertical velocity indicator is pegged at five thousand feet per minute and the fuel gauges are unwinding at very rapid rate. The fuel quantity indicator for internal fuel is moving and that means the two 120 gallon drop tanks are already empty. The machine climbs very rapidly in afterburner, but exacts a heavy price in fuel. Upon reaching assigned altitude, the fuel remaining will not be much more than half the original 5525 pounds.

As they bore on through the dense, black clouds, the only thing visible outside the cockpit is the lights from the other aircraft. The wing-man is still positioned nicely on the left wing, with nav lights blinking through the pea soup. Although the radar cannot see beyond thirty miles, the lead pilot works at fine tuning his radar and visualizing his position relative to the target. In this type interceptor there is no back seater to operate the weapons system. The complex Sabre has the highest workload of any aircraft in the inventory. Number two has a full time job for now, staying in close formation.

"Kilo Papa, this is Adcock, your target is unidentified, large, single aircraft, passing from south to north, maintaining angels forty one. We have no flight plan and no radio contact – identify – range to target now one hundred miles." Click-click.

It has now been ten minutes since the klaxons blast. Time since take-off is six minutes, but to the pilots, it seems like only a couple of minutes. They are only now becoming wide awake, having operated up to now mostly by reflexes. Lead squeezes the mike switch on the throttle and advises they have reached assigned altitude. "Adcock, Kilo Papa level, angels forty one, fuel 2550 pounds, oxygen OK. Two state fuel." "Two has 2500 pounds, oxygen OK." The fuel guzzling afterburners are shut down, but throttles are still set at about 98 percent power on the main engines to maintain .9 mach.

"Roger Kilo Papa, turn starboard two six zero, range sixty five." Click-click. The flight now breaks into the clear above the clouds and a half moon is providing some light with dim reflections off the tops of the clouds. A few stars are visible. "Two, this is One, cover me." Two now climbs two thousand feet and drops back about a mile, slightly off to one side. In the event the target is hostile, they may discover that when the lead aircraft gets shot at while making the ID. In that case, Two will survive and be in position to attack. They often swap positions for training and proficiency, but in this case, lead wants to exercise his responsibility as flight leader and take the risks involved. Lead also changes his lights from dim/steady to bright flash and looks more closely at the radar scope in the bottom center of the panel. The radar antenna is in the auto search mode, scanning high from left to right, and low from right to left, overlapping in the center. No blips yet.

"Kilo Papa, target now forty left, range thirty five." Click-click. Another minute passes while the closure rate is more than ten miles per minute. "Zero One, contact" he calls as the blip appears on his radar at twenty four miles. That is good performance for state of the art radar. *Must be a big bird, he thinks.* He notes the position is good. The controller has positioned them well. There still has been no response to radio calls on probable radio channels or the emergency channels.

The radar fire control system will not lock on beyond fifteen miles, so he takes manual control of the radar and positions the range gate marker at it's max of fifteen miles and waits for the target blip to merge with the range gate marker. The radar goes into automatic tracking, the attack display comes on, and he no longer has to manually position the antenna to spotlight the blip. "Zero One Judy", he calls to let the controller know he no longer needs positioning info from him. The controller stands by, but monitors closely in case the airborne radar breaks lock. The target may make things difficult by turning on radar jamming transmitters, dropping chaff, evasive action, or all three.

The tension builds as the pilot monitors the steering dot to make necessary corrections and wonders what the unidentified aircraft will turn out to be. A few high cloud tops are blocking his attempts to make visual contact at this distance. He will have to convert to an offset stern approach in another couple of miles and synchronize his flight path with that of the target. He is prepared to make an attack if fired upon and the wing-man is in good position to attack if necessary, but he hopes it will be friendly. As the range decreases he begins to reduce power and turn in behind and to one side of the target. He mentally reviews what has to do to arm his rockets.

There are so many safety precautions to prevent accidental firing, it is difficult to fire intentionally. Several guarded circuit breakers have to be unguarded and pushed in. Switches on the armament panel must be set and the stick grip trigger pin removed. The twenty four rockets in the pod each contains about two and a half pounds of TNT in the warhead. One of them has enough destructive power to down any aircraft.

The dim outline of a large, swept wing bomber begins to take shape in the poor light. There are some under-slung engine pods. As he moves in closer, the moonlight reflects off the side of the long, slender fuselage. The 'USAF' is plainly visible now. A USAF B-47. What is he doing here with no flight plan, or is way off his flight plan, and not monitoring military guard channel?

"Adcock, Zero One, Tallyho, target is USAF B-47." "Roger we need the tail number." So far, everything has gone easily enough, but getting a small tail number is difficult in daylight. In the dark, it is next to impossible, but control needs the number to be reported to Air Defense Command headquarters with the intercept report. A copy will go to Strategic Air Command and SAC will deny that they had an aircraft in the area. "Roger, Adcock, we will try."

The wing-man is pulling in closer now on the opposite side, looking for a tail number. Lead thinks to himself, *that is a long wing. I will have to stay slightly low and get behind that wing in order to move in closer.* Suddenly, he is blinded by a powerful white light, hitting him squarely in the face. The crew in the bomber has seen him and is trying to get a better look or just trying to run him off. No one can hold a safe position with that extremely bright light coming from the rear of the long bubble canopy. That is where the co-pilot would be.

He ducks under the wing and tries to recover some night vision. He tries to get some response on the radio. No response. Apparently they are not in trouble. There have been no known radio calls, no emergency squawk from the IFF, which would be picked up by the ground radar. Hopefully, they know what they are doing. "Adcock, bomber is blinding us with white light." "Roger, keep trying." He eases out from under the wing and drops back again. ZAP!!

More light – blinded again. Back under the wing. "Zero Two, can you see a number ?" "Negative."

The fuel gauges wait for no one. After making two more attempts with the same results, Zero One calls, "Adcock, we are at bingo fuel." "Roger, Kilo Papa, RTB, pigeons one five zero, one hundred fifteen miles, what state?" "Roger, turning to one five zero, fuel 1150 pounds, oxygen OK." "Two has 1100 pounds, Ox OK."

The flight turns toward home, having done all they can do. Although not entirely satisfied, everyone on the ground and in the air breathes easier, but there is still work to be done. There is a little matter of getting back on the ground in nasty weather. There are no alternate bases within range of their limited fuel. The present situation will require an instrument approach and will use more time and fuel than a visual approach.

Normally, they plan to enter the traffic pattern with enough fuel for one go-around, although it does not always work out that way. Tonight, they will have one shot at landing on a runway they cannot see until very close to the ground on a short final approach. Even with the cockpit cooling system working, they are already sweaty. What they do is hard work, mentally and physically. Now the recovery will be the type that causes palms to sweat. They must concentrate and make no mistakes. "Close it up Two." Two rejoins and lead again switches his running lights from bright/flash to dim/steady. Lead reviews his penetration and approach checklist, as if he didn't already know it backward and forward. He checks setting of pitot heat, defrost and anti-icing controls and calculates time and distance against fuel consumption. It will be close, but they can make it if they do everything exactly right. They have done it before.

"Kilo Papa flight, pigeons now seventy five miles, steer one five five. "Roger, one five five." A quiet couple of minutes pass, then "Kilo Papa, homeplate fifty five miles, descend to twenty thousand , contact approach control on channel fifteen, Adcock one five, out." The controller has coordinated a handover by landline. "Kilo Papa, roger – Two, speed brakes out, NOW, going to channel fifteen." Power is reduced to near idle and the engine noise subsides, but the roar and vibration of the turbulent air past the speed brakes makes up for it. The rate of descent quickly stabilizes at better than five thousand feet per minute and they plunge back into the dense cloud cover. Two is welded to his leaders' right wing.

"Approach Control, this Kilo Papa Zero One, flight of two, about fifty miles northwest, heading one five five, descending to twenty thousand." "Roger, Kilo Papa, radar contact, continue approach. You are cleared for radar vectors to the ILS (Instrument Landing System) for runway three five right. Ceiling two hundred feet, visibility one mile, moderate rain, wind northwest 15, gusts to 24, altimeter two niner eight one. Continue descent to three thousand."

The ceiling and viz have improved, but the wind has picked up. The gusts will require a higher than normal approach speed and the turbulence will make it hard on the wing-man. Wet runway, high touchdown speeds will use up a lot of runway on the roll-out for a fifteen thousand pound tricycle with brakes on two skinny wheels. At least the birds are now five thousand pounds lighter, due to fuel consumption.

"Roger approach, cut it as close as you can, we are on the fumes." "Roger Kilo Papa, continue descent and report level." Click-click. "Kilo Papa, turn left to three four five, for final approach, you are twelve miles out." "Roger three four five, level three thousand, fuel four hundred pounds, Two has less – we are receiving localizer and glide slope." "Roger Kilo Papa, cleared ILS for runway three five, tower has cleared you for landing" Click-click – "Two, speed brakes in NOW." As the airspeed bleeds off to 175 knots, the throttles are pushed back up to maintain altitude until intercepting the glide slope and lead calls for landing gear and flaps down, which requires more power.

Things are happening quickly now, and there is no margin for error. It takes strong, steady hands to maintain smooth control, in rough air, with major configuration changes taking place, causing the birds to pitch and yaw. With some power adjustments, the airspeed settles down at 152 knots, or 175 mph. The position of the wing-man does not vary more than a few inches. He risks a glance at his panel for a split second to make sure he has three green lights for his wheels. He really does not want to see the fuel quantity gauge.

Rain is pounding the windshields and the clouds are dark. Again, the only visible thing besides the glow of the instrument panel is the nav lights of the wing-man, bouncing a little in the turbulence, but holding a great position. The localizer needle slides away from center, indicating they are drifting to the right of the runway. The outer marker light flashes on indicating they are about six miles from touchdown. At the same time, the glide slope needle starts down.

Correct left! The wind must be stronger up here than on the ground. "Two, speed brakes out NOW." The added drag gives them just enough descent to keep the glide slope needle centered as they bore on in. Power settings must be kept high due to the high drag, shallow descent angle and the fuel gauges continue their movement toward the zero mark.

Make prompt, but small and precise control inputs. Concentrate on steering to keep those needles centered on glideslope and centerline. Run a rapid cross check on direction, vertical velocity, pitch and bank. Closely watch power and airspeed, which is barely above stall and can induce an insidious and fatal sink rate. At this speed the controls are sluggish with all the garbage hanging out. Thankfully, this is a pretty stable bird as fighters go.

At two hundred feet, which is getting pretty close to the ground under totally blind conditions, descending at 150 knots, questions enter the leaders mind. Are these instruments accurate? He is betting his life on it. The wing-man trusts his leader. At this point, there is no alternative. The middle marker light flashes on, indicating they are getting near the approach end of the runway, just as the clouds begin to give way to allow a dim distorted view of some pale, yellow runway marker lights through the rain streaked windshield.

Alignment is pretty good, requiring only minor correction. Lead calls "contact" so the wing-man can drop back to touchdown behind the leader. It's a little safer than touching down in close formation. The leader deliberately lands a little long, on the left side, in the event Two needs to pass on the roll-out. Brakes have been known to fail. Approach has heard the contact call and responds with "Kilo Papa, when convenient, contact ground control on channel three, goodnight sir."

"Ground control, Kilo Papa flight on the landing roll." "Roger Kilo Papa, cleared to the alert hangar." They coast to the turn-off to the alert hangar and lead taxies around back to pull into position for refueling. He will require the better part of 850 gallons. The Fuel gauge is about a needle width off the zero mark. He opens the canopy, shuts down, turns off everything, unlatches the straps, oxygen mask and takes a deep breath. His face is already marked with deep red lines where the tight fitting mask has cut into it. Then he hears the wing-man's engine die before he gets all the way into the fueling area, but coasts in. His fuel tanks are dry.

The crew chief installs the safety pins for the landing gear and climbs up the side while the pilot is re-installing the safety pins for the canopy and ejection seat. They make the necessary entries in the log book and head inside. The wing-man is just coming in from the other side. "Good Job", lead says, "Right" is the only comment in response. Lead walks over to the phone for the required debriefing and Adcock picks up on his end. Lead says, "Kilo Papa Zero One, let's debrief." "OK, good job, Kilo Papa." "Rodge, good job on your end too, Adcock. We are back on five."

The crewmen refuel and ready the birds for "cocked" status again. They are now the spare birds. The old spare birds are now primary, so there are always at least two birds on five minutes. The pilots get a drink of water and go back to whatever they were doing when the klaxons sounded, with another forty five minutes of flight time in their records.

The quiet of the night has been disturbed once more, and again a child whimpers, but the wives now sleep and the town sleeps, unaware of the effort expended on their behalf.

The End of a Good Thing

The training wing lost a lot of good men during my tour at Perrin. I did not keep an exact count, but I know we lost over twenty pilots. Even with a lot of emphasis on safety, realistic training demanded it's toll of casualties. We lost students and instructors. Some bailed out and survived. Some didn't make it. Some survived because of superior airmanship, some by dumb luck. Some just had no chance to beat the machine or the circumstances. We all knew the dangers involved but were willing to run the risk.

I don't expect everyone to understand that. For my part, I loved flying and closely related to that was a desire to serve my country. If I had the ability to do something, particularly something that most people could not do, I was obligated to do it. If I derived some satisfaction from it in the process, that was my good fortune.

Our alert unit pilots never scratched an airplane. We had the cream of the crop for maintenance people. They were the best on the base. Not much got by them. Our pilots all had a lot of experience and good judgment. It was always a pleasure to fly with any of them. In any given situation, they knew what I would do, and I knew what they would do. We often pushed the envelope, but we also knew our capabilities and limitations and tried to never exceed them. Plenty of hairy situations occurred, but the only incident I recall that really scared me was partly my fault, and partly the fault of my crew chief.

We had flown an intercept one night, and on our return, I wanted to stay in the same bird. It was quickly serviced and put back on "cocked" status. I asked the chief if he had checked everything following the refueling and said he had done so. The internal fuel was supplied through a center point, high pressure, high volume system that could pump the entire 610 gallons in a few minutes. The 120 gallon drop tanks had to be filled with individual hoses.

Although the ground crewman were usually very thorough, it was still the final responsibility of the pilot to make a walk around inspection. In all my experience, I had never found a loose or missing fuel cap. In this case, before I had to time to think anymore about it, the klaxons blew for another scramble and we were getting airborne again.

On this night, the wing-man had chosen to make an in-trail takeoff, a few seconds behind me rather than a wing take-off. We sometimes did that, practicing keeping our position on the leader with our radar. About the time I lifted off, the control tower radioed, "Kilo Papa Zero One, you are on fire!" "The wing-man, from behind also said, "LEAD, YOU ARE ON FIRE!"

No one ever wants to hear that anytime, much less just at lift-off, too far down the runway to abort and too low to eject. At that time we did not yet have zero level ejection systems. I looked back and the area was being well lighted by a huge stream of fire from each drop tank. The fuel was siphoning out of the open filler holes and had been ignited by the flame from the afterburner.

My first reaction was to jerk the throttle out the afterburner range, but instantly saw that was a mistake. As I started to slow down, the flames got closer to the tanks, so I plugged in the burner again. If I dropped the tanks, they might injure someone below, off the end of the runway. It was too dark to get a good look, so I decided to continue the status quo and hope that things didn't get any worse. They didn't and after a minute or two, that seemed much longer, the tanks emptied and the fire went out. The sortie was shortened because of my wasted fuel, and no great harm was done, except to my pride.

————

Good things often end too soon. On returning from a short leave to attend my grandmothers funeral, I found notice of re-assignment awaiting me. Larson AFB, Moses Lake, Washington, by way of Tyndall AFB, Panama City, Florida for three months of radar controller school. I was astonished! They didn't do that to fighter pilots unless they had really messed up badly.

Being a scope dope had never been one of my ambitions. The brass tried to soften the blow by telling me that ADC was desperate for radar controllers and the fastest way to get some on line was to retrain interceptor pilots, who were already familiar with the trade.

Larson AFB, Washington State

Our oldest son, Alan had just started in the first grade in Texas, but in the fall, we set out for Panama City, Florida. We decided it would be fun to live on the beach for a while and rented a house at Mexico Beach. Alan's school was in Port St. Joe, where they were on Eastern Time. Panama City and Tyndall AFB were on Central time. Alan had to get on the school bus at six AM.

In the school, my instructor, like most, had no feel for the pilots environment and the in-flight problems he faced. He and I often butted heads about how to do things, but I had to conform to the school method in order to pass the course. I could see why many controllers were not much admired by the pilots who were supposed to follow their directions. That is not to say there were not any good ones. Some were excellent. At the risk of bragging, most of the outstanding ones were the guys who wore wings on their chest. It's easier to get the most out of a pilot if you have been there and done that.

Fortunately, in addition to simulators, the school used real aircraft for targets on live intercept training. The workhorse T-bird required target pilots, so after school, I went down to the flight line and logged enough time to stay current and proficient. I didn't leave the school with the highest grade, but I graduated and we started the long trek to the northwest and Moses Lake, Washington. We had had enough sand to last us a long time.

We left warm, sunny Florida in our Jaguar 3.4 sedan, in mid December. We had no cold weather clothes and could not buy any in Florida. As far as Kansas City, the trip went well. From there on, it was terrible. There was snow and ice everywhere. We never saw a bare road surface for the next two thousand miles.

150

The car ran poorly and gave me a bad time and outwitted several mechanics because of slush accumulating in the air intake, then freezing to block air flow. I finally figured that out and we stopped in Cheyenne to buy Kathy a coat and some boots. We had to buy shoes for Scott to replace the ones that had mysteriously disappeared from the car.

After ten days of agonizingly slow progress, we arrived at Larson, only to discover that our designated sponsor had not done his job. He was to have contacted us to advise that there was no family housing available on base or in town. We lived in the Air Force guest quarters for a few days and then found a house that was available for sale. It's price tag would have been half as much in Texas. My options were to bite the bullet or send the family back east for three thousand miles, but we had come too far to do that.

We used our VA loan eligibility to purchase the house, thinking if housing was that scarce, it would easily sell when were re-assigned elsewhere. We could not know it at the time, but that was a pipe dream. We had no way to know that Larson would be closing in little more than a year. At least we were keeping the family together, but we were not yet fully aware of the shockingly high cost living in the area. As it turned out, many of the enlisted troops simply could not support their families there. The price of gasoline was twice what we had paid in other areas. Most other items were priced as bad or worse. Sales tax was levied even on labor as well as products.

I reported to the Spokane Air Defense Sector headquarters, located at Larson. It was one of several computerized air defense systems. The consoles displayed a composite air picture consisting of inputs from several ground radar sites and height finding radars. There was no raw radar displayed. It was all computer generated symbology. My next surprise came when I learned that my job was that of Air Surveillance Officer. With an enlisted crew of thirty five men, we maintained the air picture for the complex. I was ASO on a rotating shift and I was not exactly thrilled with the job.

Our primary interceptor force was at Geiger AFB, near Spokane, flying F-106s. I knew some of the pilots because they had been students when I was at Perrin. Our sector sometimes controlled aircraft from McChord AFB, at Tacoma and occasionally visiting aircraft from other sectors. Our area of responsibility extended well up into Canada. Geiger was a little too far away for me to drive to in order to fly with the 498th Fighter Interceptor Squadron.

At Larson, the SAC wing had six T-33 aircraft for utility aircraft and proficiency training for those who needed it. The KC-135 pilots and B-52 pilots either were not allowed to fly the T-birds or did not want to. I turned in my flight records to base operations at Larson. After a few flights with one of my fellow SPADS pilots, I was scheduled for a base checkout. A formal checkride with a flight examiner was needed in order for me to fly on my own or as pilot in command.

The check pilot was Captain Dysart, a very officious, do it my way or don't do it, type of person. During the local flight we did everything we were supposed to do according the regulations. We climbed right out to twenty thousand feet, which is a good maneuvering altitude and he told me to do a chandelle. Hardly anyone ever practices chandelles beyond basic pilot training. It is a maneuver designed to develop coordination in an ever changing situation of pitch, bank and airspeed. The only practical use is to gain altitude while reversing course, completing it just before you run out of airspeed.

I told Dysart we were too heavy, not having used most of our tip tank fuel, but I would do him a chandelle and modify the standard entry and recovery speeds because of our weight. He didn't much like that. Anyway, I did one and it wasn't perfect, but it was good enough. Then he told me to do a lazy eight. At the top of a lazy eight, the bird is in a steep bank, near stall, even at normal weight.

Again, I reminded him we were still too heavy, but I would do the maneuver with slightly higher than specified entry and recovery speed. Dysart was not very pleased, but at this point I had done nothing to fail the ride. After all, I had told him the correct speeds and why I had deviated. I would really have looked dumb, if we had fallen out of the sky at the top of a lazy eight. I would discover later, that he probably didn't know any better.

We did some more air work and finally were down to internal fuel. He told me to return to Larson. There was no clarification, but I had figured he would try to mess me up on the required engine flame out procedure. Some examiners try to get you in a situation where you have to think and work fast to salvage a dead stick landing. About fifteen miles out, descending through about twelve thousand, he pulled the throttle back to 55 percent, dropped the speed brakes and said. "Flameout", simulating a dead engine.

We were in good position relative to the airfield with plenty of altitude to enter the high key point over the field, and in fact had a little altitude to spare, so I continued straight on, perpendicular to the big runway and dropped the wheels a little early to compensate for the extra altitude. We hit high key right on the money and began the descending turn around to the low key point on the downwind. At the right time, I lowered the flaps, and continued right on around the base to final turn with plenty of altitude. We came over the landing spot just about right and I went around, feeling pretty good about it.

Dysart had me go out a few miles and do some more air work, including a stall series, recovery from unusual positions and a few other things that were like throwing a rabbit in a briar patch as far as I was concerned. We came on back, made a couple of landings, including a no flap landing and as the fuel ran low, a full stop. We parked and went inside.

Dysart got his pilots handbook from his desk drawer and turned to the section that describes flameout landings. The ideal pattern was depicted with a three mile initial approach lining up with the runway and turning at the high key point. However, the book stresses that is the procedure under ideal circumstances, and the pattern may be entered at any point. The pilot is executing an emergency procedure. In our case, we did not have enough altitude to go out three miles and turn back to travel three more miles to the break.

I guess he misjudged and thought he had initiated the procedure at a distance and altitude that would allow the ideal pattern. I later found out what his problem was. However, at this point in the critique, he announced that I would not have a passing grade on the flight because I screwed up the flameout pattern. He even went so far as to make some disparaging remarks about stupid ADC pilots who didn't do things by the book. My response to him was that if he wanted to bust his ass by going too far out in order to turn back in, by the book, to do it when I wasn't in the airplane with him.

I stewed about the flight with Dysart for a few days and then got a call to come over and fly with a Captain Birthisel, a flight examiner who was with one of the local missile units. At the appointed time, I showed up and we briefed for about the same routine I had done with Dysart. Everything went very smoothly and when the time came for the forced landing, I could tell that

Dysart had given him the exact details of my previous ride. The power was cut at exactly the same location and altitude as before. I flew my pattern exactly as before. I knew it was right. With a dead engine, and you want to dead stick it, you get over the field, unless you are so low you have to enter on the downwind leg at low key or on the base leg. If entry at one of those points is not feasible, then the recommended procedure is to punch out.

We continued the flight and Birthisel had me do some additional things that were not called for on a check ride. When I questioned that, he replied that he wasn't grading me on those things, just wanted to see what I would do. We finished up and parked the bird. I knew I had done well, but was wondering what standards these SAC pilots went by. When we were putting away our gear in the locker room, Birthisel turned to me and asked, "Is it OK with you if we cut orders for you to do instruction and flight examiner work?"

I replied, "Sure, I reckon that means you were satisfied with my flight?" He said, "I have flown with many pilots, but have not flown with many people who have the feel for an airplane that you have." He continued to say, "I am the chief flight examiner for this unit." Then I asked what the situation was with Dysart. Dysart had led me to believe that he was the chief flight examiner. Birthisel replied that Dysart only had a total of thirty five hours jet time and didn't know how he had managed flight examiner status. I told him I would like to administer Dysarts next check ride. He said, "you won't have the opportunity. He is going back to flying Gooney Birds."

––––––––

I flew many utility flights in my "spare time" for SAC. I made parts pick ups at other bases and flew personnel to and from other bases. One of my more memorable flights was to Hill AFB, Ogden, Utah. I got a call one evening after working all day at SPADS to go pick up a part. When I got to base ops, the supply man gave me a piece of paper with a requisition for the part. Their part numbers meant nothing to me. I had told them I would haul anything they could strap in the back seat and had done so many times.

Upon arrival at Hill AFB, I was met by a supply man from there. He asked me what kind of airplane I had brought down there. I told him it was a T-33 and he started laughing. Finally, he asks, "Do you know what that part number is?" "No", I replied. Then he says, "It's an engine cowling for a KC-135."

So, I called Larson and told them they needed to send the Gooney Bird for the part.

In the legalistic SAC culture, anytime something didn't go as it should have, there had to be a scapegoat. The next day, while I was at work, the SAC wing commander telephoned me and proceeded to eat my lunch because I had wasted the trip to Ogden. I was not insubordinate, but I stood my ground. The people who sent me to Ogden knew, or should have known what that part number represented. They knew I was in a T-bird, and I was not going to take the rap for the foul-up. As previously stated, I didn't care what the parts were if they could get them in the back seat of a T-bird.

I reminded the colonel that I had flown many trips on MY time to accommodate HIS people and I did not have to do it. Of course, I was keeping up my proficiency and enjoying some of it, but I could always go over to Geiger to fly. After the attempted reprimand, I did just that for a while. It was a long drive, but the atmosphere was totally different. There was hardly any paperwork and no Mickey Mouse.

––––––

In October of 1962, the Russians tried to call our bluff by putting missiles with nuke warheads in Cuba. The entire Air Force went on a high state of alert – ADC and SAC included. SAC had already been flying their Chromedome missions over a circuit above the Arctic Circle and back to their U.S. bases. They were loaded with a couple of those big blue dudes earmarked for a target in Russia. If the go code was received, they simply broke out of the circuit and headed for their designated target.

With increased alert status, SAC was tasked to carry a third pilot on the B-52 bombers. The local wing commander requested our Sector Commander loan him some pilots. SAC didn't say they had to be B-52 pilots, just pilots. Our boss posted a list of the rated pilots in SPADS and when we were scheduled for a turn in a B-52. I was the first one on the list and on the appointed day, I reported to the SAC command post and was assigned to a crew. I had never seen the inside of a B-52, and was not real excited at the prospect of flying an aerial truck.

———

We boarded the beast and everyone was doing their thing while I watched and tried to take in the appointments of the machine. As the aircraft commander and co-pilot were strapping in, I inquired as to where my ejection seat was. "Well we don't expect to have to egress in mid air, but if we do, the electronics warfare operator, I and the co-pilot will eject upward. The navigators in the lower deck will go downward, leaving holes in the bottom. The box you will be sitting on has no ejection system, so take your pick of the holes we leave." That was the A/C.

So, I strapped up with a seat belt and shoulder harness, sitting on a simple box with a little cushion on top. There was no backrest, much less a headrest. It was the seat used by instructor pilots and flight examiners. I also had noticed arctic survival kits on board, but could see only enough for the regular crew. I asked about where my survival kit was and was told I wouldn't need one.

About dark we departed Larson in that lumbering beast that passed for an airplane, with all eight engines laying down a smoke trail that would rival a coal burning steamship. We climbed out and leveled at about forty grand, heading east. There was another bomber in trail about a mile back. They often traveled in cells of two. The bird had good pressurization, so we took off our hard hats and masks.

The co-pilot got on the makeshift mattress stuffed between a bulkhead and the outer fuselage. I got into the left seat, and the aircraft commander got in the right seat. He showed me how to use the autopilot and how to manage the fuel system. My primary job was to keep fuel going from the correct tanks to the engines and keep a log of what had been used from which cells. Otherwise, there was not a lot to do, except to monitor the instruments and make occasional changes to the autopilot settings or throttle settings.

After three hours, we played musical chairs again, with me getting in the right seat, the AC on the mattress and the co-pilot in the left seat. Finally, my turn came to get some rest. I climbed on the mattress and it took me a while to get settled, and to figure out how to use the system. I had just dropped off to sleep, when I woke up, being shaken by the co-pilot, telling me to get up and get strapped in. It was time to rendezvous with a tanker. We were off the coast of Nova Scotia.

I never did know if the B-52 was that difficult to control, or if these two guys needed some additional formation practice. It took them too long to get connected with the tanker and they fought the controls fiercely while we were hooked up. The air was smooth and on a night refueling the twin rows of lights underneath the tanker provide a clear picture of position for the receiving bird. While hooked up the lights even show relative boom extension or compression. The AC fought the control column while the co-pilot fought the eight throttles, often going from full power to idle and back again. They had several disconnects, but finally got our fuel and I was back in the left seat.

We then turned north and proceeded up past Baffin Island on the left and Greenland on our right, but it was too dark to see anything. We were headed generally toward the North Pole. At anytime we could be diverted to Russia. However, the system is more foolproof than people are led to believe by books and movies. The "Go Code" was not initiated by a light that could malfunction. If it came, it would be via a simple but clever, self authenticating, radio transmission. I am not allowed to tell you more than that.

———

After turning more northwest and traversing thousands of miles of arctic wasteland, we turned southwest across Alaska. All of that part of the trip was in daylight and the sun was superbright, reflecting off all that ice and snow. A couple of times, the AC and co-pilot went below to the navigator deck where the coffee pot was located. When they left me up there alone in the cockpit, I felt like they were mighty brave or mighty naive.

I did not like being up there alone, not knowing much about that aluminum overcast.

Somewhere on the southwest bound leg, we hooked up with another KC-135 and the earlier refueling was great compared to this one. They wrestled the controls, with the bird wallowing all over the sky, generating several disconnects. The tanker pilot finally radioed that he was leaving. Whatever fuel we had was all we would get. He had another bird waiting to refuel and he also had to reserve enough fuel to get himself back to Fairbanks.

The crew was concerned about our fuel shortage. I didn't worry about it when I learned we were projected to have ten thousand pounds remaining over Larson. After heading south for a while, paralleling the west coast, we turned east and completed the circle by arriving back at Larson. We had been airborne for twenty hours and ten minutes. The crew had figured out a rotation system that denied me most of my rest time, but they got theirs.

Back at work, in the SPADS surveillance room, Colonel Tarbet, our director of operations came by to ask how the B-52 flight went. He had been one of my first students at Perrin, then a Lt. Col., but the rank difference didn't seem to matter much to him. Over the years we had crossed paths and he always went out of his way to be friendly. Now he was a full colonel and almost a father figure to me.

I described the flight in detail. Without comment, he went over to the bulletin board, yanked down the loaner pilot schedule, wadded it, threw it in the trash can and kept right on out the door. I would love to have heard his conversation with the SAC wing commander.

––––––––

The Russians backed down and took their nukes back to Russia. We had been very close to a shooting war and we would have evaporated the island of Cuba, but they would have done us serious damage in the process. We know now, that the Russian officers were itching to launch some nukes in our direction.

The fact that military people like Major Rudolph Anderson lost their lives by being shot down while doing recon flights seems to get lost in the major scheme of things. It was a reminder that most of us were merely expendable pawns in the game being played by the people at the top. Oh yes, the president did write a letter to Mrs. Anderson, but there was no penalty carried out against the Cubans or the Russians. As Tennyson put it in his 'Charge of the Light Brigade,' "Ours is not to reason why, but to do or die."

––––––––

Our tour at Larson turned out to be a short one. We prepared to leave the northwest, and SAC, but not ADC. According to my log book, I had flown seventy six missions for SAC in my "spare time".

We learned that we were to have a fourth child. With three boys, there was no way this one would not be a female, but we named her Thomas Brian. We had given it more than a fair chance. We jokingly told everyone that our last three children were named Eeny, Meeny, and Miney, and there would be no Mo.

The North Country

Thomas arrived on the day after Christmas in 1962. Shortly thereafter the Air Force decided I was due for another overseas assignment. My Alaska tour had exempted me for a while and most of my class mates had already been serving overseas. Someone evidently thought I liked the cold country. This time it was Labrador. Not just Labrador, but the northernmost tip at Saglek. Saglek was about as isolated as one could get. There was no local populace, just a radar station on top of a mountain, overlooking the frigid North Atlantic Ocean.

There were no roads, no power lines or telephone lines. Shipping could get into the harbor about three or four months of the year. Any other time people and supplies were transported by air. It was out of range of a helicopter. The runway down by the base of the mountain was short and ran uphill from the edge of the surf to the base of the mountain. A C-47, Gooney Bird, could make it by landing uphill and taking off down hill. The were no family quarters.

Kathy and I were not happy, but were resigned to being separated for a year and we moved her to Maryville, Tennessee, a few miles from her parents and other kin. I would get one leave for a trip home after serving six months at an isolated site. That is the way it is, sometimes, in military life.

I arrived at Goose Air Base, Goose Bay, Labrador in mid spring, expecting to go on up to Saglek, another 300 miles to the north . I didn't know that there was only one aircraft per week scheduled for that trip. As it turned out, it didn't matter. When I went into the terminal, I was met by a captain who introduced himself as my escort up to the local radar site. When I told him I was on my way to Saglek, he informed me that my assignment had been changed to Melville Air Station, adjacent to Goose Air Base. I was supposed to have been informed, but the usual military administrative efficiency had prevailed and everyone except me knew about the change.

It was quite a surprise to be re-assigned to Melville, the 641st AC & W Squadron, and certainly not an unwelcome one at this point in time. I would be close to some civilization, albeit limited civilization, and would be able to fly with the local fighter squadron. I had a choice of serving a year there unaccompanied by family, or I could opt for a two year tour and live on the main base with family. I explained the situation to Kathy and she did not hesitate in making a decision to join me. The family relationship in Tennessee had not been quite what she had expected.

For the time being, the radar site was well manned and it seemed that no one was real anxious to put me to work as a radar controller. I took my flight records down to the 59th Fighter Interceptor Squadron and it was like old home week. I knew nearly every pilot there. Some had been instructors at Perrin and others had passed through there as students, some even in our flight. I left my records with operations and took the shuttle bus back up the hill. The "hill" was a small mountain overlooking the bay from about three miles as the crow flies, and about nine miles by way of the steep, winding, muddy trail that was jokingly referred to as a road. It was a good location for a long range radar site.

Hardly an hour after I got back to the hill, fighter ops called and asked if I could fly that night. That was fine with me. Another controller from our site was rated and was scheduled that night, so we rode down together. We fired up a T-bird for a target mission with the F-102 interceptors flying against us. It was a very dark, moonless night with heavy cloud cover up to about twenty thousand. We climbed out and leveled on top with me in the back seat. After a two hour flight and two waves of deuces making practice intercepts, we made an instrument approach and landed back at Goose. I had not seen much besides the instrument panel in the back seat. I still didn't know what the airpatch looked like.

Next day fighter ops called again and asked if I could fly again that night. Our radar ops people had not put me to work yet, so I replied, "Yes, I can fly tonight. Who is the other pilot?" I was told there would not be another pilot. I would be solo. "But I have not had a base checkout". "Oh yes you have, you got that last night." So I went down there and groped my way through another flight just like the one previous. I still didn't know anything about the local area.

After several days and nights of that kind of flying, I finally got a look at the area in daylight with fairly good weather. I was to learn that good weather around there meant the field was at or above published minimum ceiling and visibility so we could fly legally.

The bay came inland from the Atlantic for nearly a hundred miles and except for the Goose and Hamilton rivers, was about the only landmark. I could see a few scrubby trees inland for a few miles and then there was nothing but rough, rocky, uneven terrain that all looked pretty much the same. Other than the road to Melville, the road to the village of Happy Valley, and road to the Goose River, which we could drive across if the river was frozen over, there was no place to drive to.

In winter, we could drive across the frozen Goose River to the Hudson's Bay Company store and an Anglican mission. There was also a Hudson's Bay Company store on the way to Happy Valley and we sometimes drove there to buy things not available in our base exchange. Anything not available there, or in the exchange or commissary, we did without or mail ordered from the states to be delivered via Air Force cargo flights.

Melville was the NORAD control center for our huge air defense sector. We had outlying stations with overlapping radar coverage at Cartwright (Susie Q) to the southeast, Hopedale, (Joe Penner) to the northeast, and Saglek, (Lonesome) to the north. They all reported to us at Melville, (Half Pint). Our interceptors had Hotel Papa call signs. The southern portion of the sector lay below the St. Lawrence River and the straits of Belle Isle including the Island of Newfoundland. Stephenville was the control center for the sub sector and had stations at St. Anthony and Gander.

We maintained a detachment of 59th aircraft at Harmon AFB, near Stephenville. Harmon was about three hundred nautical miles south of Goose. The climate wasn't much better than Goose. Maybe not quite as cold, but they got as much snow and their normal weather was just as lousy. Due to the mountains in close proximity to the air base, the ILS approach was unusually steep and a real challenge to any pilot who used it. Staying on the glide slope meant deviating from all the normal rules and techniques of instrument flying.

Each day and night, the 59th flew several training sorties as well as maintaining at least two birds on five minute alert. All pilots maintained a high level of proficiency, not only in practicing intercepts, but in dealing with a lot of nasty weather. I flew a lot of target missions and also a lot of utility flights to various places in the states and around Canada.

Eventually, I had to slack off on the flying somewhat when I was finally put to work on an operations crew at Melville. After a few days of orientation, I was senior director of a crew of three or four controllers and about thirty five enlisted troops, so the honeymoon came to a halt.

The bus schedule to and from the main base never matched my schedule, so I bought an old Goosemobile, a well worn one that had been handed down to new arrivals when the present owner was preparing to rotate back to the USA. The severe weather, the terrible roads, and driving conditions took their toll, so aesthetics were not important, only reliability was important and I needed to get back and forth between the hill and the main base.

As I was beginning a two day break on a shift change, I got a call from Sector Headquarters. A major working there had been notified that his teenage son in New Orleans was dying. Someone was needed to fly him down there. I never turned down a request from operations if I could possibly help. Of course that paid off if I requested an airplane from time to time to accommodate my schedule.

We departed Goose about mid morning in fairly good weather and refueled at Bangor. Climbing out from Bangor, my VOR indicator suddenly had a red flag appear and the needles froze in the center of the case, indicating that the system was dead. The T-bird still had a low frequency nav system because we needed it in the backward Canadian system. But in the states, most of the low frequency stations had been decommissioned. I notified Boston Center and was frantically going over my nav charts to see if there enough low freq stations to navigate by. In the northeast part of the states, traffic control was very strict because it was so crowded. I could not just stumble around in there.

Shortly, the guy at center control came back on the radio. "Dad Zero Two, would you like to have radar vectors to your destination?" Unbelievable! I am in the heaviest air traffic in the country where controllers are super busy and not much inclined to cut us any slack. "Affirmative" was my glad reply. This guy had already contacted New York and Washington Centers and made arrangements for us to be vectored all the way to Seymour Johnson AFB, Goldsboro, North Carolina. It was too easy; with someone else doing the navigating.

The next miracle occurred shortly. As soon as I figured we were in radio range of Seymour Johnson, I contacted their control tower and requested expedited maintenance and explained our problem and mission. I did not expect the word to go any further than the control tower, but I was wrong. As I was directed into a parking spot, I saw three maintenance men standing there with black boxes under their arms.

While the refueling crew did their thing, the nav-com guys replaced all my black boxes associated with the radio navigation system. They didn't spend any time troubleshooting, they just replaced everything. Transient maintenance was normally a very low priority thing, but these fellows did a super job and did it quickly.

We again took off, this time for Alvin Calendar Naval Air Station, New Orleans. Everything on the bird worked but by the time we were getting close to New Orleans, it was getting dark and the reported weather was marginal. I would have to make a precision instrument approach. The major in the back seat had not been any help all day and I was beginning to get a little tired. I requested a ground controlled approach with precision radar on the final.

They took me a long way out over the bay, at low altitude which I was not real comfortable with, being in the dark, in bad weather, to land at an airport I was not familiar with. Anyway I finally got turned inbound and made a decent approach and landing. The major wasted no time in heading for the hospital down town. We later learned that his son survived.

I was tired, and not excited at the prospect of spending the night at the Naval Air Station, so I telephoned Kathy, as she had not yet left Tennessee. I knew the Air Guard part of McGhee Tyson airport was not open to transients without prior permission. There was no other military facility located there at the time. She telephoned the commander of the guard unit and he gave me permission to land there and park for the night. So I flew one more leg that day, for a total of four, having done all the aircrew work. When I parked the bird, I could see Kathy standing off to the side by our white Rambler station wagon.

Next morning, I departed for Griffiss AFB at Rome, New York. The forecast winds promised me a good tail wind from southwest to northeast, so I could make it back in just two hops. After refueling at Griffiss, the winds lived up to the forecast and I was back at Goose in time for my evening shift as a scopedope.

———

Kathy, ever the brave soul, arrived with the boys in July, 1963, after most of the snow had melted and we had been assigned an apartment in a four unit building. It was not ideal, but the family was together. They often did not see a lot of me, but it was better than being thousands of miles away. My two primary jobs, plus some additional duties kept me quite busy. With our limited manpower, all the officers at Melville had at least two additional jobs. Mine were Motor Pool Officer and Recreational Services Officer. We had good enlisted people to run the sections, but we had to oversee them and take the flak for anything that did not please the old man.

———

During our first winter at Goose, we had 220 inches of snow fall, which was dry and loose. and the wind continually redistributed it. The runway markers were buried under several feet of snow, so small spruce trees were stuck in the snowbanks along the edge of the runway to serve as markers. Depth perception was a problem in the all white environment, so the fire trucks drove along and sprayed the edges with brightly dyed water.

Eventually, the runways would develop a sheet of ice that was not removable and braking action was zero. The primary runway was 11,500 feet long and I sometimes touched down in the first 300 feet and still slid off the end into the overrun. Our aircraft parking area was lower in elevation than the main ramp, and with no power steering, we often could not control the T-bird with differential braking. It would slide to where ever it chose to go, or we shut it down and had a tractor come and tow it in.

Indoors, we wore a regular cotton flight suit over thermal long johns. Before going out to preflight an airplane we put on a heavy insulated flight suit over the cotton suit, then a short, hooded parka. The parka hood was unzipped and lay flat on our back. On our feet, we wore insulated boots, or if it was extremely cold, we wore mukluks. A large fur hat was kept in an inside pocket. A pair of heavy mittens were dangled on a cord around the neck and hung down inside the flight suit. That way, we would not lose them on a bail out.

Our oxygen mask had to be unsnapped from the hard hat and kept in an inside coat pocket during the preflight inspection and cockpit check. It was snapped on quickly when ready to taxi because if it was exposed to the ambient air for more than a few seconds, the first breath would have enough moisture to freeze the valves closed. We had on all that clothing, a thirty five pound chute, and sat on a twenty pound survival pack, so it took two crewman, one on each side of the cockpit to stuff us in.

We carried all sorts of things in pockets. Although the survival pack was attached with a twenty foot lanyard, there was still a possibility of losing it on a bail out. Every available pocket was stuffed with candles, waterproof matches, candy bars, knives, pistol, extra ammo, socks et cetera. We could survive for a while in the snow, but not in the water. We flew a lot over the North Atlantic where survival would be doubtful if we ended up in the water. In near freezing water, hypothermia will render a person helpless in about two minutes.

We were issued survival suits, which we called poopy suits, but we seldom wore them. They were terribly uncomfortable, time consuming to get on and off, and would prolong our misery in the water for about twenty minutes. It was not likely that Air Sea Rescue could get to us within twenty minutes. However, during exercises when we had a lot of aircraft in the air, they had an aircraft airborne, ready to be diverted to a rescue. Resources did not allow for them to have a bird airborne on a continuous basis.

Later on, when I flew with the 48th Fighter Interceptor Squadron out of Langley AFB, Virginia, we were required to wear the poopy suits for over water flights, but the water was warmer there and our chances of survival much greater. It required two personal equipment specialists to get us into and out of the things and by the time we got in the airplane, we were stewing in our own personal sauna.

––––––––

One of my early sorties out of Goose was a target flight during a war exercise, and my instructions were to simply fly out to Fort Chimo and return at an assigned altitude – at night. The only problem with that was the total lack of radio navigational aids three hundred miles to the northwest. We had been taught dead reckoning navigation, but had hardly ever used it, since there was an abundance of nav aids in the states. Canada was very different. Radio nav aids were few and far between.

It turned out to be a good experience though, because it bolstered my confidence in dead reckoning navigation. Outbound, I tracked on the 310 degree radial of the Goose VOR for about 90 miles and the signal, as expected, faded. Maintaining a heading, corrected for drift based on the forecast wind, and keeping airspeed constant, I flew until the clock indicated I was over Fort Chimo. The weather was fairly clear, but I had not seen any lights on the ground for the last hundred miles. I had seen only three or four dim lights on the ground since departing Goose.

I could see one dim light on the ground as I flew out the calculated time. There was no way to verify my location, so assuming I was over Ft. Chimo, I reversed course. I could receive nothing on the VOR, low frequency radio compass, or the UHF communications radio. Still maintaining altitude, airspeed and course, corrected for wind, I headed back in.

When I calculated that I was one hundred miles out, I called the target controller at Half Pint, and told him I was estimating my position at one hundred miles northwest. "Dad Zero Two, Half Pint, standby." After about a minute, during which I am sure he was verifying my radar return, and I had traveled about six miles, the voice came back, "Dad Zero Two, you are on the 310 radial of the Goose VOR at 96 miles."

After flying three hundred miles out and two hundred miles back, I had miscalculated my position by only a couple of miles. The variances in wind speed and direction could easily account for that. After that, I was much more confident in dead reckoning and had many more opportunities to use it.

———————

Limited fuel and bad weather made for constant challenge. We nearly always had to sweat the fuel and the instrument approaches. I am taking off for a local target mission, with full internal fuel, two 230 gallon tip tanks, two chaff dispensers under the wing pylons and a radar reflector on the JATO hooks underneath the airplane. The airborne radar of the era did not see a T-bird well at more than a few miles. The chaff dispensers are as large as the 230 gallon tip tanks, and add another thousand pounds of gross weight. The T-33 looks more like a B-33 and now weighs more than 16,000 pounds.

Breaking ground, as the wheels come up at 125 knots, accelerating and looking for 140 knots to get the flaps up, I am enveloped in thick wet clouds. Water is streaking back over the windshield and canopy. A couple of hundred feet higher up, that water is supercooled and will turn to ice when disturbed. As the flaps come up, I change from tower frequency, to Half Pint control. "Half Pint, Dad Zero Four, airborne, squawking mode three low, heading 350." "Roger Dad Zero Four, this is Half Pint One Eight, radar contact, port two seven zero, climb to angels 33." "Zero Four, roger." The cloud tops are reported to be at 28,000.

Pitot heat is on, to prevent icing of the airspeed indicator system. Without correct airspeed indication, I would be in big trouble. There is no anti-icing system for the wings and engine intake. There is a windshield anti-icing system I will use on the return descent. Hopefully, my climb through the worst icing area will be quick and I won't accrue much ice. My present climb speed is 270 knots, which I will allow to decrease during the climb to a minimum of two hundred knots in the thinner air.

Passing through ten grand, the zero delay lanyard is disconnected, and all systems are normal. Cockpit heat, bled from the engine compressor is left on high, although I don't need that much heat for comfort, with all the clothing I am wearing. I don't want the windshield and canopy to get cold soaked, but they will. The tip tanks are feeding. I know they are because I have turned off all the boost pumps for the wing tanks and the fuselage gauge is indicating full. For take-off, all fuel systems were activated as a precaution.

At about 27,000 feet, the clouds begin to let a little light through and soon I begin breaking out of the cloud tops. It is blinding bright up here. The sun was there all the time, but you would not think so when on the ground or in the clouds. I level off at 33,000 and throttle back to cruise power. "Half Pint, Dad Zero Four level." "Roger Four, port, one six zero, you have two fighters, Hotel Papa Zero Three and Four, at twenty four miles, crossing left to right and two more, Hotel Papa Zero Five and Six, at thirty six miles, report visual contact."

I strain to get a sighting on what will initially appear to be two tiny dots on the canopy. Just as the controller is calling range info to the interceptors at fourteen miles, I begin to detect two dots that could have been easily mistaken for specks of dirt on the canopy. The dots don't appear to change position, even though we are closing at several hundred knots. That is because they are on a collision course for now and their angle will be constant. It has been calculated to be like that. About three miles out they will convert to a stern approach, to simulate launching their heat seeking missiles. I call, "Dad Zero Four, Tallyho."

The interceptor pilots don't know I have chaff on board. It is time to turn it on and I can see the bundles being spit out of the dispensers, knowing the tiny aluminum slivers will disperse into a large cloud and generate a very large, bright return on their airborne radar and on the ground radar. To make it even more fun, I turn thirty degrees. They can't pick me out of the clutter and the controller is dead reckoning them. He doesn't know I have turned either. His only clue is to look at the head of the chaff stream and if he is good he will soon figure out my position.

We all know each other, but that makes no difference as to how the game is played. I am the bad guy and won't make it easy for the controller or the interceptors. We are practicing a deadly game and won't make it easy for the shooters to rack up a good score.

The interceptors carry a mixed load of radar missiles and heat seekers. Some also carry an additional twenty four 2.5 inch rockets. The deuce is a lethal machine. I figure that by now they have switched to the infra red mode on their scope display and are ignoring the chaff and I turn back to my original heading. If I want to cause additional trouble, I can hold down my mike button and open my mask to generate a horrendous noise on the radio channel to block directions from the controller. I'll save that for later.

The first two have locked on, calling "Judy", but the controller does not relax. He keeps a close watch in case he is needed again. In a few seconds, the interceptor pilots call their, "MA" for mission accomplished. In a real battle, I, the bomber, would be destroyed. They break off to reposition for another attack as the second pair bore in. "Tallyho Five and Six". The second pair complete their attack and break off. The two pairs continue the drill until they are low on fuel and RTB.

By this time, my tip tanks have stopped feeding because they are empty. Four hundred sixty gallons expended; three hundred fifty remaining. I know because the low pressure light for the tip tanks is on and the gauge for the ninety five gallon fuselage tank is moving down. I switch on the boost pumps for the leading edge tanks. The fuselage tank again shows full. Satisfied that the leading edge wing tanks will feed, for weight and balance purposes, I switch them off and turn on the main wing tank boost pumps. The fuselage tank indicates that it is staying full.

The controller is informed of my fuel state. He must remain aware of the fuel state of target aircraft as well as interceptors under his control. Another flight of interceptors appears and make their attacks as I travel back and forth in a pattern designed to allow the maximum number of intercepts and also to keep us a reasonable distance from home plate.

After a couple of passes, the low pressure light comes on for the main wing tanks. Now I have 110 gallons remaining in the leading edge wing tanks plus the fuselage tank. I need to start home soon. "Half Pint, Dad Zero Four, 200 gallons, oxygen OK." "Roger Dad Zero Four, we will do one more pass and RTB. Pigeons three zero five, eighty five miles." The interceptors do their thing and leave for home.

"Dad Zero Four, steer three one zero, descend to twenty thousand, home plate eighty miles." Click-click. The hot air windshield defrost is turned on. The auxiliary electric powered windshield defrost is turned on and it fries my eyeballs, but I need to try to keep the windshield clear for the landing and I know I will collect a lot of ice in the lower clouds.

Entering the black clouds, I am back on the gauges and there is a dramatic change from the bright sunlight above the clouds. I turn up the instrument lights, and it takes several seconds for my eyes to adjust.

The engine speed is back to around sixty five percent. At this altitude, it won't go much lower and the speed brakes are out, creating a roar and lots of vibration. The altimeter is unwinding rapidly and going through twenty one thousand, so I break the descent and start easing the nose up. At a couple of hundred feet above twenty grand, I bring in the speed brakes and push the power back up to maintain altitude. "Dad Zero Four, starboard zero niner zero, distance to home plate now fifty miles. Goose weather 200 feet, half mile viz, wind zero eight zero, 8 knots, altimeter 2985. Approach will be from the west gate, braking action poor." Click-click. The west gate is thirty miles from the runway in use. The reported ceiling and visibility is at published minimums for Goose Air Base, but it really doesn't matter. I can't go anywhere else with my remaining fuel.

About three minutes later – "Dad Zero Four, steer zero eight zero, descend to twelve thousand and contact Goose Approach on channel fifteen." "Dad Zero Four, roger." Again, I pull the throttle back, drop the speed brakes and change radio channels.

"Goose Approach, Dad Zero Four, approaching the west gate at twelve thousand." "This is Goose Approach, Dad Zero Four, cleared for ILS to runway zero eight, descend to three thousand and continue approach."

The ice is really building now. The windshield is completely iced over. The center panel must have two inches of ice on it. The canopy is covered completely in the front and nearly all the way back. Only the rear portion is clear. A pilot qualified for back seat landings would have a little vision out the sides, but there is no one back there. I make sure the nav radio is tuned to the Goose ILS and the localizer and glide slope needles are active and there are no red flags in the case. "Approach, Dad Zero four, level three thousand and receiving the ILS." "Roger four, tower has cleared you for landing."

My butt hurts, but I cannot move it or reach it. Two hours in the same position is beginning to make for a lot of discomfort. I can feel the .22 Hornet/410 shotgun through the thin foam rubber pad covering the survival pack. My head hurts from some imperfection in the hard-hat padding. My mask is cutting my face but I can do nothing about any of these discomforts except to try to tune them out and concentrate on controlling the bird. There is no autopilot and no relief pilot in the back seat.

I am down to some real precision flying now. I must concentrate to maintain exact heading and altitude until intercepting the glide slope. Keep that rapid cross check going. Check bank, pitch, heading, altitude, speed, power, vertical velocity (rate of descent) and periodically include engine instruments. I have done this many times, but the requirement for extreme concentration is still there.

I have the landing gear down, flaps at twenty percent and the speed brakes are still out, carrying fairly high power. My eyeballs hurt, but I cannot turn off the defrosters. I am beginning to see a little clear spot at the bottom of the windshield center panel. The wings are loaded up with ice and I wonder if I am carrying enough airspeed. The glide slope needle starts down and I must follow it. I have left the flaps at twenty percent for the last few miles. Now I position the handle for full down flaps and let the nose drop, not changing the power setting.

The technique works. The nose drops about a bar width on the attitude indicator, the vertical velocity goes from zero down to four hundred fifty feet per minute. I don't have to touch anything else. As the localizer needle starts off center, I make very small heading corrections – like one or two degrees with hardly any perceptible bank. More of a pressure change than actual stick movements.

I am going a little below glidepath. The ice is requiring additional power. I add five percent power, and slow the rate of descent a few feet per minute. The glideslope needle is again centered, so I back off two percent on the power and hope I have made a correction on power that will hold me on the glide path. Make sure I haven't messed up the airspeed. Like everything else, it is critical. If I get too slow, the bird will stall. If it gets too high, I won't be able to stop on the icy runway. I try to keep it within two knots of the airspeed I have calculated for the situation.

Rate of descent is controlled with power and speed controlled with pitch attitude. I am good on fuel, the fuselage tank gauge is showing 85 gallons, but all the other tanks are empty. Low pressure lights are on for the main wing, leading edge, and tip tanks. To conserve electrical power, I could turn off the boost pumps for the empty tanks, but on final approach, using the last of my fuel, I want nothing left in those other tanks.

There is no distance information furnished on this type approach, but I know that when I get down to a couple of hundred feet I should be seeing some lead-in strobes, if not some glimpses of the runway. This part of the approach is always a little tense. I can't see through the iced over canopy and if I could see through it, I would not be able to see past my wing tips in these dense clouds. I am getting close to the ground and there is always that nagging doubt that maybe something is wrong and you don't know what it is and it will be too late when you find out. On the instrument panel, the low fuel warning light comes on and the fuselage tank gauge is now showing 70 gallons. No problem, if I don't have to make a missed approach.

Finally, the glow begins to appear through the murk; faintly at first. The powerful flashing strobe lights are pointing the way to the runway and they are dead off the nose. The localizer is only a half needle width off center and the glide slope needle is dead on. I am OK. Hold what you have and look through that little clear spot at the bottom of the windshield. The flashing strobes disappear under the nose and the threshold lights come into view. They are a beautiful sight. Hunkered down to look through my little hole in the iced over windshield, I ease off on the power as the main wheels touch and I am on the runway, but I wonder how far I will slide. The nose wheel is held off as long as it will stay up for maximum aerodynamic braking. The wheel brakes are not going to do me much good.

Approach says, "Dad Zero Four, cleared to ground control channel." "Roger" I don't have time to talk to anyone right now. I am busy keeping this tricycle pointed down an icy slab and it doesn't want to stop. At the last turn-off, after using more than eleven thousand feet of runway, I am slow enough to turn and the ice is starting to melt and slide off the canopy and windshield. I can look out and see slabs of ice coming off the wings. I can turn off the defrosters now. I also must remember to turn off the pitot heat so some maintenance man won't get a nasty burn when he puts the cover on the pitot tube.

I park, log my time, make any entries needed for the maintenance people and head up the hill for a shift as a scope dope.

Radar Operations

In the darkened operations room, we sat at consoles watching the trace go around every twelve seconds, in sync with the huge antenna housed in a separate building with a geodesic dome. The late evening training missions have been completed and the fighter squadron will not require any radar controllers until morning, unless there is an active air scramble for the five minute birds. The airbase is quiet. There is a fleet of KC-135 tankers on standby for any air to air refueling that might be needed For B-52 and B-47 aircraft, but they are all quiet for the time being.

Our huge, vertical plotting board shows several friendly tracks, which are mostly airliners taking advantage of the strong tailwind from west to east as they head for European destinations. Our radar coverage overlaps with the outlying stations, and we have cross tell with them. Their tracks are plotted on our board and vice versa.

We have settled down for a quiet night when a track appears on our plotting board with a symbol classifying it's status as "unknown". The letter prefix on the track number indicates that is from Susie Q, our station at Cartwright, on the southeast coast. The unknown classification means that no one in our system has a flight plan that can be correlated with the track. Our crew chief calls Susie Q to verify that they are cross telling us an "unknown" track. They are.

Calls to Air Route Traffic Control shed no light on the track. Susie Q has made several attempts to make radio contact and gotten no response. The track is 150 miles off the coast, heading straight for Goose Bay at about 500 mph. I tell my enlisted assistant to give the alert pilots a heads up. They are always ready for instant action, but a courtesy call is appreciated. They might want to make a last minute visit to the sandbox before blasting off.

I have decided if we have no identification when the track is within one hundred miles of the coast, I will scramble the five minute birds. We have excellent long range radar and every twelve seconds, as the trace comes around, I can see the blip is two miles closer to us and we cannot verify what it is. The course, speed and altitude does not change.

As the track crosses the hundred mile mark, my tech pushes the scramble button. In about four minutes a new blip appears on my scope and the voice of my good friend, Captain Lehman breaks the silence in my headphones. "Half Pint, Hotel Papa, Zero One and Two, airborne." I give them heading and altitude instructions, and they head east into the night.

My crew continues making every effort to identify the track. The echelons of command above us are notified of the track and our action taken. We always hope that there will be a happy ending to the scenario, but one never knows and we must be prepared for the worst, while hoping for the best.

If the track turns out to be a friendly in need of assistance, our birds can lead them to a safe landing or mark the location if it goes down, and assist in a rescue operation. If it appears to be friendly and has gotten too far off course and time to match a flight plan, let it go on it's way. In the worst case, shoot it down.

I could hand over control of the deuces to Susie Q, but prefer to handle it myself unless they get out of range. The birds are vectored toward the target with enough offset for a 180 degree turn to parallel and join up with it while we continue to attempt radio contact.

It was another one of those cloudy, moonless nights with moderate snowfall. At the appropriate time, the interceptors are given the turn to parallel and join up on the target, with the wing-man taking up the standard position to cover the leader.

They established radar contact and moved in, but were in and out of clouds, preventing decent visual contact. Lehman reported that it appeared to be a large commercial airliner, but he could not get a really good look at it. At that distance, radio communications were getting poor and we had to repeat several calls. He asked me if I wanted a tail number. Under the circumstances

I didn't want him to get that close, but due to the poor communications, he misunderstood and moved in with his landing light on.

The radio channel erupted with some rapid fire chatter in Italian. We never did know if the airliner captain had been sitting there listening to us and declining to answer, or just did not know what was happening. When he saw the two fighters close on him, we couldn't shut him up. The aircraft was an Alitalia, bound for Goose Bay, so I pulled off the fighters and brought them home.

In a little while, Goose Center called and told me that an Alitalia captain wanted to file a formal complaint about our interceptors harassing him. I told them, "Fine, tell him to go ahead and we will file an airspace violation against him and charge Alitalia for the expense of dispatching the interceptors to identify him." As usual, that was the end of the deal.

We made a lot of ID passes on wayward aircraft and we often suspected what the true identity was, but if a plot did not match certain criteria, it was our job to do whatever was necessary to get a positive ID. Sometimes they were airliners, sometimes SAC B-47s, as they seemed to have more navigation problems than any other military traffic, especially on their way back from over the Atlantic. We had a lot of B-52 aircraft traversing the area, but they rarely, if ever, were off time and course. The early warning system never slept.

———

I did get to see Saglek, from the ground. I had seen it a couple of times from the air on rare days when the weather allowed visual contact. The call sign, Lonesome, was truly appropriate. The high, bare, windswept, mountaintop site was quite alone. There was no visible civilization closer than Hopedale, a hundred fifty miles down the rugged coast. I was told that a few indigenous types were in the area, but I never saw any evidence. I was sent up there for a week to monitor their operation during some war games.

The gooney bird made a long, shallow approach from out over the Atlantic, set up for a short field landing. The water was rough, with high, whitecapped waves crashing over the rocks at the approach end of the strip. The pilot put it down as near the end as he could and we rolled up hill with the steep base of the mountain looming in the windshield, but he got it stopped just short of the far end. Not a job for a novice pilot. On departure, he would take off down hill, toward those rocks and monster waves.

Several guys from the radar site were waiting for us with a couple of four wheel drive vehicles. The steep, winding trail up the mountain was no place for two wheel drive. We off loaded some supplies, and watched the C-47 taxi into position at the base of the mountain, run up the engines to full power and release the brakes. In a few moments it was disappearing in a turn to the south. I felt like I had just been stranded and cut off from the outside world.

My week went by fairly well and at the appointed time on Saturday, I was happy to be told that the C-47 was inbound. Several of the local guys accompanied me down to the airstrip. I now knew that the arrival of the Gooney Bird was the highlight of their week and it reminded me of my days at Farewell, Alaska.

———

On a rare, three day break, I hitched a ride on the a C-97 cargo plane, piloted by a member of the SAC contingent at Goose, who had been in my upper class at Hondo. At Thule Greenland, I got to visit the Ballistic Missile Early Warning site, with its monster antenna system looking toward the Soviet Union, tracking missiles and space garbage. We had a squadron of F-102 interceptors there, which I visited and renewed acquaintances with some of the pilots. There was a radar site at P mountain, eighteen miles out on the ice, but that did not interest me.

We doglegged back by way of Sondestrom Air Base, midway down the Greenland coast and I was able to buy some Danish tableware we wanted, but had not been able to buy at Goose. Our sector commander was with us and took a side trip to one of the radar sites out on the ice fields on a C-130 fitted with skis. That didn't interest me either. A three day visit to Greenland was quite enough.

———

Back at Goose, the grueling routine continued. I never did really like my work at the radar station, but figured it would be better for me and everyone else if I just did the best job I could and tried not to be bitter about it. The flying with the 59th was a lot of extra work, but it was a break from the scope and it was what I really wanted to do. My family paid a price for that, but they endured it well.

Kathy and the boys could not leave Goose except by commercial air and we could not afford that. I felt a little guilty because many of my trips by air were back to the states. In most cases, I did not get off a military installation, but at least I saw some civilization. Kathy was confined to the base, and her circle of friends, consisting of the wives of other military people. Except for a chartered Dehaviland Beaver for a fishing trip to an outlying lake, she did not leave Goose for over two years.

———

On a day when we had a massive exercise going, and for some strange reason, I was not required to be at the site, Fred Caldwell, assistant operations officer for the 59th, and I took off on a T-bird target mission. We were scheduled to fly from Goose to Harmon, by way of St. Anthony, on the northeast coast of Newfoundland. We would refuel at Harmon and fly back to Goose acting as an intruder from the south. Weather at Goose was not good, but that was not unusual.

The flight was going OK, over a high, thick overcast, with Fred in the back seat, and as we passed over St. Anthony, I requested Harmon weather. It was bad. Ceiling zero. Visibility zero. High wind, blowing snow. It was not a good idea to continue in that direction. If we turned directly back toward home immediately, we could make it. I called Moncton Center and was cleared direct from present position, to Goose at present altitude. We went back across the St. Lawrence Seaway, but couldn't see it because of the bad weather.

About fifty miles out, I called Goose Approach and they gave us an approach time several minutes past our zero fuel time. The radio channel was saturated with aircraft converging on Goose wanting to land. We had interceptors returning from their missions, low on fuel. We had visiting interceptors coming up from Maine and New Brunswick. They were all low on fuel and needing to land. The weather was getting worse by the minute and was slowing recoveries. I complained until they gave us a better approach time. We absolutely had no fuel for a holding pattern.

We made the penetration with the low fuel warning light on. The Canadian system of using a thirty mile gate for instrument landings required more fuel and caused us to pick up more ice in the lower clouds. Because of the direction of the runway in use, we had to turn off on the RCAF side. We needed to get back across the active runway, but with so many birds landing, and low on fuel, approach was really packing them in. Normal spacing had to be disregarded.

There was always someone on the landing roll, and ground control would not clear us across. I kept badgering them, but still they delayed. I had already turned on the starting fuel and stopcocked the throttle to keep the engine running with a bare minimum of fuel consumption. At that low engine speed, the generator was inoperative and it was a question of whether we would run out of fuel or battery first. With about a minutes worth of fuel remaining, I finally told them, if they didn't clear us across, we would flame out and be blocking the taxiway. they finally cleared us across and we made it to the other side just as the engine died.

———

We had been briefed to expect radio contact with Soviet vessels in the Atlantic and the St. Lawrence Seaway and I didn't think much about it until, on my way back from Harmon on a rare clear day, I swung to the east to get a look at St. Anthony. We didn't get many opportunities to see the ground in the consistently bad weather. As I was passing abeam St. Anthony, with a good view of the Atlantic to the east and the Straits of Belle Isle to the north, the radio inquiry began. The transmissions were very strong and very clear and in excellent English. "Aircraft passing St. Anthony, what is your call sign?" We had been briefed that we were not to acknowledge that we heard such transmissions. Any of our people would know my call sign and my mission. Therefore I made no reply.

"Aircraft now northwest of St. Anthony, what is your mission?" No reply. "Aircraft continuing northwest and crossing the seaway, what is pilots name? Why do you not answer? We know you are there. What is your mission? What is your call sign?" Only an idiot would have given them a reply, but I reckon they thought they might snag an idiot if they tried long enough. I had a strong urge to tell them to stick it, but remembered the instructions to ignore them altogether.

On that particular flight, there were no Trawlers or submarines in sight, but later in a similar situation, I spotted a Soviet submarine in the straits, unloading what appeared to be large wooden crates on an ice floe. By the time our navy people got there, the sub and all the crates had disappeared.

———————

On a rare Saturday morning off, the 59th called me at home. They had a pilot down at North Bay with a broken F-102 in need of parts and a mechanic. I told them OK. With the mechanic in the back seat we would have to take a bird with chaff dispensers under the wing pylons and carry the spare parts in them. The mechanic had not been through physiological training and therefore was not allowed above 18,000 feet. That limited my range because of the higher fuel consumption. At normal cruise altitude, I could make North Bay in one leg.

I would have to dogleg to the RCAF base at Baggotville to refuel. We did that and after some delay in getting refueled, we finally arrived at North Bay. The mechanic got the parts changed out and the deuce pilot was able to go on his way. We started back late in the afternoon and thunderstorms had developed along our return route. Eighteen thousand is a terrible altitude for cruising in thunderstorm activity, but it was that or violate the rules. If I took the enlisted guy up to 35,000 and he developed problems, We would both be in trouble.

So, I played by the rules and filed a flight plan for eighteen grand. Sure enough, the ride was pretty bumpy and the mechanic probably would have been better off at a higher altitude above the thunderstorms. My bird was equipped with an old fashioned low frequency receiver because that was mostly what the Canadians still used. Baggotville was one of the few RCAF bases that had a Tactical Navigation System (TACAN), but my bird was not equipped for that. I could receive their low freq station, but the static was so bad, the automatic direction finder was useless. The only thing left was the manual mode of direction finding, which required using a left/right switch on the right console to position the loop antenna and hope I could hear a null.

It was a full time job to keep the bird right side up in the rough air, and I had to use my right hand on the loop switch most of the time. That meant using my left hand on the control stick, which is a clumsy way to do things. As we got closer to Baggotville, I realized I would not get a precise bearing on the station to make a safe approach and we had only enough fuel for one approach. I had worn holes in the thumb and forefinger of the glove on my right hand, from almost continuous operation of the loop switch. My only distance information was based on time and computed ground speed, assuming the wind forecast had been accurate.

Estimating about fifty miles out, I called approach control and got a reply right away. It always makes a pilot feel better to be able to talk to someone on the ground when things are getting sticky. Baggotville advised me that they had no precision radar and the IFF on their surveillance radar was inoperative. A little T-bird is hard enough to see on raw radar in good weather. With no IFF to make our blip stand out, we were going to be very hard to see in the cloud clutter. I told the operator our circumstances and he said he would try to help. *Try? How hard would he try?*

He gave me an identifying turn, and said, "I think I see you." He gave me an inbound heading, saying, "I think I see you." The *I think* was beginning to bother me. We Let down to initial approach altitude for a downwind leg to the active runway. By this time, it had gotten dark and in the clouds or not, I could not see anything outside the cockpit. In due time we were turned on to a base leg and eventually a final approach heading. This was the continuing story of my flying career; unfamiliar territory, in the dark, bad weather and low on fuel.

There was no alternative, so I put down the landing gear and flaps and hoped the guy knew what he was doing. The brightest thing I could see was the low fuel warning light. At about three hundred feet and a mile out, we started breaking out of the clouds, and dead ahead was a beautiful double row of runway lights. While being refueled, I phoned the approach control operator and thanked him for his effort and expertise. His job had not been an easy one and he had saved my posterior.

The last leg, back to Goose, was an easy one, because I could receive the VOR from a hundred miles out, plus, if I was so inclined, I could call one of my radar controllers at Half Pint and get radar vectors from more than two hundred miles out.

———

Every major command had it's own culture and ADC was no exception. The bases were mostly in desolate, remote locations with bad weather, away from family and without the amenities that most people take for granted. Therefore, morale was more of a problem than in other commands. The pilots had morale problems, although their locations were usually not as remote as the radar sites, they sat for long hours in alert hangars with poor heating and knew if the horn blew they would go, regardless of weather conditions.

They took off in airport conditions and weather conditions that most pilots would not consider flying in. When returning from a mission, low on fuel, often after having identified a wayward airliner, they would have one shot at an instrument approach to an ice covered, windswept runway. They were not just good pilots. They were outstanding pilots, otherwise they would not have survived. Although few of them were ever in the spotlight, nor achieved fame and glory as the day fighter pilots did, they are to be ranked with the best.

———

Although many thousands of training sorties, in addition to the active air scrambles that were flown during my stay at Goose, we only lost two aircraft and one pilot. It is tragic to lose anyone, but considering the amount of flying we did under very adverse conditions, our record was outstanding. One of the aircraft was lost due to a failure of the constant speed drive system, causing loss of control and forcing the pilot to bail out. The reason for the other loss of aircraft and death of the pilot was never determined.

———

As is so often the case with military people, a good sense of humor made life a little less difficult, and most of the higher ranking officers cut us some slack. The evening training sorties were usually completed by about ten p.m. and if weather conditions would allow, the pilot leading the last flight would ask to go VFR when he had the base in sight. The radar controller would release him to recover as he pleased and we could count on the gaggle picking up speed and flying down the Hamilton River at tree top level. The senior officers, including the fighter squadron commander, lived in their single unit houses down by the river. A flight of four deuces, low level, at max throttle would really rattle some windows and startle the occupants.

Sometimes, when returning from a mission in VFR conditions, I would ask the controller, "Is the grass green?" If the reply was affirmative, it meant that no senior officers were present and a buzz job would be approved. If the grass was not green, it meant that a buzz job was not advisable. Even a T-bird coming across the ops site at full throttle, barely a hundred feet in the air, made quite a racket.

The SAC wing had a couple of twin engined Grumman Amphibians. One of them landed at Hopedale with engine problems. Not being able to repair the engine on site, they decided to lighten the bird as much as possible and fly it back to Goose on one engine. The pilot was a bit skittish, but agreed to do it. I happened to be airborne and listening on the radio while he was inbound with the Grumman.

The pilot made progress reports every minute or two and ended each and every transmission with his call sign and the words, "SINGLE ENGINE". After several such transmissions, heard by several of us who had never flown anything except single engine birds, one of our deuce pilots entering the landing pattern, and called on initial approach: "Goose Tower, Hotel Papa Zero Six, initial, Single Engine." The radio was quiet for several minutes.

A few other things compensated for our lifestyle in the far north. Since we maintained a detachment at Harmon AFB, there was frequent traffic between Goose and Harmon. Often, when I flew down there, transferring parts or personnel, I would call the guys at the detachment before I departed Goose and ask them to get me some lobster, which was plentiful and cheap down there.

Upon arrival, and while being refueled for the return trip, I would stuff several large lobster in the nose of the aircraft under the gun bay doors. There was no baggage space per se, so I put them into nooks and crannies in, on, around the equipment in there. Surprisingly, they would still be alive on arrival back at Goose. It was a mystery as to how they could survive the cold and thin air at 35,000 feet or better.

The SAC wing maintained a fish camp under the guise of a "survival camp" and we could get a three day trip out there if we were lucky. My turn was pre-empted several times by visiting dignitaries, but I figured out how to get out there.

I learned that for most scheduled trips there were "no shows" and no attempt was made to find last minute replacements. So, when I had a scheduled break from work, I would just go down there a few minutes before take-off time for the seaplane and fill a spot left by a no-show.

I also learned that the camp, located about seventy five miles out on Lake No-Name, was supplied on weekends by the SAC pilots, using a DeHaviland Otter on floats. The Otter did not require a co-pilot and usually flew without one. If I had some weekend time off, I could go down to SAC ops, find the Otter pilot and ride with him in the right seat. He usually was at the lake for at least two or three hours before heading back, which provided me enough time to catch some nice trout and pike. If a trout was under five pounds, we put it back.

Kathy had been pretty much home-bound for two years and I wanted her to see some of the outlying country and experience some outstanding fishing. We rented a DeHaviland Beaver, smaller than the Otter, and landed in the middle of No-Name Lake. The lake was so large, we just drifted and stood on the pontoons to fish. On every cast, the fish would fight over the lure.

———

One of the 59th pilots took off in the left seat of the TF-102, called the "Tub" because of the wide side by side seating arrangement. An instructor pilot was in the right seat to do a periodic evaluation on the one in the left seat. The weather was solid from a couple of hundred feet all the way up to forty thousand. Just as they broke out on top, the right windshield blew out, or rather "in" striking the right side guy in the head. The air blast was horrendous and the outside air temp was about fifty below zero. The pilot immediately began a let down through the solid weather and notified the radar controller. The controller vectored him directly to the west gate for an instrument approach. The cockpit was incredibly cold with the air blast coming through the hole in the right side.

Just as they got established inbound at twelve thousand, to begin an ILS approach, a tremendous explosion occurred somewhere in the rear. The aircraft began to vibrate so badly the instruments were unreadable. There was no way the approach could be completed in bad weather with useless instruments. The radio still worked and the controller advised the pilot to climb to a good ejection altitude and get out. He declined, in case the guy in the right seat might still be alive, and he was too busy fighting the bird to try to check or to render any aid. He did try to pull the instrument panel hood up to block some of the air blast, but with little success.

There were other birds airborne at the time, already on top of the overcast and they were advised to standby for a join up with the damaged Tub. The Tub pilot managed to keep his bird under control well enough to climb back up through the mess and break out on top again. The controller then had one of the other birds join up with the crippled one and take the lead. They again descended through the weather with the damaged bird on the wing. He was fighting for control, but managed to keep the leader in sight in the dense clouds.

In that fashion, they flew an ILS approach and landed without any further mishap. The injured pilot was first thought to be dead. He had suffered a major blow to the head and had been exposed to an extremely frigid air blast for something like forty minutes. However, he was thawed out and recovered, eventually to fly again. This is the kind of people who put their lives on the line every day, even though no one is shooting at them.

These were the kind of emergencies our controllers and pilots responded to and kept their cool.

The F102 was designed to be started without an APU by an on-board high pressure air bottle. Examination of the TF revealed that the air bottle had exploded and caused structural damage.

———

After serving a little over a year at Larson and a little more than two years at Melville and Goose, I was looking forward to the Air Force keeping its promise to return us to primary cockpit duty. I knew a few pilots that had made it, but in my case, they reneged. The personnel managers were still whining about not having enough radar controllers. Actually, it was difficult, because I never knew anyone who really liked a constant series of remote assignments and there were few if any volunteers. Most of the people in the system who could get out of the controller field did so, creating a constant shortage.

In July of 1965 we were pleased to be heading back to the USA. Our assignment turned out to be Cape Charles, Virginia, another isolated radar station. While at Goose, I had logged seven hundred fifty nine live intercepts, countless hundreds of supervised intercepts, training new people, and a hundred seventy eight missions for the 59th FIS in my "off" time.

Cape Charles

Cape Charles was a nice place to be if you didn't mind being isolated from urban development and liked to hunt and fish. At the southern tip of the DelMarVA Peninsula, we were separated from Norfolk by the Chesapeake Bay. Otherwise, the nearest town of any size was Salisbury, Maryland, a hundred miles to the north. The little town of Cape Charles had only a few small independently owned stores. The local industry consisted mostly of fishing and farming.

The telephone system was so antiquated, the open wire lines had several parties on each line. When I would try to call home from Langley AFB, I would ask for Cape Charles, number 417-J, with two long and two short rings, the Norfolk operator would officiously inform me there was no such number. So, I would say, "Just get me the Cape Charles operator." Upon telling the Cape Charles operator what I wanted, she likely as not, would proceed to tell me, "Mrs. Wade is not home. I know she is on her way to the drugstore." or "She is over at the Stinsons, do you want me to ring them?" It was like Mayberry USA.

Upon arrival at the radar station, I was informed that I had two jobs. The primary one was radar operations officer. The secondary one was station security officer. There was no airstrip, but we had a level field large enough for a Dehaviland Beaver to operate out of. I knew some of the small stations had one when rated pilots were assigned there, but I was never able to get one for us. I would have to go over to Langley AFB to fly with the 48th Fighter Interceptor Squadron.

We were required to live in the adjacent base housing because my jobs required me to be close by. It didn't matter because I don't think anything else was available locally. We got Kathy and the boys settled in and I had to leave for Tyndall AFB for a months training on our new computerized air defense system. The blockhouse (Sector headquarters) for the Washington Sector was located at Fort Lee and our radar, along with two others fed information to them. However, we had our own local capability for interceptor control when the central system was down. We practiced daily with live aircraft and with simulation.

Although I was well versed in the manual system like we used at Melville, I had never seen the equipment that was about to go on line at our site. So, I drove down to Tyndall AFB for a month of school. Kathy and the boys would have to fend for themselves, but she was an old hand at that. Due to the move, some leave time, getting into a new job et cetera, I had not flown except as a passenger for several weeks. So I took my flight records over to operations at Tyndall.

––––––––

Fred Caldwell, who had been in the 59th at Goose, was in one of the flying units at Tyndall and he got me scheduled with an instructor for a base check-out. Because of my day school schedule, we did it at night and it went well. From then on, I flew as often as I wanted to, mostly on night target missions. After a month of school, I drove back to Cape Charles.

The work there was demanding since we were keeping proficient in interceptor control by practicing every day with the F-106s out of Langley, Navy F-4s out of Virginia Beach and anyone else who wanted to use us. At the same time we were practicing on the new computerized system and trying to work out the bugs in that system. The squadron commander didn't help, rather he hindered our progress and frustrated us because he couldn't make up his mind on the new procedures over which he had approval authority.

The radar maintenance officer was having the same problem with the boss. We would show him a draft of procedures one day and he would red pencil changes all over it. The next day, we would take it back with HIS changes incorporated, only to have him rant and rave about what a bunch of dummies we were. He never liked anything we showed him. We knew he had some mental disorder, but proving that about a commander is next to impossible.

That eventually came to a head, but only after I had departed for my next assignment.

My station security officer job required some time, but was really not as bad as it could have been because I had a good NCO. He took care of the routine stuff as much as he could because he knew I had my hands full. I had not given up on flying. I just didn't know any better, so I paid a visit to the 48th FIS operations officer. Trips to Langley involved crossing the Chesapeake Bridge Tunnel, plus the Hampton Bridge Tunnel and paying about ten bucks in toll for the round trip. The Air Force would not pay for my toll.

The 48th was glad to get any assistance I could provide and I made a few trips over there each month, usually on weekends or even holidays, when I could get away from CC. It was a chore, and it was expensive, paying my own toll. Our commander could have given me government tickets for the toll, but he did not consider my trips to be government business.

One of the extra benefits of helping out the 48th, was getting an occasional ride in the F-106B, a mach two airplane. It was an awesome performer. If we needed it to go faster, all that was needed was a nudge on the throttle and it went faster. It was the first of the interceptors with an on-board digital computer.

———

One of my flights for the 48th was for radar evaluation of the long range sites. I was to fly out east, over the Atlantic for about two hundred miles at twenty thousand and return at five thousand. Except for the misery of sweating gallons in the sealed, unvented poopy suit, everything was OK on the outbound leg. It was late in the day, and by the time I turned around and dropped down to five thousand, the sun was setting. The bird was well trimmed and easing along, in smooth air, not requiring much effort on my part. Five thousand was not a good cruise altitude for fuel consumption, but that was what someone had ordered for the mission.

As the sun dipped below the horizon, I let go the control stick to reach over on the right console to turn on the nav lights. The instant I flipped the switch, I was pulling negative Gs with the nose pointing straight down and the ocean was coming up at me quite rapidly.

It didn't take me long to get both hands on the stick and start bringing the nose up, but it was not coming up fast enough and I was running out of altitude and ideas. Then I realized I had a runaway trim situation caused by a short between the light wiring and trim motor. I turned off the nav light switch and held the thumb switch on the stick grip for nose up trim.

I got it leveled off down in the wave tops and started breathing again. Then climbed back up to five grand to continue without any running lights. It was full dark with no moon by the time I got back. The control tower people at Langley could not see me in the traffic pattern until I turned final with the landing light on, but I was not about to turn on the nav light switch again, knowing there was a short circuit to the pitch trim motor. I did not check to see how much body waste the personal equipment technicians had to clean out from the poopy suit.

———————

After several months, the overall grind was wearing me down, and it was not good for family life. On returning from an overnight trip to the 48th, I decided I didn't have to do everything I was doing. The extra flight pay was nice, but we could make it without that. The thing that really discouraged me was a new policy recently announced from Headquarters, U.S. Air Force.

Before leaving Melville, I had received a letter, along with several hundred other officers, that our indefinite status was being revoked. We now had a separation date. Some elitist group had decided to purge the service of all us who had prior enlisted service. They were being generous though. They would allow us to serve a total of twenty years, including our enlisted time. For me and many others, that meant being too close to separation to qualify for promotion. We were now officially second class members of the service.

The proponents of that move were a lot less intelligent than they supposed themselves to be. There had always been a few officers who looked upon enlisted types as inferior beings and made no secret of it. The loss was theirs. I believed then as well as later, that we were not inferior, but the better for it. However, someone had gotten the power to rid the service of us and were proceeding to do it. I knew a lot of ex-enlisted officers, and would not hesitate to rate them as highly as any of the snobs who were now putting us down. If the self appointed superiors really understood the morale implications, they were cruel indeed. If they did not understand, they were mentally deficient.

———————

While pondering my situation and resigning myself to serving the remainder of my military career in my present location, job and rank, good news arrived, in the form of a personal letter from Captain Zerbe, Craig AFB, Selma, Alabama. Zerbe was telling me that personnel had promised his section, Flight Test, that the next qualified pilot to arrive on base would be assigned there. They were short on help, and to hurry on down.

If the people at Craig knew about my assignment to Craig, I wondered why I had not known. The AF normally gave us pretty decent lead time on transfers. So, I hurried over to our administrative office. No one goes through his personal file everyday and I had no reason to check mine earlier. That day, I asked the clerk for my file, and sure enough, there was the transfer order that had been there for weeks. I asked the clerk why I had not been informed, as they normally would have done, and he told me the commander had instructed him not to tell me.

I usually observed proper protocol when reporting to the head guy for the station, but on that day, I kicked open his office door, flung the paper on his desk and demanded to know why I was not informed. His face turned a deep shade of red and he hemmed and hawed around for a while and finally told me. He had been afraid that once I found out I was leaving, I would not do a good job for him. I asked just when he had planned on telling me about the transfer. I never got an answer. We had about a week to get things in order and make arrangements for a move.

I was glad to be off that station with a lunatic in charge, but felt sorry for the guys who were left there to deal with him. I learned later than he got canned, but not before a lot of other idiotic things happened. It seems that my persistence in keeping up my flying proficiency had not gone unnoticed in Washington. Although we had some eggheads there like the ones who gave us separation dates, we also had some people with some sense.

Someone up there had been comparing individual flight records with those of the flying units we were attached to. They didn't match. The organizations were not reporting attached pilots as part of their personnel strength, and the head shed was not pleased. It was announced that I and forty nine other pilots around the service were being given directed duty assignments to the cockpit, not from ADC, but from Headquarters AF. Mine was to Air Training Command, Craig AFB. I chuckled at the part of the order that stated no rebuttals from lower commands would be accepted.

Training Command would not have been my first choice, but I was thrilled to be headed for a flying job again, and from Zerbe's letter, I knew I would not be a basic pilot instructor. I could do that, but would not be as thrilled as I would be with some other flying job.

Flight Test

Selma, Alabama is about fifty miles west of Montgomery on highway 80. In 1966 there was little industry there and it was a relatively poor area. The Alabama River snaked it's way past the town, through the red clay and green pine trees.

Craig Air Force Base was by far the largest economic factor in the community. The mission of the base was to operate a pilot training wing for Air Training Command, headquartered at Randolph AFB, near San Antonio, Texas. The base facilities were old and mostly of WWII vintage. Family housing was scarce and mostly of poor quality. Many personnel, including some pretty high ranking officers, were living in duplexes and quadplexes that were just plain ratty. Housing in town and the neighboring community was almost non-existent.

I had left the family with my parents in Commerce, Georgia until we could find a place to live. There was nothing immediately available, on or off base. I put our name on the waiting list for base housing and reported for work at Maintenance Flight Test where Major Mitchell was in charge. He was preparing to leave for a new assignment in Alaska. Three other captains were assigned to the section, which was really a part of maintenance quality control.

We had a secretary and about fifteen enlisted and civilian inspectors. A master sergeant was in charge of the inspectors and he reported to the chief pilot. Our boss was Lt. Colonel Cowgill, chief of aircraft maintenance, who had an office with his staff on the opposite side of the hangar, upstairs, as mine was. He was the type person we could talk with, if need be, but he was a no nonsense guy. He expected everything to be done right the first time, and if not an explanation was required. He was a good pilot and stayed current, flying an occasional test flight.

Not many of the troops knew it, but Cowgill had served in the enlisted ranks during WWII and had survived the Bataan death march and a stint as a prisoner of the Japanese. After the Bataan march, he had been sent to Japan to work in the Japanese machine shops. His insistence on strict maintenance procedures stemmed, at least in part, from his hope that none of his countrymen would ever be subjected to the treatment he and his comrades had experienced during WWII.

The fighting in Viet Nam was escalating and the Air Force has never had it's pilot production in sync with it's needs. Now the demand exceeded the supply and we were under pressure to produce more than we were equipped for. Training flights were conducted from six in the morning until midnight, making utilization of aircraft very high.

The aircraft had to stand down some time for servicing and the mechanics needed some time to catch up. The flight line crews and the field maintenance guys were more than slightly overworked. They have long been the unsung heroes of the Air Force.

Initial pilot training was conducted with a T-41 prop driven airplane, a military two seat version of the Cessna 172. They were not compatible with the jets in the traffic pattern and operated out of the civilian airport across town. We had nothing to do with them. Our aircraft were T-37 and T-33. The Cessna T-37 was a small, unpressurized, twin engine jet, with side by side seating for primary training. The Lockheed T-33 was the familiar old workhorse trainer and utility aircraft that been in the inventory for nearly twenty years.

All the other pilot training wings were already using the Northrop, twin engine, supersonic, T-38 as a replacement for the T-bird. Craig was beginning to get some.

Roger McClure, one of our test pilots, was already checked out in the T-38 and I climbed in the back seat for one of his test flights. I was surprised that the Air Force was using such a hot bird for a trainer. I knew the type had been around for a while, but had no idea it was such an eye popping performer. Comparing the T-bird to the T-38 was like comparing a Mustang to a Ferrari.

It was pretty much the same airplane as the F-5, Freedom Fighter, except there were no external stores or tanks. It was extremely clean aerodynamically, very agile and very fast. It was said to have performance comparable to the MIG

21. It was easy to fly if one could stay ahead of it. Anyone who could not, was in deep doo-doo.

One of the interesting performance features of the T-38 is it's ability to do a rudder roll. The rudder is quite large and very effective at landing speeds. However, it can be too effective at high speeds and when the nose gear is retracted, a mechanical lock limits rudder travel to six degrees either side of center. Even with the restricted deflection, at speeds of three or four hundred knots, with hands off the stick, continued rudder deflection will produce a complete 360 degree roll.

I flew a few test flights in the T-33 and that was old hat. I had flown test flights at Larson and knew the routine. It was really good flying, usually alone, in fairly good weather most of the time and I was pretty much my own boss in the air. It was also nice in that we rarely had to sweat the fuel. I had done more than enough of that. The systems performed correctly or I wrote them up in a manner that the mechanics would know what to look for. There were endless reasons for the test flights. Things like engine changes, major work on landing gear, student pilot or instructor complaints on systems that malfuntioned in the air, but checked OK on the ground and so on.

One thing that caused a fairly high frequency of T-38 test flights was the little hotrod General Electric J-85 engines. Rigging was so critical and wear rate was so high, they were pulled for major inspection every two hundred hours, if they made it that far.

There was no school for T-38 maintenance flight test pilots. The closest thing to it was the instructor upgrade course at Randolph AFB, so I went down there for six weeks, flying the T-38, attending academics on engineering, normal procedures and emergency procedures. Following the course, I hung out with their flight test section for a week and rode with some of their pilots.

The timing was good. We had been assigned a house on base, so we had our goods taken out of storage and delivered to Craig. The house was small and cramped, but the family was finally together again. Kathy and the kids had about worn out their welcome in Commerce, being even more cramped with my parents there.

Arriving back at Craig, I found that Major Mitchell had made his departure and I was now chief pilot of maintenance flight test. The pilot training class that had begun in the T-33 had to complete their training in the T-33. We were getting new T-38s and the students coming in were starting their training in the T-38. We had three types of aircraft to maintain and would at one point have over two hundred airplanes to tend.

We went out to the Northrop factory at Palmdale, California and picked up our new airplanes. They usually had about one hour of total flight time on the engines and airframe. That was incurred during one production test flight. I had never flown brand new airplanes before, but was to learn that they still had bugs to be worked out. For the first few months, our people put in a lot of overtime.

The first one I picked up at Palmdale did OK for the first leg to Kirtland AFB at Albuquerque, where I stopped for fuel. After about a thousand feet of take off roll, the right afterburner blew out. Each time I tried to relight, it promptly blew out. I was supposed to abort, but I had a lot of runway in front of me and I knew that Kirtland had no maintenance facilities for that type. So, I continued the take-off, left engine in full afterburner and the right engine at full military power. It was another one of those instant decisions that pilots have to make.

The situation was not all that bad. At Randolph, my instructor had tailored my training toward my work at Craig as much as he could. He was older and wiser than the average bear. I remembered that he had let me do an illegal, single engine take-off just to see what it was like. Of course, in that instance the dead engine wasn't dead. It was at idle and could be brought up at anytime. It was good experience.

I had filed a flight plan to Randolph for my next refueling stop and I knew I could get the engine fixed there by experienced people. It required an overnight stay, but I left the next morning with both engines humming at full power for an uneventful trip back to Craig.

When I say uneventful, that means no major problems. Not many flights are completed without some level of difficulty. Halfway between Randolph and Craig, the towering cumulus are really towering. Cleared for flight level 450 (45,000 feet adjusted for standard altimeter setting of 29.92), some of the cloud tops are above me. The J-85 engines are not very tolerant of ice and hail, so I don't want to bore right through those clouds. I ask for and receive clearance for flight level 490.

Many published specifications for military aircraft performance are more than a little conservative. The T-38 is in that category. The books list the service ceiling as 50,000 feet. Technically, service ceiling is the altitude at which the aircraft will climb at no more than one hundred feet per minute. Rate of climb is still quite good up here. The real problem is indicated airspeed versus mach. If I cruise slower than 240 knots indicated, the increased angle of attack induces enough drag to require more power and fuel than is required at 250 knots.

If I maintain 250 knots indicated, true airspeed 530 knots, at this altitude, the ratio of my speed to the speed of sound gets me into the transonic range of about .95, where handling begins to get difficult because of instability. Therefore, I have a cruise speed envelope of about five knots, 240 to 245. Supersonic cruise is not practical as it requires afterburner power and makes too much noise on the ground. To complicate the situation, some cloud tops are still above me.

So, I have the power to climb some more, but I will have to fight the controls because of the instability in the transonic range. Also, we are not allowed above 50,000 because we are not wearing pressure suits. A pressure suit is not the same thing as a G suit. I am willing to take my chances, but don't want it a matter of record. The probability of anyone else being up here is not very great. My other option is to remain at FL490 and risk damaging the engines. I opt for a higher altitude without clearance. The throttles are pushed up another notch and the engines easily zip me up to 52,000, above the clouds. If I lose cockpit pressurization up here, I am probably a dead duck. 98 degree blood boils at this very low atmospheric pressure. In another fifty miles or so the clouds are not so high and I ease back down to assigned altitude.

––––––––

Back at the ranch, as soon as we could get one airplane flown and off the test board, another one would appear. We were allowed to fly test flights only during daylight hours and each pilot was limited to five. Actually, that was a pretty good days work. It was not unusual to preflight as many as seven, and abort a couple. The aborts didn't count. The ground guys did a good job, but sometimes put a bird up for test flight that we wouldn't pass on a ground run-up.

That was no big reflection on the mechanics, we were just more experienced and more critical than they were.

A T-bird was on the board for engine change. I signed for it and found it on test row. After the usual walk around inspection and cockpit check, I fired it up. On most flights we did not do a full power run up prior taking the runway, but on engine changes, we did a thorough engine check while still on the ramp. This one did not sound quite right and I could feel a faint vibration that did not belong. An engine specialist was standing by and I motioned for him to climb alongside the cockpit. I asked him, "Do you hear that weird sound?" He says, "No sir, sounds OK to me." I knew this guy was one of our better engine men, but I had misgivings about flying the bird, so I gave it thumbs down to undergo some more checking.

Next day I followed up on it. I would feel bad if I had made the hard working maintenance troops pull an engine for no good reason, but the test pilot was God as far as they were concerned. If we had any doubt, it didn't pass. The engine shop supervisor told me that they had found two pairs of mismatched turbine blades. The balancing was so critical, each turbine blade and it's opposite had to match within a few milligrams.

One of the things we checked on a T-33 full profile, was the accuracy of the mach meter. Accuracy was important, because the specified critical mach was indeed critical, as it is with straight wing aircraft. If exceeded, the aircraft would literally self destruct. We had a simple way to check it. The critical mach listed for the T-bird was .80, and the corresponding airspeed would vary considerably with altitude. That is why there was a separate indicator for mach or percentage of the speed of sound.

Usually at a medium altitude, in level flight, we would accelerate to about .78 and then continue to slowly accelerate while watching the ailerons and paying particular attention to any vibration in the rudder pedals. As the critical mach was reached, we could feel a definite buzz in the rudder as it vibrated rapidly and we could see the trailing edge of the ailerons appear to be about four inches thick due to rapid flutter. If those conditions coincided with an indication of .80, we knew the instrument was calibrated accurately. As soon as we were satisfied with the condition, we quickly backed off on the power and dropped the speed brakes to get below a speed where damage could occur.

A T-38 was on the test board following some electrical work. I found it on the line and when making my cockpit check, noticed a square control panel on the left console was oriented ninety degrees from what I had seen previously. I wondered if I had missed a technical order revision, and made a note to check it when I got back to the office. The orientation of the switches was logical, so I was not concerned about it and proceeded to fire up the engines.

On bringing up the throttles from cut-off to idle, I noticed they were unusually stiff, but that feature is adjustable and I made a note to have the mechanics check it. As I pushed up the throttles to begin the trip out to the runway, the throttles were really difficult to move, but I decided to live with it for the duration of this flight.

I taxied off the parking row and headed for the main ramp, which was slightly up hill, requiring a little more power. As I reached the ramp, made the ninety degree turn onto it, I brought the throttles back to idle. That was when so many trouble lights started coming on, I could not keep track of them. The master caution light was on, bar lights on the right console were lighting up like a Christmas tree, and smoke was billowing from somewhere, filling up the cockpit so badly I couldn't see much.

I didn't know if the radio was still operational, but I took time to make a quick transmission to ground control, telling them I was on fire as I hurriedly re-installed the ejection seat and canopy pins, unlatched the seat belt and shoulder harness. I went over the side while the bird was still rolling straight down the ramp, but it came to a stop by the time the fire wagons got there. Ground control had heard my radio transmission.

I immediately went upstairs to Cowgills office to tell him I had done some serious damage to the bird. It turned out that an electrician had installed the panel incorrectly and the throttle cables had sawed through a major bundle of electrical wiring. Since the panel was square the holes were located so that it could easily be installed incorrectly. The electrician still lost a major portion of his backside and surprisingly, I was not chastised for my part in the fiasco, because Cowgill allowed he would have treated the incident the same way I did.

Inexperienced instructors and low time students generated their share of unnecessary work for us. An instructor wrote up a T-38 for "Number two generator light comes on at four Gs." He was in the back seat with a student in the front. I put on my G suit, flew the bird and really wrung it out. There were no trouble lights and I signed off the bird to be put back on the line. On the next training flight, the bird was written up for the same problem.

By that time, I had gotten a little wiser. I managed to get the instructor on the phone to ask if the student had gotten a warning light in the front cockpit. No, he had not. He had not bothered to state in his write up that the light came on in the rear cockpit only. So, I grabbed one of our enlisted men who was authorized to fly with us and put him in the back seat. Sure enough, in a hard turn, at four Gs, the master caution light and the number two generator light came on in the rear cockpit. There were no warning lights on in front, so I made the push to test check and my warning lights came on. I knew then that the problem was really just a chafed wire, affecting the rear cockpit only. Two test flights could have been avoided by the instructor making a proper write up. We liked to fly, and that was our job, but we were being overworked to keep operations supplied with enough airplanes.

My flights were alternated between the T-38 and T-33. We were allowed to be current in only two aircraft types. Other pilots were current in the T-37 and T-33. Two were current in the only other combination, T-37 and T-38. I had flown in the T-37, Tweetie Bird, with other pilots and was not highly impressed with it, but any flying was better than walking.

My days would go something like this: Go by the weather office next to base ops and get a briefing from the meteorologist on duty. Check the status board in our office upstairs and put my name by the aircraft I intended to fly. Get my flight gear from the room next door and head for the flight line. If the bird was near by, walk to it. If it was a considerable distance away, grab one of the line men with a pickup or tug (tractor) and ride to save time.

As I arrive at the aircraft, the first streaks of light are penetrating the cool, gray dawn. Do the walk around inspection with a checklist about four times longer than the standard pilots checklist. Start up and head for the runway. "Craig Ground, Mukluk Four, taxi."

"Roger, Mukluk Four, active runway three two left, wind calm, altimeter two niner niner eight." "Roger, 29.98."

On the way to the 8,000 foot long, outside runway, designated for the T-38s and T-33s, many things are checked and discrepancies noted on my knee pad. Minor adjustments can be cleared without requiring another test flight. This bird is just back from periodic inspection, requiring major teardown and inspection. Both engines have been replaced with overhauled ones.

Official sunrise has just occurred as the tower clears me on the runway to "Hold." the sweeper has not yet cleared the far end. Every reasonable effort is made to prevent foreign objects from being picked up by the turbojet engines. They do not tolerate, rocks, nuts, bolts and miscellaneous junk. The sweeper turns off at the far end of the runway.

"Mukluk Four, cleared for take-off." Heavy pressure is applied to the brake pedals, as there is no hydraulic boost for brakes on the T-38. Both throttles are brought up smartly to the military detent. Normally, I would be smoother, but we want to be sure the engines can respond to demands for rapid power increase from idle to full power. Therefore, they are not babied. The dual set of engine instruments, indicating oil pressure, hydraulic pressure, RPM, exhaust nozzle position, exhaust temp and fuel flow are scanned and are normal. No red or amber lights are on. No trouble lights on the bar light panel on the right console. All systems are "go."

The tachometers are reading one hundred percent. The engines are screaming at maximum RPM, so the brakes are released as the throttles are pushed past the detents into the full afterburner range. The burners light and the clock is punched to start the recording hand. Acceleration is quick, but not neck snapping at this point, since the General Electric J-85 engines have a soft lighting A/B. The acceleration is building at an exponential rate, and just keeps on building.

Passing the 1000 foot marker, I have my pre-calculated acceleration check speed of 94 knots and a couple of seconds later, the critical engine failure speed of 114 knots. Passing 125 knots, the stick is eased back to raise the nose about three degrees. The air is cool and dense, so 2500 feet down the runway, at 155 knots, the right hand nudges the stick back slightly, while reaching for the gear handle with the left hand. The handle is snapped up as the bird breaks ground and the hand transfers to the flap handle just outboard and to the rear of the throttles. By the time the gear doors are thumping closed, the far end of the asphalt disappears under the nose and the airspeed is passing through 240 knots, which is max for open gear doors. I am still accelerating like a turpentined cat and the throttles are eased back to about eighty percent, to level temporarily at 3,000 feet maintaining 300 knots, per departure procedure.

The radio is switched to the channel for Atlanta Center. "Atlanta Center, Mukluk Four, airborne from Craig, request max climb to flight level four five zero." "Roger Mukluk Four, cleared flight level four five zero, via Thomasville Departure, report Thomasville VORTAC." I turn toward the radio nav-aid a few miles to the southwest. Technically, present speed and altitude are supposed to be maintained until crossing the nav-aid. Actually, a little fudging takes place.

Approaching the radio fix, the throttles are pushed back up to full military power, and as the indicator shows station passage, the bird is whistling along at better than five hundred knots. The nose is pointed up about twenty five degrees as the throttles are shoved into the full afterburner range. With all that air being crammed into the intakes, plus what the eight stage compressors are sucking in, the engines can burn a whopping amount of fuel and produce some real power.

This time, when the burners light, my shoulders are slammed against the seat back, my head is snapped against the headrest and the bird accelerates and climbs like a rocket. "Atlanta, Mukluk Four departing Thomasville." "Roger Four, report APC." (Area of positive control – 24,000 feet, later lowered to 18,000).

In less than four minutes, I am passing 43,000 feet and beginning the level off, fifty four miles southwest of the base. If I wait any later to lower the nose, I will overshoot my assigned 45,000 feet. "Atlanta, Mukluk Four, flight level four five zero." "Roger Four."

Due to the very thin air, at .93 mach, the indicated speed is now only 250 knots, but true airspeed is 525 knots, better than 600 mph.

I leave the left throttle in full A/B and retard the right one to a hundred percent military as I watch to make sure the exhaust nozzles close down, and then back it on down to idle. As soon as it stabilizes at idle, I bring it back to full power – max A/B and it lights off OK. the procedure is repeated with the left engine. Both burners relight on a throttle burst, at high altitude – the acid test for engine performance. All the gauges are in the green. I recheck the oxygen system OK. There is not much air up here and the temperature is minus forty five.

"Atlanta, Mukluk Four requests flight level three zero zero." "Roger, cleared flight level three zero zero, report level." Click-click. The nose is eased down, as I turn ninety degrees to stay in our local area, and the mach meter winds up to 1.2 as the altimeter begins to unwind. I do a roll to the right, a roll to the left, retard the throttles to ninety percent and drop the speed brakes while still supersonic. I level at 30,000 and report to Atlanta. The right throttle is brought back to idle, then to cut off. The left engine is kept at a hundred percent to maintain altitude while operating single engine. The dead engine winds down and windmills at fourteen percent. The right airstart button is punched and the throttle brought back up to idle position.

The EGT flickers and then rises rapidly to a few hundred degrees as the fuel flow meter increases and the rpm begins to increase. OK, bring it on back up to full military power and retard the left throttle to idle. Let it stabilize and then cut it off. "Mukluk Four, Atlanta, traffic your ten o'clock position at twelve miles." "Roger, I have visual." The airstart procedure is repeated for the left engine, but there is no increase in EGT or RPM. I have fuel flow, but no fire. I stopcock the throttle and try another start, but no luck. "Atlanta, Mukluk request flight level two eight zero." "Roger, cleared two eight zero."

I descend to 28,000 to try another airstart on the dead engine. Optimally, it should airstart at 30,000, but is acceptable if it will light off at 28 grand. I am careful to maintain an indicated 250 knots, as the envelope for airstarting is narrow; 240 to 260 knots indicated airspeed. This time it lights off and the remainder of the checks are to be made at lower altitudes. "Atlanta, Mukluk Four, out of APC." "Roger Mukluk four, squawk mode three, code 1200, (IFF codes) Atlanta out."

At 15,000 feet, several more checks are made to insure that everything operates as advertised. Aircraft collect all sorts of junk that cannot be found through normal inspection, so we do an in-flight junk check. I roll it inverted and maintain one G, level flight for several seconds. All the pencils, hardware, safety wire clippings and miscellaneous junk can be picked off the top of the canopy while I am hanging in the belt and harness.

Up to about ten thousand, the sky is full of big fluffy cotton balls. The cumulus is building, as usual in the warm, humid climate, but I can see plenty of real estate below. I can see that big gash in the red clay where the new interstate highway is being built between Montgomery and Mobile.

The radio comes alive again. "Mukluk five entering the test area." "Roger, Four is departing the west side." McClure has taken off a few minutes behind me in a T-37. A "Tweety Bird" is the world's most efficient converter. It converts JP-4 jet fuel into noise. The little Continental J-69 engines make so much high pitched noise, we have to wear ear muffs plus ear plugs when we are around them on the flight line.

I switch radio channels again to Craig Feeder Control, who spaces me in between other traffic entering the pattern., and after a few miles switch again to Craig tower. In the gaps between the puff balls, I can see stretches of the Alabama River, with it's red banks, winding through the green pine forests dotted with a few plowed fields. Three miles out, lined up with the runway, tower is notified, "Craig, Mukluk Four, initial, full stop." "Roger Mukluk Four, wind two niner zero, eight knots, altimeter two niner niner six, report base leg."

Level, 1500 feet above the ground, at 280 knots, 2000 feet down the runway, I retard power slightly, bank into a hard left turn to roll out on the downwind leg at 240 knots. The landing gear and flap handles go down and the throttles are pushed back up to about eighty five percent. I keep a firm hand on the stick as the bird tries to pitch and yaw from the configuration changes taking place. The three green lights for landing gear are shining brightly, but just to be extra sure, I look at the rear view mirrors and see the bottoms of the main gear tires below the wings.

Looking back over my shoulder at the landing spot, the descending turn to base leg and final approach is begun at 175 knots. "Mukluk Four, base, gear checked." I roll out on the final approach, line up the slab and reduce power to about 75 percent to maintain airspeed at 155 knots. I point the nose at the over run about 300 feet short of the actual runway. Over the fence a few feet in the air, and the tires chirp, touching down a couple of hundred feet down the runway and the throttles are eased back to idle. As soon as the speed gets below 130, the stick is brought full back to induce as much drag as possible to slow the bird with aerodynamic braking. The nose comes up and I quickly decelerate to a hundred knots so the brakes can now be used without skidding and blowing tires.

Forty two minutes from take-off, the aircraft is back on the line, functional check completed. The forms are signed and it is cleared for flight as soon as it can be refueled. No doubt, someone will be along in a few minutes to fly it on a training mission.

Trudging back up to the office, I sign for a T-33 that is on the board for a test flight after having some work done on the hydraulic landing gear system. It has had a retraction test on the jacks, but the boss wants it flown, so I go find it on the ramp and fire it up. As soon as I can get airborne and up to a safe altitude, I put it through a series of simulated traffic patterns to cycle the landing gear, flaps, and speed brakes at landing speeds. Everything works, so I have it back to the airpatch in less than twenty five minutes. Fortunately, the 230 gallon tip tanks were only fueled to 125 gallons each and now there is only internal fuel remaining. Landing weight and getting it stopped will not be a problem.

Back in the office, it is nearing eight AM, the time for the morning maintenance meeting. I walk down a hundred yards or so to the building where all the maintenance supervisors meet with L/C Cowgill, our boss. Every missed or delayed take-off, or air abort that involved maintenance problems the previous day, is discussed in detail. Especially if there is a second occurrence of a particular problem. We find out who or what messed up. The problem has to be identified, whether it relates to flight line maintenance, field maintenance, supply, or a policy or procedure. In-house policies and procedures are modified on the spot, if need be. Others will be dealt with through proper channels.

Cowgill likes for one of our pilots to attend, because in-flight problems are our specialty, and we can often shed some light on problems the ground people cannot. The meeting ends and everyone goes back to work, and there is no shortage of work for any of us. On the way back to the office I stop at the mobile canteen, parked between the hangars and grab a cup of coffee to go.

Upstairs again, the flight test board is filling up. More aircraft are coming out of maintenance that need to be test flown. My secretary is filling up my IN basket with paperwork, but that will have to wait until after sundown. I sign for the next bird listed on the board. All my other pilots are already in the air on the ramp getting ready to fly. My next bird is a T-38 that has been written up by a pilot for vibration problems. I try to phone him to get more specific information, but cannot track him down, so it's on to the flight line again.

I preflight the aircraft and strap in, make a cockpit check and signal for air to the right engine. The right engine must be started first because its instruments are powered by the dinky on-board battery. The left engine instruments are dead for now. I punch the start button, and hear the hiss of high powered air from the start cart. The six inch diameter air hose jumps and stiffens on the ground. As the right engine tach eases up to fourteen percent, the throttle is brought up to the idle detent, I have fuel flow and the EGT gauge comes alive. There is fire back there. The engine stabilizes at 43 percent and the right generator comes on line. Now there is electrical power to everything, including the left engine instruments.

I signal for air to the left engine and punch the start button. The engine winds up and the left generator comes on line and we go through some checks assisted by the crew chief. He visually verifies speed brakes retracted, flaps at take-off setting of sixty percent and stabilator trim correct, matching an index mark that the pilot cannot see. Radios are turned on, the air line is disconnected, and the chocks are pulled.

With taxi information from ground control, I again head for the active runway. There is no need to go the full route on this flight, considering the nature of the write up. I already have a strong suspicion about what the problem is, if there is one. Students and low time instructors could save a lot of time and expense by making better write ups

At fifteen thousand feet, I level off and at about 300 knots, ease the right throttle back to idle, paying close attention as the engine speed decelerates through the 75 to 65 percent range, and back up to 100 percent. Smooth – no problems. I repeat the procedure on the left engine, and sure enough, at 72 percent, there is an erratic rattle and low frequency vibration. The two speed gear box driving the generator and hydraulic pump on the left side can't make up it's mind whether to stay in high or low. Seventy to seventy three percent is the shift point. I will tell the mechanics only that I got vibration at seventy two percent on the left engine. They will say, "We know what that is. We'll change out the two speed gear box coupling." I like to let them think they are involved in the problem solving process.

Back in the traffic pattern, I have to calculate speeds for the base turn and final approach. After such a short flight, I am still heavy with fuel. I could stay up and mess around for a while, but I know that ops needs the bird, so I will make a heavy weight landing. My final turn airspeed will be 190 knots and final approach speed will have to be 170 knots. I will have to plant it right on the end, do maximum aerodynamic braking and still the brakes will be smoking when I turn off at the far end.

With the wheels and flaps down, coming around the turn to line up with the slab, the air is smooth, and I can feel a little buffeting. The wings are trying to tell me they are loaded to the max at that speed, and any increase in bank to tighten the turn, or any further loss of speed will result in them delivering too little lift to offset the aircraft weight. There is a very thin margin between flying and stalling.

I point the nose at the overrun and touch down in the first twenty feet of asphalt, barely missing the barrier webbing lying flat, which would be raised if we were landing from the opposite direction. Eight thousand feet sounds like a lot of runway, but it is barely enough for this type landing. Mobile control, manned by training squadron instructors will call operations and complain that I touched down on the webbing – again. We never did, but they often thought we did. I suspected they were slightly envious of us who got to do a little more challenging types of flying than they did.

I go back upstairs to find that we are not catching up. The board is still filling up faster than we can fly the aircraft. Ryan is out in a T-33, McClure in a T-38, Zerbe in a T-37 and Mink is getting a no-notice standardization check ride. I pick the next airplane on the list and find it on the ramp. It has a history of engine problems, but has been reworked and is on test row again. I fire it up, and in view of it's history, give it a thorough run-up by taking it over to the edge of the ramp, away from the main flight line with the tail pipes pointing away from everything. On the first throttle burst, the left engine compressor stalls, with a bang, instant RPM rollback, and fire shooting out the intake. It is a reject without even leaving the ground.

———

People with decent working hours went to the mess hall, the officers club, or home for lunch. With so much to do, and so little time to do it all, we rarely had that luxury. So, I go by the flight line snack bar for a sandwich and a coke that will pass for lunch.

As I enter the office, my secretary is on the phone and motions for me to pick up the extension on my desk. A solo student pilot is trying to make it back with one engine out and the other one damaged. Part of our job was to investigate every incident involving our aircraft, regardless of who the pilots were, so I hurried outside and got a ride on a flight line truck to the taxiway where the crippled bird was just turning off. He had made it. There was no Plexiglas in the front canopy frame, but the frame was intact. He said while cruising at about three hundred knots, the canopy had simply ripped loose on the left side, rotated over to the right and shattered, with chunks of Plexiglas going into the engine intakes. It wiped out the right engine and slightly damaged the left one. He had done an outstanding job, getting it back on the ground.

We decided to inspect all the T-38 canopies. We had just gotten some new X-ray equipment that allowed us to look at a lot of things without tearing them apart. In the case of the canopy problem, the seal strips covered the area where the locking rods ran all the way from front to back to hold the canopy in the frame. With the X-ray equipment we could check them quickly and discovered that some had cracks where the locking rods had been forced in and overstressed the Plexiglas. Another base lost a T-38 when the instructor and student had to bail out after losing both engines because of the same problem.

After much investigation, and a hassle with Northrop, we found that they had a bad canopy jig, turning out warped units and the assemblers were forcing in the locking rods when they should have been a hand fit. With continued overstress, it was only a matter of time before they let go. On our aircraft, we found several units that had cracked and were about to come loose.

———

I get a call from Maintenance Control. One of the training squadron pilots volunteered to help us out by flying over to Shaw AFB, Sumter, South Carolina to pick up a part. He has called back to say he has a tire that is worn beyond limits and Shaw does not have any of that type. Will I take him a tire? Now we have an aircraft out of commission because he either did not check remaining tire tread before leaving Craig, or he has skidded one by braking too hard or too early and wiped it out and we still don't have the part we need for another aircraft.

With a wheel and new tire strapped in the back seat, I blast off for Shaw in a T-38. It has been a typical hot and humid day and my flight suit is soaked. I am glad to have the engines up to speed and have some cold air coming from the vents. It is a good flight and I arrive at Shaw late in the afternoon.

While the transient maintenance people change his wheel, and refuel my airplane, we file a flight plan back to Craig. The sun is setting as I walk past his airplane on the way to where mine is parked. Without really thinking about it, I automatically count the exposed threads on the axle of his right main wheel. That's the one they just replaced. Wrong number! The wheel bearing has been installed incorrectly. The local mechanics don't know that the bearing can be installed backwards and will fail on take-off.

I am tired and too aggravated to wait on him and fly formation with him.. I put the new part we desperately need in the back seat of my bird and head on back to Craig. The other pilot can bring back his bad tire and wheel.

After a uneventful trip back home, my fifth flight of the day, I drag my tired butt up the stairs to the office one more time. The IN basket is full. Most items are time sensitive and must be dealt with by morning. The administrative people can be a month behind in their work and overtime is not in their vocabulary, but excuses for delays from maintenance are not accepted.

About nine thirty PM, I knock it off and go home, I flop on the couch, take off my boots, and consume a large quantity of iced tea. The kids are already in bed. About one thirty in the morning, I wake up, still on the couch in my grungy flight suit. If I go to sleep like that the wife does not wake me. I get a shower and go to bed until five AM, when it's time to get up and start over.

I park my 250cc Honda in the hangar by the foot of the stairs. I long ago gave up driving my MGB and always finding someone in my reserved parking spot. I don't have time to fight with them and the Air Police. The Air Police could not care less that there are too few parking spots. All they cared about was writing tickets. As a part-time, temporary maintenance squadron commander, I am constantly pestered with citations to my 330 GIs over petty things.

I have to endorse each one and send it back to the Provost Marshall with action taken. My standard endorsement was a rubber stamped, "Library card revoked for three days." The Air Police just didn't get it.

As I get to the top of the stairs a few steps from the office, I hear the phone ringing. I am the first one there, so I pick it up. Maintenance Control is calling. One of our instructors and his student left a T-bird over at Maxwell AFB yesterday afternoon. There is a blue AF car with a motor pool driver and a mechanic waiting for me outside. I leave my secretary a note, get my flight gear and head back down the stairs to the waiting vehicle. The instructors story is that the engine died on him and he had to do an airstart and landed at the nearest airport, which happened to be Maxwell.

It takes us over an hour for the drive to Montgomery and the Maxwell flightline. I am pretty sure of what caused the instructor to think he had a problem with the T-33. The throttle in the front cockpit has an idle detent. The rear cockpit throttle has no detent, but being interconnected to the front one, it doesn't need one. If the detent gets worn, or out of adjustment, a hard pull on the rear one can make it slip past and both throttles go to cutoff.

Years previously, when flying as an instructor in the back seat, I had inadvertently shut one down while making a landing. Fortunately, we were touching down when it happened. I had learned not to jerk the rear throttle to the idle stop.

The mechanic fired up the T-bird engine and could find nothing out of order. He made some adjustment on the idle detent and declared there was nothing more he could do. I agreed and told him to go on back to Craig in our vehicle. Then I fired up the T-bird and beat him back to Craig. For the rest of his life, that instructor will tell war stories about how he flamed out at 15,000 feet and had to do an airstart. The Form 781 write up: Engine flamed out at 15,000 feet on retarding throttle to idle." The corrective action entry read: "Adjusted idle detent."

On the way back I have to remind myself that the traffic pattern speeds are different from the T-38 and turn onto initial approach at 250 knots, 1500 feet above the ground. Down the runway a couple of thousand feet, I roll into a steep bank, retard the power to 55 percent, and drop the speed brakes, all at the same time. The bird goes into a three G turn with roaring and turbulence from the speed brakes. Speed is bleeding off rapidly, and I thumb in a lot of pitch trim change.

Rolling out of the 180 degree turn on the downwind leg, landing gear and flaps come down and power pushed back up enough to maintain 140 knots in the descending final turn. I have three green lights for the wheels, the runway is coming around to line up with me and I reach down in the floor to shake the gear handle one more time, to make sure it is locked. Then I am over the fence and the tires are chirping on the black top runway. I park and sign off the bird as being ready for operational flight.

———————

Back at the office, the test board is filling up and the other guys are in the air or out on the ramp getting ready to fly. I select a T-38 that has a long history of problems with the starboard engine. The little J-85 engines have a very critical setup to operate at max performance. The combination of variable inlet guide vanes, variable exhaust nozzles, compressor bleed ports, under a wide variety of conditions are not easy to deal with.

Everything went just fine up to forty five grand and back down to thirty. It was time to make the airstart checks. The hangar queen in the right hole did well. It fired right up at thirty. *I am thinking, I can finally sign off this bear. They have fixed it.* The left engine had no history of trouble, so without a second thought, I shut it down. It is windmilling at the usual fourteen percent, 250 knots, in the middle of the envelope and the fuel pressure is good. No light. The EGT does not budge. There is no increase in RPM. It still does not light off after another attempt.

"Atlanta Center, Mukluk Four, request flight level two eight zero." "Roger Mukluk, cleared to flight level two eight zero." The airstart procedure is repeated twice more and it does not respond. The left engine is now a reject. I thought it surely would light off at some lower altitude, but it would not. I figure it's time to practice my single engine landings.

If done right, a single engine approach and landing is no sweat. If you mess up, it can be fatal. The bird flies quite well on one engine, but in a three sixty overhead traffic pattern, close attention must paid to speed, bank angles, and power settings on the good engine. If you ever get behind the power curve, you may not recover. With steep bank angles, the lift may decrease to the point where there is not enough power to overcome the weight and drag. Flaps are set to sixty percent instead of full down to reduce drag and allow for a possible go-around.

The cross feed and boost pump switches are used to juggle the fuel and weight and balance, since the dead engine is not using any fuel. Some pilots prefer a long, straight-in final on one engine. I don't like being out there, low and slow for a long time, and prefer the overhead pattern. The landing goes OK. The notoriously bad actor in the right hole has brought me home. The engine men find a bad igniter plug in the left engine, but it will still have to be test flown again.

We are short of qualified enlisted men to start, taxi and runup aircraft. Two of them who have completed training are waiting in the office for their final check. Zerbe takes one and I take one. We will give them an oral exam and then go out to the line and ride in the back seat while they fire up a bird and drive around the ramp for a while. Mine does OK and I sign his license and head back to the office to take care of some of the most urgent paperwork and get it out of my IN box and into the OUT box.

Headquarters AF has tagged us to do an equipment evaluation project for some additional electronics for the T-38. I am the project officer. I really need something to fill in my spare time! I make a little progress and decide to break routine and go home for lunch. The test board is not too far behind, so I call Kathy and zip home on the Honda for a quick lunch. The boys, except for Thomas, are in school. Some days I don't get to see them at all, since I leave before they are up and get home after they are bedded down for the night.

Back at work, I pick a T-bird and find it has a low strut. Somebody on the line has not done a thorough preflight. The crew chief has to find an air cart. I can't taxi with a low strut because the fifteen thousand pound tricycle will only go in circles. There is no power nose wheel steering on the T-33. The nose wheel free swivels from differential braking. The brakes have no hydraulic boost and it takes a lot of foot pressure even for normal steering.

We finally get a high pressure air cart and I get airborne to go through a full profile, which will take the better part of an hour. While finishing the routine, doing a rigging check, all the garbage out, power at idle, full nose up trim, hands off the controls, falling out of the sky at 119 knots, "Tat, tat, tat, tat," Ryan goes whizzing by in a Tweety Bird. He is playing dirty, pretending to shoot me down while I am unable to maneuver. He knows I will wax his posterior if he takes me on under more normal circumstances. Not because of my superior piloting, but because the T-37 performance is worlds apart from the T-33. The ops weenies would have us on the carpet if they knew about some of the things we do out there, and they have probably done it too, but they can't officially approve of it now.

Back at the office, Lt. Mink comes in and tells me maintenance control has requested him to take a pilot over to Columbus, Mississippi to recover a T-38 that was left there with problems. Everyone else is out somewhere, and it is getting late in the day, so I tell him, "OK, let's go," and we fire up a T-37 and depart for Columbus. On arrival, Mink lets me practice a landing in the T-37. I am not officially checked out, but that does not prevent me from flying it with a pilot who is.

We file flight plans back to Craig, and I tell Mink not to depart until he knows I have departed in the T-38, in case I need a ride back. I don't want to be stuck there overnight. I do my walk-around and strap in. I signal for starting air to the right engine and it fires up OK. I signal for air to the left engine and punch the start button. Nothing happens and I look around to see the power-man standing there with a puzzled look on his face. About the same time, I look out toward the runway and see the T-37 breaking ground. I am not happy with Lt. Mink.

I shut down the right engine, unstrap and climb down. After thinking about the start system for a moment, I ask the crewman for a nine sixteenths wrench and climb under the bird. The air diverter valve can be shifted from one engine position to the other one manually, and I show him how to do it. Getting strapped up again, I get both engines fired up and head out.

Technically, the aircraft needs a test flight before it can fly another mission. I can do that on the way back to Craig, but the sun is setting. I am not remaining at Columbus overnight so I can log a test flight tomorrow morning after sun up. Therefore, I proceed to make the necessary checks on the way back and land well after dark. I note in the log that the electric actuator for the diverter valve is not working. That will not require another test flight. When I fill out the log, I simply enter the time for the flight as taking place an hour earlier. No one will ask, and I won't tell. I am home for the night, late. Late is better than not at all, which is often the case.

After another short night, early morning flight, and eight o'clock maintenance meeting, I go back to the office in time to hear the deep roar of the big engines that power the crash trucks, and the siren of an ambulance. I look out the office window and see a black column of smoke off the approach end of runway 14 Right. The phone is ringing. The pilots in flight test serve as maintenance engineering officers on accident investigations and we do it on a rotating basis. A student pilot in a T-38 has augered in on the final turn. It is McClure's turn and he hurriedly leaves to join the team that will be converging on the crash site.

He will tell me tomorrow that they found enough evidence in the wreckage to determine that the flaps were full up. That is a fatal mistake unless enough airspeed is added to compensate for the loss of lift. Stall recovery is impossible at low altitude. Very sad, but the training must go on, and it does.

I go out to fly a T-38 that needs a full profile. It has had some engine problems. At forty five grand, I begin the high altitude checks for afterburner relights. The right engine relights OK. I retard the throttle for the left engine, stabilize and go back to full power. Military power is OK. As I shove the throttle past the detent for A/B the handle sort of snaps and goes limp. The engine stays in full afterburner, no matter where I position the throttle handle.

I can't land the thing with full power on one engine and would probably run out of fuel before I could get back anyway. That leaves only one option. I pull up the guard over the main fuel shutoff switch for the left engine and push it to "off." It works. The engine abruptly winds down to the usual fourteen percent. It will run the hydraulics for the landing gear and speed brakes until in the landing flare. At that point it will wind down, and the right side engine pump will also power the flight controls, but not the landing gear, which will already be down and locked. Now the master caution light is on. The left generator failure light is on. I cancel the master caution so it will be armed to tell me if any more trouble lights illuminate on the bar light panel on the right console.

I have more practice on single engine landings coming up. As the airspeed bleeds off in the flare, the master caution light comes on again. Hydraulic pressure from the left pump is too low, but I am on the runway now. On the ground the maintenance types tell me the throttle cable broke. First and last time I ever heard of that. While dismounting and looking back toward the right rear, I notice one of the linemen opening a panel back there. I walk around there and the entire right side of the bird is streaked with red hydraulic fluid. The reservoir sight glass indicates an empty fluid tank. Someone did not properly secure a filler cap prior to take-off. It is under a panel and not an item on the pilots check list. Fortunately, between the left and right sides, I had somehow maintained enough hydraulics to get it on the ground. There is no need to report it, the line chief will have a big chunk of someone's backside.

It is lunch time, so I stop by the flight line snack bar, but can't have a quick lunch, because I run into one of the standardization pilots who likes to pick my brains for information they don't normally have. I don't know if he is really interested in knowing more about the aircraft systems, or just wants to be able to ask questions he thinks the pilot being checked doesn't know. Check pilots like to ask questions they think the checkee cannot answer. Overall, they do good job, but it is a little irksome to get a check ride from some young, fast rising pilot who is trying to intimidate someone with three times his own experience. Anyway, it takes too long to get away from him.

It is way past noon and the paper pile is too high and I have only flown two birds so far. I decide to put most of the flying on the other pilots and tackle some of the most urgent paper for a while. By mid afternoon, I have had enough paper shuffling and pick out a T-38 that needs a full profile. The flight was pretty routine and while finishing up my checklist at about 20,000, I look up a see an F-4, smoking along, level, on a quartering head-on, unauthorized intercept. It is probably out of Eglin or Hurlburt. I roll inverted for a second, pull hard and roll back rightside up to keep him in sight. He does a hard break, up and away, hightailing it out of our area. He probably thinks he has bounced a student in the little trainer who will meekly go on his way.

I don't have any guns or radar, but we can still play. I am not short on maneuverability. I plug in the burners and follow the smoke trail. You could be half blind and still follow an F-4. The speck on the windscreen, begins to grow into a full sized airplane as I overtake him at close to mach one. I am probably out of our local area by now, but no one is keeping track. I do a roll around him, completing it where he cannot fail to notice, then break hard right, back toward home. He probably knows he can't turn with me and doesn't try. So there, I had to let him know he wasn't picking on some student who was just stumbling around out there. Back to work.

Back on the ground, I am hot and sweaty. To save time, I call the office from a line shack and get the tail number of another T-38. The take-off and climb goes well and just as I am leveling off at forty five grand, I am jolted by a tremendous BANG! the cockpit filled up with vapor, which I first thought to be smoke. My mask was being blown away from my face by the massive involuntary exhalation that takes place when the pressurization instantly drops to a very low value – like, nearly zero. Something ricocheted off the canopy and back down to the floor. The water wings inflated under my chute harness and had my body in a vise.

The vapor was clearing out and I could see the gauges and that everything was normal except the cockpit altimeter, reading 45,000 feet, same as the flight altimeter. The canopy seal had blown out and caused an explosive decompression. The automatic oxygen regulator was doing it's job and was forcing air down my intake, making it very difficult to talk against it, but I told Atlanta Center, I needed a lower altitude and they obliged. I could survive up there, but it was too uncomfortable to stay if I didn't have to. I got my heart back down in my chest where it belonged and finished up the mission.

A little later, when I looked at my watch, I realized what it was that had bounced off the canopy. The instant depressurization had blown my watch crystal off. When I pulled out my ball point pen, I saw that all the ink had been blown out and all over my pocket. Having the air in ones lungs equalize with the atmospheric pressure at that altitude is a weird experience. It's a little like letting the air out of an inflated balloon. It is uncontrollable and any attempt to control it would probably result in ruptured lungs.

Sundown brought a halt to the test flying for the day. Training flights continued on into the night. After doing all the paperwork I could stand, I went home for some rest so I could do it all over again the next day. Our work often continued on into Saturday and even on Sunday afternoons. If there were airplanes on test row, we were expected to fly them as soon as possible, regardless of the day of the week. I never asked anyone, I just took Sunday mornings off and went to church with my family.

———

Eventually, all the T-33 aircraft left Craig for other units, some of them going to other countries. The overall workload of the training wing was still heavy due to high production quotas imposed by headquarters. At least the maintenance problems were simplified, in that we now maintained two types rather than three.

Roger McClure was promoted to major and although I had slightly more time in grade, I had known I was not on the list for consideration. My involuntary separation date triggered that and the date was drawing closer. I certainly did not envy Roger and all the other captains who were promoted at that time. They had earned it and deserved it but I felt more than ever, that I was being treated unfairly. Except for that, I was pleased that I had worked mostly at jobs I liked and felt I had earned my keep. As was always my personal policy, I would do my best at whatever I was doing while it lasted.

One week later, insult was added to injury. After having to swallow the bitter pill of being left off the promotion list, I was called over to the personnel office. The colonel in charge showed me a letter he wanted me to sign. It was an offer to remain on active duty for an indefinite period. (Strange. That had been the status of my choice before HQ AF changed it for me.) Of course, the deck was stacked. They could decide to dismiss me at any time with six months notice and I knew I would never be promoted under those conditions.

I didn't have to have a PH.D. in Human Resources to know what was happening. The snobs who had engineered my separation date, along with several hundred other pilots, had made a huge mistake and pilots were badly needed in Viet Nam. I could reconcile my going to Nam, but it would only be fair if I went with the same privileges as everyone else. The AF was not about to promote me retroactively or any other way now, but wanted me to be cannon fodder. I told the colonel "No." They had prepared me for separation over the past two and a half years, and now they could live with it. Besides, my sons needed a father.

For the last few months, Roger became chief of flight test as my immediate boss and we got along fine, as we always had. The good part was that I was relieved of a lot of responsibility and although I still worked hard, it was a little more enjoyable. I still flew as much and made a lot of trips to pick up broken airplanes and some trips with Cowgill. He liked to have me fly with him on afternoon and evening cross country flights to keep up his proficiency on instrument flying and navigation. Two of our pilots left for airline work and we got in some new ones.

Lt. Mink broke a T-38 and broke the flight test sections long record of accident free flying. Fortunately he was not hurt, but was charged with the accident and was grounded for a year. We never did know exactly what caused it, but accident boards tend to lean toward pilot error if they can't find some other obvious reason.

On a test flight I had a similar experience to Mink's, but salvaged the airplane and found out exactly what caused the difficulty. A student pilot had written up a T-38 for flight control problems on a solo formation flight. That was not an uncommon gripe if a student had done poorly on a formation flight, but we very rarely verified any flight control problems.

With this particular bird, I had that thought in mind, but was obligated to flight test it. The run up and initial take-off roll was normal. At 155 knots, as I nudged the stick back slightly to rotate, with my left hand already on the gear handle, the bird pitched up violently to a very nose high attitude. My reaction was to push the stick forward to prevent the developing stall. I over controlled and then the nose was pointing steeply down at the asphalt.

I had enough training and experience to recognize a porpoise, so I held the stick slightly aft for a slight nose up attitude and held it with both hands, because it was very difficult to overcome the instinctive reaction to fight the porpoise. If you fight it, you will never get in sync and it will only get worse. With the stick absolutely rigid, the nose was oscillating up and down several degrees, but I had achieved my temporary goal of maintaining a climb. After the initial shock started to wear off, I started trying to analyze the situation and was embarrassed to realize that the gear was up, but the flaps were still down and both engines were still in full afterburner. My heart rate was probably off the chart.

I shut down the burners, got the flaps up and leveled at 15,000 to assess the situation. On that particular flight a T-37 instructor was in the back seat for his first ride in a T-38. I don't know what he was thinking. Probably thought he had an idiot for a pilot. The nose was still rising and falling with no control input, but less so than before. The left side hydraulic pressure was slightly high, but not alarmingly so. The right side pressure was normal.

While making a wide circle around the base, I made some large stick inputs and both hydraulic gauges dipped a little and returned to normal, but I had begun to suspect the high pressure on the left side had something to do with my problem. Both engine driven pumps supplied pressure to the dual, supposedly fail-safe flight control system. Thinking the left side might be overriding the right, I cycled the speed brakes several times and the left side pressure dropped slightly but went right back to the previous reading. Anyway, there was no steady state fluctuation of either pressure gauge, so I could not account for the erratic pitch.

Again, to try to deal with the high pressure on the left side, I shut down the left engine, but even with only windmill speed, the hydraulic pressure was too high and the flight conditions remained unchanged, so I restarted the left engine.

Now, I am faced with a question. Is controllability good enough for landing? I was not one to go around looking for an opportunity for a nylon letdown. The guy in the back seat had no experience in a T-38 and could not be of any help. I felt sorry for him, but had no time to hold his hand. After making some simulated traffic patterns in landing configuration, I decided to land it. We made a normal three sixty, overhead pattern because as I said earlier, I did not like long, straight in approaches unless necessary. The bird behaved well enough for me to make a pretty good landing. I told the T-37 instructor I would give him a rain check, but he was not interested.

On the ground, we checked the flight control system and found two problems, Both were rare, and unheard of in combination. The servo for the slab actuator on the left side was loose, allowing the actuator to wander around, and the slightly higher pressure was overcoming the right side actuator, moving the slab randomly. The left side pump was suspect and was removed and put on the test stand. At the lowest speed we could run it, the output pressure was still 4200 psi., a high reading. Certain failure modes of a variable volume, constant pressure pump can cause that.

We immediately checked all our other T-38s and found several with loose servo couplings. We also notified all the other bases with that type aircraft. I never did know exactly how close I came to the ground on that first down swing following the pitchup, but I know it was close. Mink had a similar problem and his bird did make contact with the runway on the downswing. Unfortunately, we were never able to determine what caused it in his case.

———————

There were so many aircraft accidents, at any given time, at least one of us was working with an accident investigation team. We only had a small Kaman H-43 helicopter for search and rescue work and the crew did their work well. They were quick to be on the scene when needed, but could only carry a limited load. I rode with them to crash sites a few times, but usually only after they had already made an initial trip.

Due to the need for some of us to be on the scene quickly, we had an arrangement with the Alabama Highway Patrol. Anytime they were notified of a need, they dispatched two patrol cars to our base ops for the flight safety officer, a chaplain, security personnel , and one or more of us from maintenance. We would pile into the cars and they would drive us as close to the crash site as they could. We did not have to ask them to hurry. Those guys evidently got a charge from having an excuse to put the pedal to the metal. They gave us some wild rides.

The training operations people had sustained a very large number of accidents. If I am remembering correctly, we lost eleven aircraft while I was at Craig. Unfortunately, some lives were lost too. A couple of wing commanders were fired, but they were not the problem, just the scapegoats. We were being pushed too hard, by headquarters, to do too much, too fast, with too little. Then we were chastised for being less than perfect.

The Training Command rules regarding flying at Craig were a lot different from what they had been at Perrin. Of course, at Craig, the overall levels of experience and proficiency were much lower. As the pressure to produce more pilots increased, so did the accident rate. The response was to add more rules and procedures. After a while, everyone was so busy trying to comply, attention was diverted from flying the airplanes.

Each training flight was assigned a small area and a block of altitudes to operate in. Entry and departure was by a specified narrow corridor. Too much time was required to comply with the space restrictions. The flight test section had it's own operating area, which was large enough for us to operate in without undue space restrictions.

Eventually, the heads of flying operations felt like they needed to micromanage every flight, including the test flights. They grudgingly allowed us to take off and land, in between their training flights. If we wanted to practice precision instrument approaches for our own proficiency requirements, we had to go to another base to do it. They even required us to get permission from the deputy wing commander for ops to fly our missions if the weather called for anything less than unrestricted student flights. They never declined, but having to ask was demeaning for a group of pilots who had far more experience than most of the instructors.

————

Someone has said that a wing commanders' primary concern is that his career rests on his pilots ability to fly their missions without mishap, and the pilots only make a small contribution by betting their lives on it.

It has also been said that one of two things will happen to a fighter pilot. He will walk out to his airplane not knowing it will be his last flight, or he will walk out to his airplane knowing it will be his last flight. I had the good fortune to know.

My last flight as a military pilot was to conduct a test flight in a T-38. I knew it was my last flight and I had some pretty strong feelings about it, but said nothing to anyone. I wanted it to be a routine flight, if there was any such thing, and it was. At least I knew I was making my last flight in a military airplane. Too many pilots had begun their last flight, not knowing it was their last.

Reflections

Our family departed Craig AFB on the first day of November, 1967 with Kathy driving the Rambler wagon, carrying three boys and a dog. I followed her to Commerce, Georgia, with the other son in our MGB roadster. We had our household goods shipped to Charleston, South Carolina, but at the time, did not know exactly where we would live. After a few days rest, with my parents, we headed on down to Charleston.

From the time I was a teenager, I had held to a firm belief that the creator of heaven and earth, Almighty God, was in control of his creation. I believe that he looked after fools who entered into situations where angels fear to tread, preserving them for some future purpose. I was one of those fools. I had wished to be a military pilot and my wish had been granted, so how could I complain? Only time would tell for what purpose I had been preserved.

At the time, I did not know the term, "burnout", but looking back I think I was close to that point. All my work for several years had been hard, demanding, high stress types of work, requiring long hours. I was in need of some mental and physical rest. Half my base pay for retirement would not support us, but would make our new lifestyle a lot less demanding.

At Craig, I had flown over five hundred test flights, supervised other pilots and our quality control inspection team, participated in numerous aircraft accident investigations, reported on countless incidents, and special projects. For one three month period, I was commander of the field maintenance squadron, as an additional duty. The Air Force had gotten it's money's worth from me.

The things I have described here, by no means cover every interesting situation in my experience. They are merely representative and are intended to provide a general idea of what some of us did as enlisted men and as pilots. Not

223

many flights were truly "routine." One thing I could be sure of; those of us who were leaving, were leaving everything in good hands.

———

Over the years past, I am privileged to have worked with and flown with a lot of good men. To a man, I could trust my life with them. Any one of them would, without hesitation, put his life on the line to help another. Many of them did pay with their lives; some in accidents, some in combat. Some experienced the horror and indescribable misery of POW camps. My hat is off to all of them. Because of them, the world is a better place.

Glossary

ADC – Air Defense Command

ADF – Automatic Direction Finder. Low frequency radio that indicates bearing to the station. Subject to atmospheric noise and static crashes from lightning.

APC – Area of Positive Control. Floor originally at 24,000 ft, later 18,000 ft.

APU – Auxiliary Power Unit. Provides starting power and electrical power to aircraft prior to engine start. Most turbine powered fighters require external power for starting. Early ones used electric starters. Later ones use air for starting.

Attitude Indicator – Gyro powered artificial horizon. Indicates pitch and bank.

EGT – Exhaust Gas Temperature. A critical parameter on jet engines.

GCA – Ground Controlled Approach – with precision radar.

G Force – One G is normal pull of gravity. Accelerated turns will simulate increased gravity force.

IFF – Identification Friend from Foe. Transponder in the aircraft that responds with coded radar pulses when triggered by ground radar. Military jargon for unit in aircraft – "parrot" Instructions might be "squawk low" or "strangle parrot".

IFR – Instrument Flight Rules

ILS – Instrument Landing System. Ground transmitters located at end of runway send signals to aircraft receiver. Vertical needle indicates left or right of course, horizontal needle indicates above or below glideslope.

Knot – One nautical mile per hour. A nautical mile is 1.15 statue miles.

Mach – Percentage of speed of sound. Related to airspeed, but changes greatly with respect to altitude. Mach One = speed of sound. Some aircraft have critical mach limits, which if exceeded, will result in destruction of the aircraft.

RTB – Return to Base

SAC – Strategic Air Command

Slats – Wing leading edge devices that automatically extend to increase lift and decrease stall speed at low speeds.

Speed Brakes – Electrically controlled, hydraulic operated, sections of metal that are normally faired into the fuselage. When deployed to slow the aircraft, or to prevent speed build up, they extend into the slipstream.

T-Bird – Lockheed T-33 trainer/utility aircraft. Tandem two place cockpit. Top speed limited to 505 knots. Design derived from the single seat F-80.

TACAN – Tactical Navigation. Aircraft transmits signal to the ground radio system which transmits distance and bearing information to aircraft. The distance function is called DME, Distance Measuring Equipment.

VFR – Visual Flight Rules

VOR – Very high frequency Omni Range. Ground radio system transmits bearing information to aircraft. No distance info.

ISBN 141203202-4

51298222R00129

Made in the USA
San Bernardino, CA
19 July 2017